Music First!

FIFTH EDITION

WITHDRAWN

Gary C. White
Iowa State University Emeritus

Boston   Burr Ridge, IL   Dubuque, IA   Madison, WI   New York   San Francisco   St. Louis
Bangkok   Bogotá   Caracas   Kuala Lumpur   Lisbon   London   Madrid   Mexico City
Milan   Montreal   New Delhi   Santiago   Seoul   Singapore   Sydney   Taipei   Toronto

Higher Education

Published by McGraw-Hill, an imprint of The McGraw-Hill Companies, Inc., 1221 Avenue of the Americas, New York, NY 10020. Copyright © 2007. All rights reserved. No part of this publication may be reproduced or distributed in any form or by any means, or stored in a database or retrieval system, without the prior written consent of The McGraw-Hill Companies, Inc., including, but not limited to, in any network or other electronic storage or transmission, or broadcast for distance learning.

1 2 3 4 5 6 7 8 9 0 VLP/VLP 0 9 8 7 6

ISBN-13: 978-0-07-313774-2
ISBN-10: 0-07-313774-X

Editor in Chief: *Emily Barrosse*
Publisher and Sponsoring Editor: *Christopher Freitag*
Developmental Editor: *Barbara Gerr*
Associate Developmental Editor: *Beth Ebenstein*
Project Manager: *Carey Eisner*
Manuscript Editor: *Michael O'Neal*
Cover Designer: *Kim Menning*
Text Designer: *Glenda King*
Production Supervisor: *Richard DeVitto*
Composition: *12/14 Times Roman by Thompson Type*
Printing: *50# Plainfield Opaque Plus, Vicks Lithographics*

Cover: Darren Hopes/Getty Images

Library of Congress Cataloging-in-Publication Data
White, Gary C., 1937–
    Music first! / Gary White.--5th ed.
        p. cm.
    Includes index.
    ISBN 0-07-313774-X
        1. Music theory--Textbooks. I. Title.

MT6.W4146M9 2006
781--dc22   2006041993

The Internet addresses listed in the text were accurate at the time of publication. The inclusion of a Web site does not indicate an endorsement by the authors or McGraw-Hill, and McGraw-Hill does not guarantee the accuracy of the information presented at these sites.

www.mhhe.com

Contents

CHAPTER FOUR
Compound Meter   71

Interlude 2   *91*

CHAPTER FIVE
The Keyboard   92

CHAPTER SIX
Major Scales/Major Keys   109

Interlude 3   *131*

CHAPTER SEVEN
Intervals   132

Preface

Music First! is an introduction to the fundamentals of music for students who are beginning their formal music education. The premise of this book is that intellectual understanding of music should follow direct experience—that **music** should come **first!** Thus, the study of fundamentals is combined with considerable experience in music reading to get the student involved with music through performance. Other forms of musical involvement such as listening, composing, and some formal ear training are suggested in the text; the individual instructor can select from these musical experiences according to the level of the class and his/her own tastes.

The sequence of chapters has been carefully reconsidered. A primary consideration has always been to introduce both pitch and rhythm notation as near to the beginning of the book as practicable. The reason for this is to get students involved with reading music and performing as early as possible. Thus the first two chapters deal with notation of pitch and notation of rhythm. These chapters are the basis for activities that will continue throughout the book, particularly in sections near the end of chapters that are designated "Using What You Have Learned." It is hoped that a major part of class time will be devoted to performing. Each chapter presents multiple opportunities to do so while the student is developing fundamental concepts.

The order of chapters is further influenced by the need to introduce certain principles and concepts before they are used in succeeding chapters. An example of this is the insertion of the chapter on intervals between the chapters on major scales and minor scales. The concept of the major scale is important to the definition of interval qualities, and the interval qualities are convenient when discussing the relative relationship between the major and minor scales and in describing the various forms of the minor scale. While the chapter on intervals might otherwise seem out of place, its placement at this location is intentional, since it makes for an orderly and·compact presentation.

Much consideration is given to the performing media that the students may need if they become classroom teachers or if they wish to continue their musical education. The voice, of course, is primary, and a large repertoire of songs is provided to give a variety of singing experiences. The primary accompanying instruments are likely to be the keyboard and the guitar. A foldout keyboard is provided in the back of the book to aid in the development of keyboard skills, and a section of Chapter 1 and all of Appendix 4 are devoted to gaining basic keyboard skills. Appendix 3 presents information on tuning the guitar and reading guitar tablature. Guitar tablature is provided for all songs that are to be accompanied.

Since a music fundamentals course is often considered to be a part of the "general education" of a student, I have included five "Interludes" that encourage thought and discussion about a broad range of topics and relate music to other areas of study. The interludes have been updated in the fifth edition to include a larger number of quotations from living musicians.

Providing a body of suitable music for individual and class study is critical to a broad-based approach to music learning. The songbook includes over seventy songs with guitar chords and popular-music chord symbols. These songs represent a cross section of musical styles and, for the most part, are songs that are familiar to students and teachers. A new feature in the fifth edition is the inclusion of more than one verse for many of the songs.

The accompanying compact disk provides a complete musical background for the student's early experiences with rhythm and pitch as well as recordings of all the songs in the songbook. The CD has been newly recorded for the fifth edition.

A feature introduced in the fourth edition of *Music First!* is the Online Learning Center, which contains many activities designed to enhance the student's learning experience. Included are activities designed to reinforce specific concepts in the chapters, to allow students to create their own musical compositions using only the computer keyboard, and to give students opportunities to listen to all the songs in the songbook. In the fifth edition, specific activities in the Online Learning Center are suggested at the appropriate place in each chapter. If students avail themselves of these activities, they will find their learning of music fundamentals much expedited. The Online Learning Center can be found at

www.mhhe.com/musicfirst5

An **Instructor's Manual,** which includes suggestions for using the materials of each chapter, grading keys for all assignments, sample tests, and a set of overhead projector masters to facilitate class work, is available from McGraw-Hill.

The reviewers of the previous editions have contributed many helpful suggestions over the years, and I credit them for making major contributions to the development of this book. They have been my sounding board and gentle critics, and I remember their comments with appreciation. I am also deeply indebted to Dr. Steven G. Estrella, who created the software for *Music First!* (which you will find in the Online Learning Center at the URL listed above). His imagination and sound pedagogical approach have made a major contribution to *Music First!* The author is indebted to Mark Anderman, Santa Rosa Junior College; Beth K. Aracena, Eastern Mennonite University; Dan Barnard, Penn State, Erie, The Behrand College; Ralph D. Converse, Western New Mexico University; Pamela Buckheit, MSU Great Falls, College of Technology; Anita Hanawalt, University of La Verne; Daniel McCarthy, University of Akron; Darleen Mitchell, University of Nebraska, Kearney; Carolyn Sanders, University of Alabama at Huntsville; Sandra Starr, Minot State University, whose valuable input has helped to further polish the pedagogy of the fifth edition and make the package more useful to students and teachers alike. I hope you will find the result to your liking.

To the Student

"The art of music is so deep and profound that to approach it very seriously only, is not enough. One must approach music with a serious vigor and, at the same time, with a great, affectionate joy." — NADIA BOULANGER

You are reading this book because you want to know more about music. Music is an important part of your life, and you may want to increase your enjoyment, improve your performance, or better understand how music is put together. If you will make the effort to do what this book recommends, I feel sure that you can make significant progress toward the following goals:

1. Learn to read, or improve your ability to read music.

2. Broaden your enjoyment of the whole range of music, from the classics and folk music to the latest rock and pop music.

3. Gain an understanding of the structure of music that will lead to an awareness of how music creates the emotional responses that we all feel.

4. Learn to transpose music.

5. Learn how to provide a simple accompaniment to a melody.

6. Compose your own music.

If these goals match your needs, then let's get started.

—Gary C. White

CHAPTER ONE
Elements of Music: Pitch

"The song is ended, but the melody lingers on."

— *Irving Berlin*

The term *pitch* refers to the "highness" or "lowness" of a musical sound.

It is important that you experience pitch firsthand by listening and playing, so take out the keyboard chart or sit at a piano or an electronic keyboard. On any keyboard the "higher" pitches are to your right as you face the keyboard and the "lower" pitches are to your left.

figure 1.1

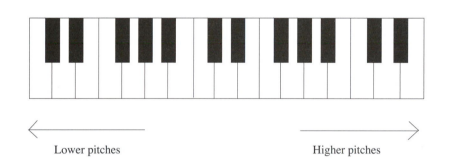

Lower pitches   Higher pitches

The white keys are named using the first seven letters of the alphabet (**A B C D E F G**), as you can see on the keyboard chart. Notice that the black keys are in groups of two and three, and that **C** is the white key to the left of each group of two black keys.

figure 1.2

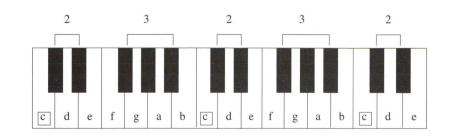

This pattern of the black keys will aid you in finding various pitches on the keyboard. It is important that you memorize the names of the keys on the keyboard.

Explore the white keys of the keyboard to hear high and low pitches. Now play all the Cs on the keyboard. All the Cs sound similar (except for their highness or lowness) and for this reason they are given the same name.

Middle C

The **C** nearest the center of the piano keyboard is called *middle C.* This is the **C** nearest the manufacturer's name, which often appears on the inside of the keyboard cover. This is an important reference point as you learn the keyboard.

figure 1.3

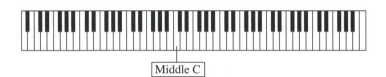

On electronic keyboards with shorter keyboards (often forty-nine keys as opposed to the eighty-eight on the standard keyboard, you will still find *middle C* in the middle of the keyboard.

figure 1.4

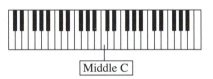

The Octave

The relationship or interval between two adjacent notes of the same name is called an *octave.* "Octave" refers to the eight white keys contained in the interval.

figure 1.5

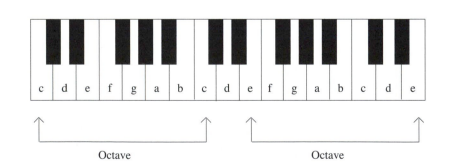

Play octaves all over the keyboard and listen to the similarity of the two pitches. When boys' voices change, the effect is a difference of an octave between women's and men's voices, which means that men and women naturally sing in octaves.

Name the notes marked on the keyboards below. Try to do this from memory without referring to the keyboard chart.

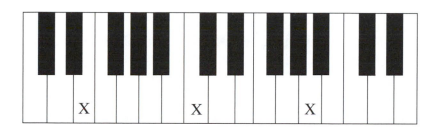

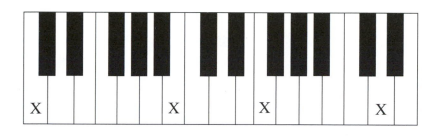

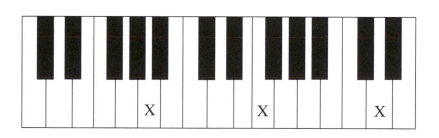

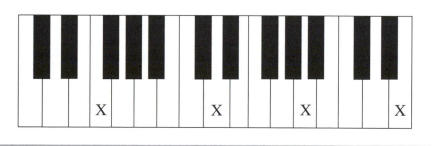

Musical Notation

Play the following series of notes (try to find the notes from memory):

G E G   G E G   A G F E D E F

This is the beginning of the familiar song "This Old Man." If you know this song, try to play the rest of it on the keyboard. (You will need only the white keys.) Perhaps the words will help:

> This old man, he played one,
> He played nick-nack on my thumb,
> With a nick-nack paddy whack give the dog a bone!
> This old man came rolling home.

As you try to pick out "This Old Man" at the keyboard, you are "playing by ear." Some people are better at this than others, but your skill will improve with practice. Another way of playing music is called "playing by note." Everyone can become skilled in playing and singing by note, and it is not necessary to know a melody in advance to be able to play it if you can read musical notation. The following is the musical notation for "This Old Man."

figure 1.6

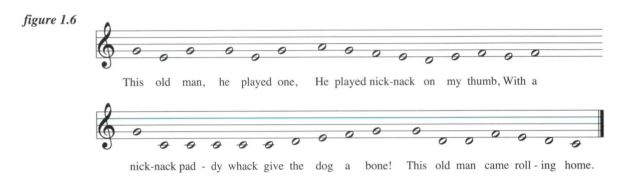

Even if you didn't happen to know this melody, or had difficulty picking it out on the keyboard, you will be able to play it as soon as you know the meaning of the various symbols in musical notation. The example below is the first part of "This Old Man" with the clef and staff labeled:

figure 1.7

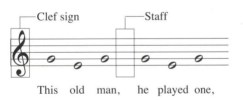

The Staff

The *staff* consists of five parallel lines that indicate the pitch (the highness or lowness) of sounds. The lines and spaces are numbered from the lowest to the highest.

figure 1.8

Notes are written on the staff so that their heads either are between two lines or cross a line. Note heads between two lines are said to be "on a space," while those crossing a line are said to be "on a line."

Try to use this position whenever you are asked to play on a keyboard and you will soon find it to be quite comfortable. It may be a good idea to have someone skilled in keyboard performance check your hand position at this point to correct any problems before they become habitual.

In the beginning, fluency in playing the keyboard comes when the hand seldom has to move over large distances. This means that most of the notes of a melody should be "under the fingers." The position for the right hand below places **C, D, E, F,** and **G** under the fingers.

To develop keyboard proficiency, it is important that you work out a good fingering for each melody you play. The melodies in this book have fingerings written in. The fingerings in keyboard music are indicated using the following numbering system:

figure 1.21

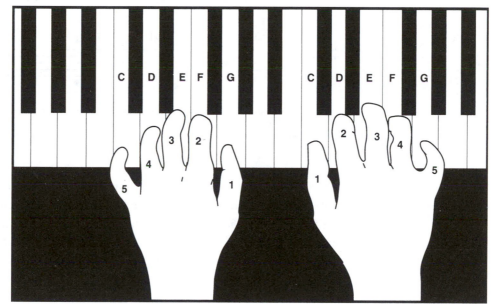

Fingerings for the right hand are indicated **R.H.** Those for the left hand are indicated **L.H.** Place your right thumb on middle **C** on a keyboard. Your fingers should be in the position of the right hand in figure 1.21 (1=**C**, 2=**D**, 3=**E**, 4=**F**, 5=**G**). Now play the following melodic patterns, making all the notes the same length.

3 3 4 5 5 4 3 2 1	5 3 3 4 2 2 1	1 1 2 3 3 2 2 5	1 2 3 4 5 5 5
5 3 3 4 2 2 1	1 1 3 3 5 5 3	1 1 2 3 2 1 1	1 4 3 2 1 5 1

Quick Check

Play the following pitches on the keyboard. Try to develop both speed and accuracy in finding the right note and playing it. To get used to playing notes with both hands, play all bass staff notes with the left hand and all treble staff notes with the right hand. Play this exercise several times, increasing your speed with each playing. (Note: this exercise will not "lie under the fingers"!)

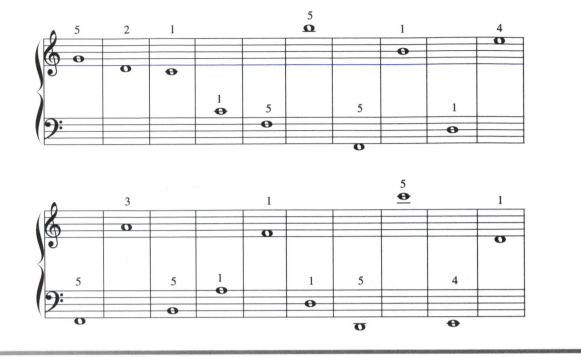

This would be a perfect time to check into the online activities found at www.mhhe.com/musicfirst5. When you reach the opening page of this site, click on the Student Center in the left column. Now click on Chapter 1. You will see a list of two activities. Click on 1.1 Keyboard Note Reading white keys. Read the instructions in the upper-left corner of the window. You will find that this game is very helpful in teaching you to read music. The more you practice, the faster you will become at identifying and playing notes on the keyboard.

Drawing Musical Symbols

You can draw musical symbols easily if you follow the step-by-step instructions below:

Treble Clef

You can draw the treble clef in one continuous line beginning with the tail below the staff.

figure 1.22

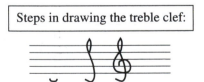

Steps in drawing the treble clef:

Notice that the curves cross on the fourth line of the staff, and that the spiral is around the second line of the staff.

Bass Clef

Draw the bass clef as follows:

figure 1.23

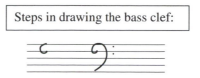

Steps in drawing the bass clef:

Notice that the symbol spirals around the fourth line of the staff and that the dots are in the third and fourth spaces.

Note Heads

Note heads in spaces should be drawn to fill the space between two lines, while those on lines should occupy half of the spaces above and below a line:

figure 1.24

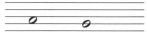

◆ **ASSIGNMENT 1.4, PAGE 19**

KEY TERMS

Define the following terms in your own words:

Pitch _____

Middle C _____

Octave _____

Clef _____

Staff _____

Treble clef _____

Bass clef _____

Grand staff _____

Ledger line _____

LISTENING

The following melodies contain only the white keys in the octave from middle **C** to the **C** one octave higher than middle **C**. Listen to them and try to find the starting note on a keyboard. Find the final note on the keyboard. Can you find the other pitches and play the melody? Check your perceptions by looking in the songbook.

"Love Somebody" (p. 288, CD track 38, or the Web site)

"Lullaby" (p. 289, CD track 39, or the Web site)

"My Hat" (p. 291, CD track 42, or the Web site)

"Over the River and Through the Wood" (p. 294, CD track 45, or the Web site)

"Twinkle, Twinkle Little Star" (p. 309, CD track 69, or the Web site)

USING WHAT YOU HAVE LEARNED

These sections, which will appear near the end of each chapter, are intended to reinforce the materials you have learned in previous chapters. They are partly review sections, but often they allow you to build on the skills you have already acquired.

 Two exercises on the Web site (www.mhhe.com/musicfirst5) will provide excellent practice and fun for your further enjoyment. You may have already experienced Exercise 1.1 (see page 10). Exercise 1.2, Pitch Pattern Matching, will test your knowledge of pitch patterns. This exercise gives you an opportunity to listen to and identify simple pitch patterns. I strongly urge you to make use of these online activities.

Name _____

Section _____

Date _____

Write the names of each of the following notes in the blanks below:

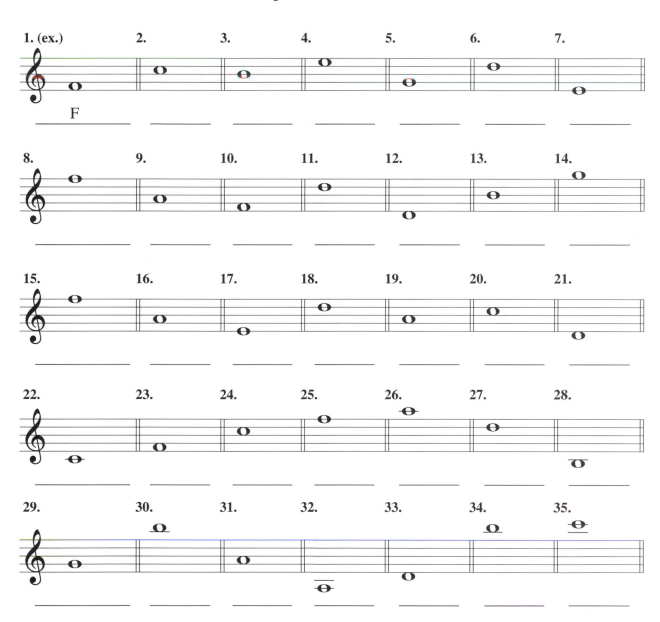

Octaves in the Treble Staff

Write notes an octave above the given notes:

Write notes an octave below the given notes:

CHAPTER 1 — ASSIGNMENT 1.2a
Names of Notes in the Bass Staff

Name _____

Section _____

Date _____

Write the names of each of the following notes in the blanks below:

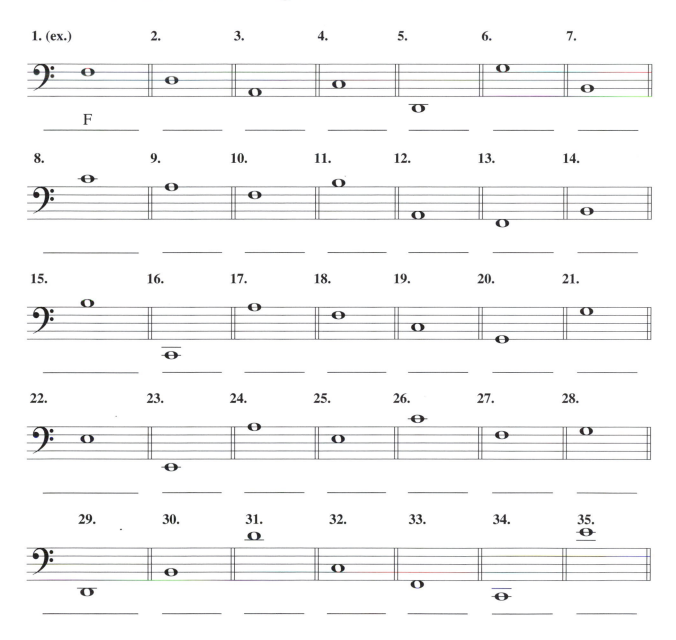

Octaves in the Bass Staff

Write notes an octave above each of the given notes:

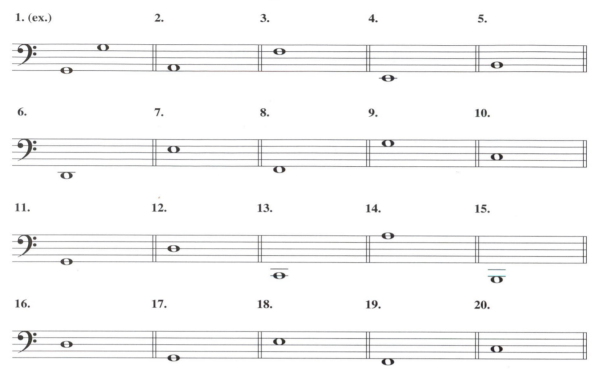

Write notes an octave below and in the bass staff from each of the treble staff notes:

CHAPTER 1 — ASSIGNMENT 1.3a
Names of Notes on the Grand Staff

Name _____

Section _____

Date _____

Write the name of each note in the blank below it:

Octaves on the Grand Staff

Write notes in other octaves for each of the given notes on the grand staff. You should write at least three notes for each problem. (See example.)

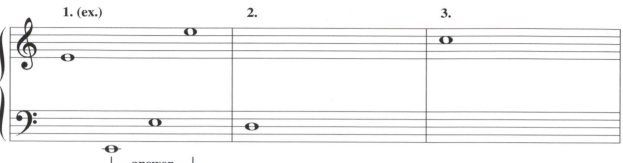

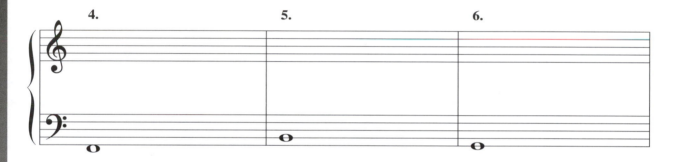

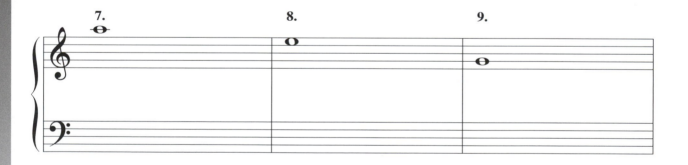

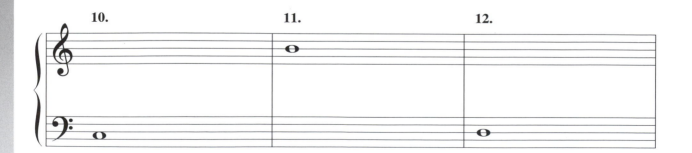

Name _____

Section _____

Date _____

Draw five each of the following symbols. Compare your work with the symbols in figures 1.22 through 1.24.

Treble clefs:

Bass clefs:

Notes on lines:

Notes on spaces:

ASSIGNMENT

CHAPTER TWO
Elements of Music: Rhythm

"Time is nature's way of keeping everything from happening at once."

— *Anonymous*

"In the beginning was rhythm."
— *Hans von Bülow*

"Jazz without the beat, most musicians know, is a telephone yanked from the wall; it just can't communicate."

— *Leonard Feather*

Trying to learn music by reading a book is a little like reading about food when you are hungry—it's interesting, but not satisfying. For this reason it is important that you get involved in music—by singing, clapping, listening, playing, and creating music. If this experience is going to be musically satisfying, you must overcome your inhibitions and join in freely. Relax and enjoy these musical experiences.

Play example 1 on the accompanying CD if you are working alone. (If you are in a class your instructor may choose to perform at the keyboard.) You will hear a series of chords. Clap along with the chords, trying to stay precisely in time with them. This will require careful attention, but remain relaxed about it. Relaxed attention promotes a more musical result. Stay with this exercise until you feel comfortable. You are experiencing a fundamental element of music: the beat.

In this chapter we will be dealing with two fundamental elements: beat and rhythm. You have just been experiencing the *beat* by clapping along with example 1. Beats are regular pulses that provide a framework that organizes music in time. The terms *beat* and *pulse* are roughly the same, and musicians use them interchangeably. If you have watched a large ensemble, such as an orchestra or a band, you may have seen a conductor who helps the ensemble play together by marking the beats with a baton.

Rhythm, on the other hand, is a pattern of longer and shorter durations that forms the basis for the life of a musical composition. When you were clapping along with example 1, you may have been aware that the drummer was playing a much more complicated pattern along with your clapping. All these patterns, plus the patterns played by the other instruments, create a sense of flow that accounts for much of our response to music. For this reason, rhythm has been called the lifeblood of music.

The Beat

Beats are the basis for measuring time in music. A *beat* is not a specific duration, as is the minute or second, but rather a unit established by musicians themselves, who choose the speed based on their understanding of music style and indications in the printed music. In music notation the beat is indicated by a note, often a quarter note.

figure 2.1

(Notes may be drawn with their stems in an upward or downward direction. This is purely an editorial decision and has no effect on the meaning of the symbol.)

Thus your clapping could be notated as follows:

figure 2.2

The speed of the beat varies from one piece of music to another, and *tempo* is the term used to describe the various speeds. Tempo can be measured in the number of beats per minute, or described in general terms. The following is a partial list of common terms that refer to tempo:

The terms above are Italian terms to indicate tempo, since Italian is considered to be the international language of music. They are generally placed above the music at the beginning of a composition and wherever the tempo changes. (For definitions of these terms see the glossary.)

 It is important that you learn to sense and respond to beats in music. For this reason I urge you to go to the online activities at www.mhhe.com/musicfirst5. Click on Chapter 2. 2.1 Tap the Tempo will help you understand common tempo terms. Tap along with the music and see your tempo displayed. This exercise allows you to tap along with some music while the computer checks how well you are able to keep a steady tempo.

Simple Division of the Beat

Play example 1 again. This time clap twice for each chord. At first your clapping may be uneven, but continue to practice until you can clap in a smooth and steady flow of equal time units. You are experiencing the division of the beat. When the beat is divided into two equal parts we call it *simple* (or *binary*) *division*. If the beat is assigned to the quarter note, then the division of the beat will be indicated by eighth notes.

figure 2.3

Eighth note:

Parts of eighth note:

Thus we could indicate your clapping with the chords as follows:

figure 2.4

When a series of eighth notes is written it is common to substitute beams for the flags:

figure 2.5

Beams connect eighth notes that are in the same beat, so figure 2.4 could have been written:

figure 2.6

Music for instruments generally uses beams, whereas vocal music often does not.

Rhythm Patterns

The beat and divisions of the beat provide a regular framework that supports the rhythmic life of a piece of music. The patterns of longer and shorter durations are called *rhythm patterns* or simply *rhythms*. Thus the beat is generally made up of regular time units, while rhythms involve irregular units of time with the beat as a background.

figure 2.7

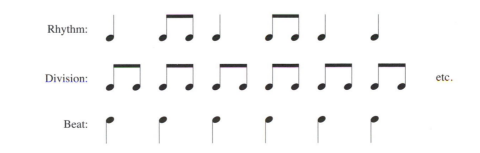

Repeat Sign

When a section of music is to be repeated it is enclosed in *repeat signs:*

figure 2.8

With an understanding of these musical symbols, you are ready to begin reading some rhythm patterns. Count each quarter note in a pattern using 1, 2, 3, 4. For eighth notes count the first note in the beat as you would a quarter note and say "and" for the second eighth note:

figure 2.9

Quick Check

If you choose to sing, let the chords guide your voice. Concentrate at first on the rhythm and don't be particularly concerned about the melody you sing. Play example 1 again and sing or speak the following rhythms. Now tap the beat as you sing the rhythm.

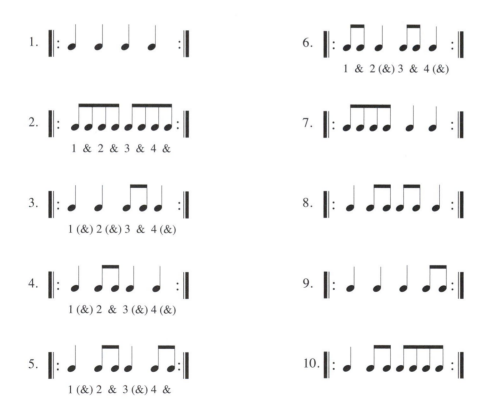

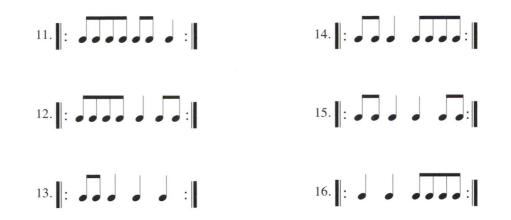

Select any two of the rhythms above to perform at the same time as a duet with a friend. Take turns clapping one part and speaking the other.

Drawing Quarter Notes and Eighth Notes

Note Heads

Quarter notes and eighth notes have black note heads. These heads may be somewhat difficult to draw with a pencil or pen, but you can do it quite neatly with a little practice. Notice that the note heads are not circles but ovals with a slight upward slant.

figure 2.10

Avoid either large-circle note heads or single-line note heads because they are difficult to read.

figure 2.11

Stems

The stems of notes whose heads are within the staff should be one octave in length.

figure 2.12

Stems go down on those notes on or above the middle line and up when the notes are below the middle line. If the surrounding notes have their stems up, then it is proper for the stem of a note on the middle line to go up.

figure 2.13

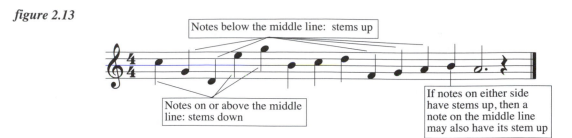

When stemmed notes are in ledger lines, the stems should extend to the middle line of the staff. Unbeamed stems always touch or cross the center line of the staff.

figure 2.14

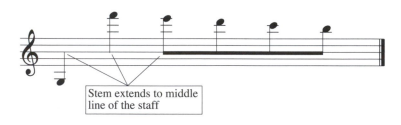

Improving Your Ear

While regular practice in reading music will improve your ability to relate music notation to the sound of music, the reverse process—relating sound to music notation—is equally effective. This reverse process is often called ear training. Use the following three exercises throughout the book to develop your ability to relate the sound of music to its notation.

Ear-Training Exercise I

A friend or classmate or your teacher selects one of the patterns in the exercise on page 24, establishes a steady beat, and sings or plays the pattern two or three times. The other person should choose a neutral syllable like "Ta" and sing on a single pitch or choose a single key to play the pattern. The remaining students look through the patterns and select the one that was played. Your answer will be the number of the pattern.

Ear-Training Exercise II

This is an exercise in echoing a musical pattern. The group establishes a steady beat by tapping a finger or toe. When the beat is clearly established, a designated leader (a student or the teacher) sings or plays one of the patterns above and the rest of the group echoes this pattern immediately, without skipping a beat. Repeat this process until everyone echoes the pattern accurately.

Ear-Training Exercise III

A friend, classmate, or your teacher selects one of the patterns in the exercise above, establishes a steady beat, and plays or sings the pattern two or three times, allowing a pause of approximately ten seconds between each playing. Listen to the pattern played and in the pauses, notate the pattern on a piece of blank music paper. (You will find several sheets of music paper at the end of the book.) The leader then announces the number of the pattern played. Check your work by comparing it with the pattern as printed in the book. (Also be sure to check to see if you have written the symbols properly.)

Longer Note Values

The half note is equal to two quarter notes:

figure 2.15

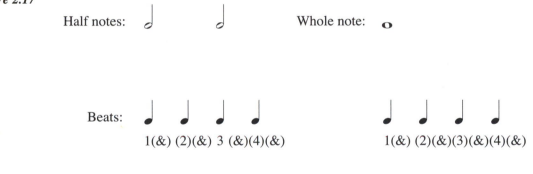

The whole note is equal to four quarter notes:

figure 2.16

Thus, when a quarter note indicates the beat, a half note is played or sung on the first beat and sustained through the next beat. A whole note would be played on the first beat and sustained through the next three beats.

In counting these longer notes, whisper the counts through which the note is sustained. (The beats to be whispered are indicated in parentheses.)

figure 2.17

Half notes: 𝅗𝅥   𝅗𝅥   Whole note: 𝅝

Beats: ♩ ♩ ♩ ♩   ♩ ♩ ♩ ♩
1(&) (2)(&) 3 (&)(4)(&)   1(&) (2)(&)(3)(&)(4)(&)

Quick Check

Play example 1 again and sing or speak the following rhythms involving half and whole notes. Tap or conduct the beat as you sing the rhythm.

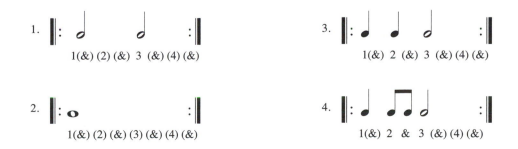

1. ‖: 𝅗𝅥   𝅗𝅥 :‖
   1(&) (2) (&) 3 (&) (4) (&)

2. ‖: 𝅝 :‖
   1(&) (2) (&) (3) (&) (4) (&)

3. ‖: 𝅗𝅥 ♩ 𝅗𝅥 :‖
   1(&) 2 (&) 3 (&) (4) (&)

4. ‖: 𝅗𝅥 ♫ 𝅗𝅥 :‖
   1(&) 2 & 3 (&) (4) (&)

5. ‖: 𝅗𝅥   ♩ ♪♪♪ :‖

7. ‖: ♪♪♪♪ 𝅗𝅥 :‖

6. ‖: 𝅗𝅥 ♪♪♪♪ :‖

8. ‖: 𝅗𝅥 ♪♪♩ :‖

Clap, tap, or speak pairs of these rhythms as a duet with a friend.

Do Ear-Training Exercises I, II, and III (p. 26) using the patterns above.

Rests

Silence is an important aspect of music. There are complete silences from time to time within compositions, but more often one part will be silent while others continue. Silences are indicated by *rests*. There is a rest symbol for each note value. The chart below shows the whole rest, half rest, quarter rest, and eighth rest.

figure 2.18

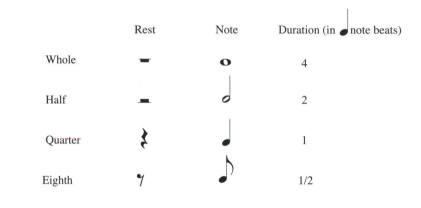

	Rest	Note	Duration (in ♩ note beats)
Whole	▬	𝅝	4
Half	▬	𝅗𝅥	2
Quarter	𝄽	♩	1
Eighth	𝄾	♪	1/2

◆ **ASSIGNMENT 2.1, PAGE 39**

Speak or sing the following patterns with example 1. Try conducting or tapping the beat while you speak the rhythm.

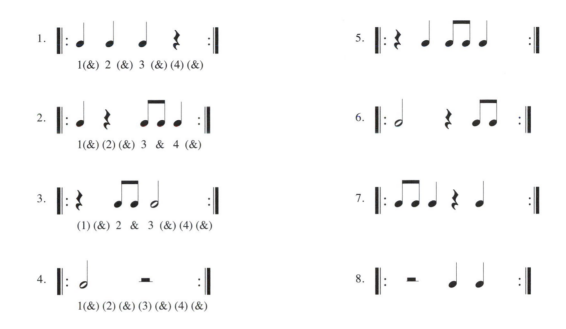

Make duets from pairs of the rhythms above.

Do Ear-Training Exercises I, II, and III (p. 26) using the patterns above.

The Tie

The *tie* is a curved line connecting two notes:

figure 2.19

Tie

When two notes (of the same pitch) are tied together, they are to be considered as a single note, a single sound. Thus, two quarter notes tied together have the duration of a half note.

figure 2.20

♩ ♩ = ♩ (2 beats)

A quarter note tied to an eighth note has a duration of 1 1/2 beats:

figure 2.21

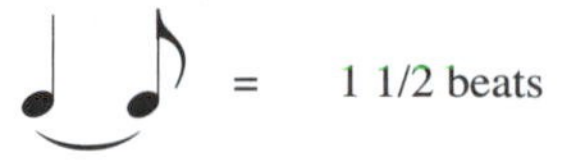

 = 1 1/2 beats

Practice clapping, tapping, and speaking this pattern with example 1.

figure 2.22

1(&) (2) & 3 (&) (4) &

The Dot

A *dot* placed to the right of a note head increases by one-half the value of the note.

figure 2.23

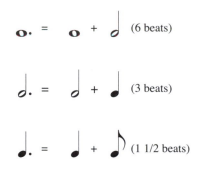

Sometimes ties are used in music and sometimes dots are used, depending on the musical situation. Dotted notes can often be used in place of ties.

Thus you could also write the pattern in figure 2.22 using dotted note values.

figure 2.24

1(&) (2) & 3 (&) (4) &

◆ **ASSIGNMENT 2.2, PAGES 41–42**

The following patterns contain dotted notes and ties. Speak, tap, or clap them with example 1. Perform them again without the musical background. Create duets from any two patterns.

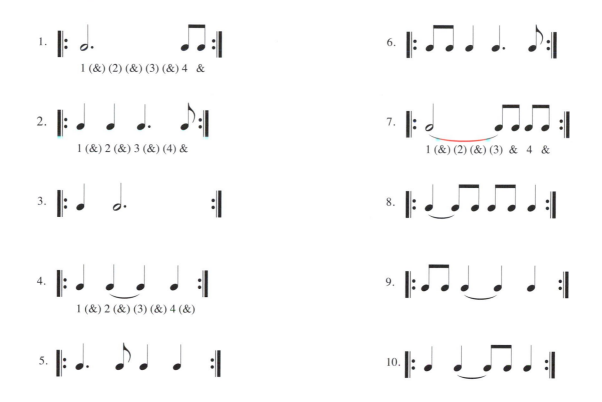

Do Ear-Training Exercises I, II, and III (p. 26) using the patterns above.

Compound Division of the Beat

Play example 2 on the CD. Clap along with the chords until you feel comfortable with the beat. Now clap three times for each chord. Stay with it until your clapping is smooth and steady.

When the beat is divided in three equal parts as you have been doing, we call it *compound* (or *ternary*) *division*. Simple and compound division are the two basic divisions of the beat. They are often referred to as simple and compound *time*. The divisions in compound time are often indicated using eighth notes.

figure 2.25

In this case, since there will be three eighth notes for each beat, a dotted quarter note is used to indicate the beat.

figure 2.26

Thus we could indicate your clapping with the chords in example 2 as follows:

figure 2.27

Quick Check

Now you are ready to begin reading rhythmic patterns in compound time. For the beats (which will be dotted quarters), count as you have before: 1, 2, 3, etc. For the division of the beats (eighth notes), say "la-lee." (Your instructor may prefer another counting system.) Use example 2 to accompany your speaking.

Try clapping or tapping these rhythms without the musical background.

Combine any two of the patterns above to form a duet.

Do Ear-Training Exercises I, II, and III (p. 26) using the patterns above.

Dotted Rests

Since the beat in compound time is indicated with dotted notes, a symbol is needed to indicate an equal number of silent beats. The *dotted rest* serves this purpose. Figure 2.28 shows the common dotted rests:

figure 2.28

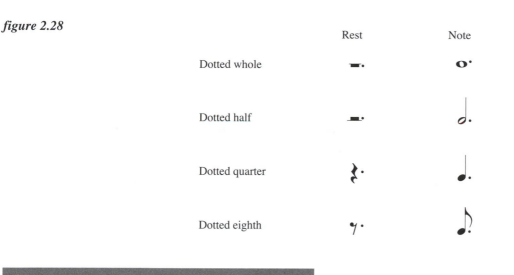

♦ **ASSIGNMENT 2.3, PAGES 43–44**

Quick Check

Sing or speak the following patterns using example 2. Clap or tap these rhythms without the musical background. Make duets of any two patterns.

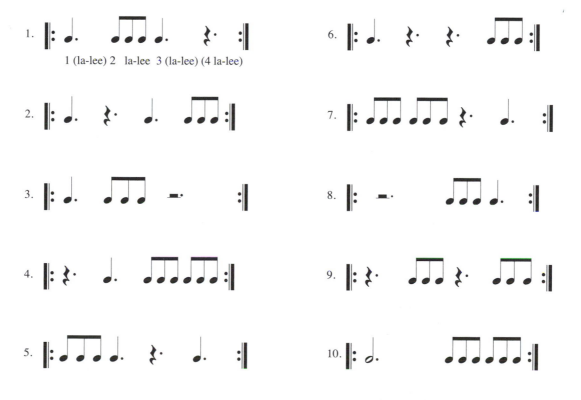

Do Ear-Training Exercises I, II, and III (p. 26) using the patterns on page 33.

Summary of Relative Note and Rest Values

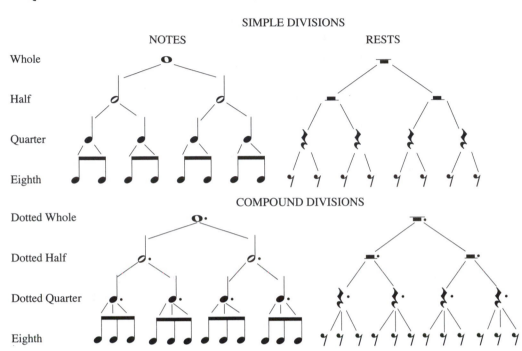

KEY TERMS

Define the following terms in your own words:

Beat _____

Rhythm _____

Rhythmic pattern _____

Note _____

Tempo _____

Repeat signs _____

Simple division _____

Note head _____

Flag _____

Beam _____

Stem _____

Rest _____

Tie _____

Dot _____

Compound division _____

LISTENING

Listen to some of the songs listed below on the CD of songs from your songbook, and clap or tap the beat. When you feel comfortable with the beat, try to determine if the music has simple or compound divisions. Sometimes the division shifts from simple to compound or vice versa, but one division usually predominates. Do this listening exercise using music you hear on the radio, television, or stereo. You hear music several times each day, and you can improve your musicianship with careful listening.

"Are You Sleeping" (p. 266, CD track 11, or the Web site)

"Billy Boy" (p. 270, CD track 17, or the Web site)

"Down in the Valley" (p. 277, CD track 24, or the Web site)

"I've Got to Know" (p. 283, CD track 33, or the Web site)

"Lavender's Blue" (p. 285, CD track 35, or the Web site)

"Love Somebody" (p. 288, CD track 38, or the Web site)

"Over the River and Through the Wood" (p. 294, CD track 45, or the Web site)

"Pawpaw Patch" (p. 295, CD track 47, or the Web site)

"Row, Row, Row Your Boat" (p. 298, CD track 50, or the Web site)

"Simple Gifts" (p. 302, CD track 55, or the Web site)

"Three Blind Mice" (p. 306, CD track 64, or the Web site)

"White Coral Bells" (p. 312, CD track 73, or the Web site)

USING WHAT YOU HAVE LEARNED

There are four learning activities for Chapter 2 on the Web site at www.mhhe.com/musicfirst5. Spending time with all these activities will ensure that your musical skills will increase. The activities are:

2.1 Tap the Tempo will help you understand common tempo terms. Tap along with the music and see your tempo displayed.

2.2 Rhythm Pattern Matching will test your knowledge of rhythm patterns.

2.3 Rhythm Pattern Jam is a fun activity to help you apply your knowledge of rhythm patterns in a musical context.

2.4 White Key Pitch Pattern Jam is a fun activity to allow you to apply your knowledge of pitch patterns in a musical context.

1. Clap, speak, or tap the following rhythms, using example 1:

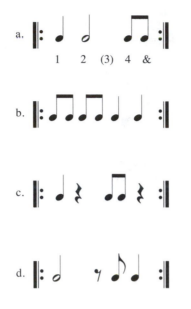

2. Clap, tap, or speak the following rhythms, using example 2:

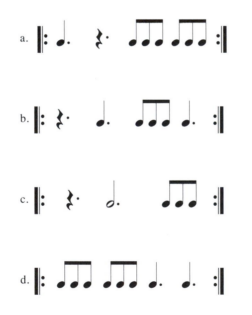

3. Do Ear-Training Exercises I, II, III (p. 26), using the patterns above.

4. Play the following melodies on the keyboard. (Notice the suggested fingerings.) First, listen to the song, then work out the pitches and rhythms separately. When you can play the melody, play along with the recording. Now sing the melodies and check yourself by playing on the keyboard. **Enjoy yourself!**

Important advice:

a. Practice the rhythm separately from the pitches. Reading both rhythm and pitch at the same time will come only after you have perfected your ability to deal with the pitches and rhythms separately.

b. Sing the melodies. Singing is extremely important because singing will improve your musical ear. (See also *Interlude 1,* p. 45.)

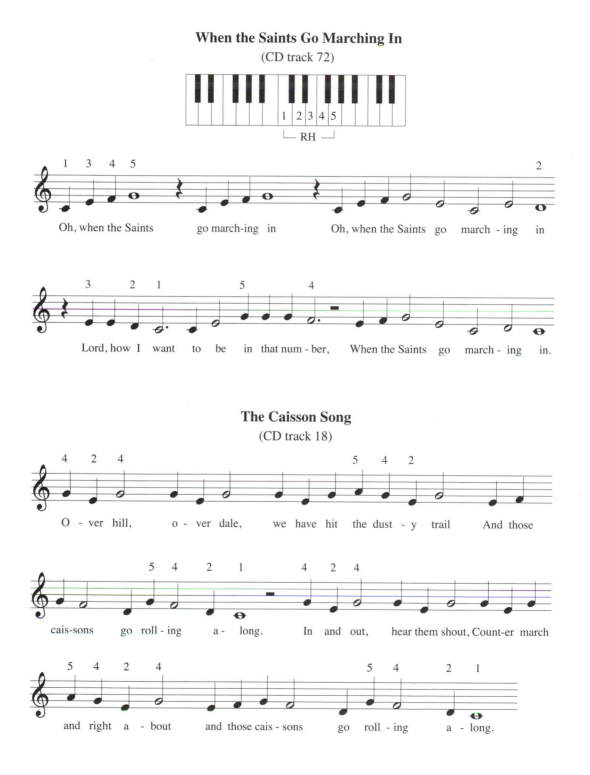

When the Saints Go Marching In
(CD track 72)

Oh, when the Saints go march-ing in Oh, when the Saints go march - ing in

Lord, how I want to be in that num - ber, When the Saints go march - ing in.

The Caisson Song
(CD track 18)

O - ver hill, o - ver dale, we have hit the dust - y trail And those

cais-sons go roll - ing a - long. In and out, hear them shout, Count-er march

and right a - bout and those cais - sons go roll - ing a - long.

5. Listen to at least three of your favorite pieces of music. Try to identify whether the music has simple or compound divisions of the beat. To do this, establish the beat by tapping or clapping and try speaking "one-and, two-and" or "one-la-lee, two-la-lee" along with the music. One of these patterns should fit better than the other. If, after listening to three pieces, you haven't found an example of both simple and compound division, try listening to additional examples until you hear both simple and compound divisions. If your instructor asks, bring an example of simple and compound division to share with the class.

CHAPTER 2 — ASSIGNMENT 2.1
Note Values

Name _____

Section _____

Date _____

The two groups of notes and rests in each following question contain different numbers of beats. Add up the number of quarter-note beats in each group, identify the shorter group in the blank at the right, and give the number of beats it is shorter than the longer group. (See example.)

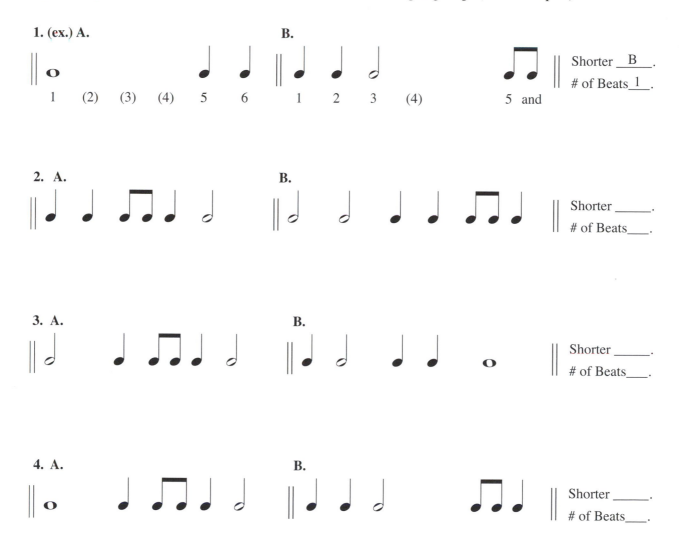

1. (ex.) A.   B.
   1 (2) (3) (4) 5 6   1 2 3 (4)   5 and   Shorter __B__.
                                            # of Beats _1_.

2. A.   B.   Shorter _____.
                              # of Beats ___.

3. A.   B.   Shorter _____.
                              # of Beats ___.

4. A.   B.   Shorter _____.
                              # of Beats ___.

CHAPTER 2 — ASSIGNMENT 2.2a
Ties and Dots

Rewrite the following rhythms, replacing all ties. (See example.)

CHAPTER 2 — ASSIGNMENT 2.2b
Ties and Dots

Rewrite the following rhythms, replacing all dotted notes with tied notes. (See example.)

CHAPTER 2 — ASSIGNMENT 2.3a
Rests in Simple Time

Name _____

Section _____

Date _____

Replace each note with the equivalent rest. (See example.)

Replace each note with the equivalent rest. (See example.)

 *Interlude 1*

"Reasons Briefly Set Down by the Author, to Persuade Everyone to Learn to Sing," by William Byrd. (Introduction to *Psalms, Sonnets, and Songs of Sadness and Piety*, 1588)

1. First it is a knowledge easily taught, and quickly learned, where there is a good master and an apt scholar.
2. The exercise of singing is delightful to nature, and good to preserve the health.
3. It strengthens all parts of the breast, and opens the pipes.
4. It is a singularly good remedy for a stuttering and stammering in the speech.
5. It is the best means to procure a perfect pronunciation, and to make a good orator.
6. It is the only way to know where nature has bestowed the benefit of a good voice; which gift is so rare, as there are not one among a thousand that has it. And in many that excellent gift is lost, because they want art to express nature.
7. For instruments there is no music whatsoever, comparable to that which is made for the voices, where the voices are good and the same, well sorted and ordered.
8. The better the voice is, the more fitting it is to honor and serve God therewith. And the voice is chiefly to be employed to that end. *Omnis spiritus laudet Dominum.*

Since singing is so good a thing,
I wish all people would learn to sing.

—*William Byrd, 1543–1623 (English composer)*

I have always been very fond of music. I would not change my little knowledge of music for a great deal. Whoever is proficient in this art is a good man, fit for all things. Hence it is absolutely necessary to have it taught in the schools. A schoolmaster must know how to sing or I shan't tolerate him. Nor must one ordain young fellows in the priesthood unless they have learned and practiced the art during their schooling.

—*Martin Luther, 1483–1546 (founder of the Lutheran church)*

The ability to sing and to read music was considered to be a part of the accomplishments of any lady or gentleman in earlier times. Much of the music of William Byrd and other composers of the time was intended for performance in informal settings in the home and at social occasions. Amateur performance (singing and playing on instruments) was an important part of our own culture well into the twentieth century. Why do you think that the practice of informal social singing has largely died out in our time? Have we lost something important to us in the process? Examine Byrd's reasons again and consider whether they may have validity today.

CHAPTER THREE
Simple Meter

 It is important that you continually practice keeping a steady tempo. Go to the Online Learning Center and click on Chapter 3. Use activity 3.1, Tapping a Steady Beat, to practice this important skill. Return to this exercise as often as necessary to improve your skills.

Establish a steady beat by clapping. Now clap louder on every other beat:

Clap Clap **Clap** Clap **Clap** Clap etc.

Accent

Sounds that are stressed (your louder claps, for example) are said to be accented. The musical symbol for an *accent* is >.

The pattern you were clapping could be notated as follows:

figure 3.1

etc.

Meter

Meter is a regular pattern of accented and unaccented beats. Most music has these regular patterns of stress, and meter can be classified by the number of beats in the pattern. There are two beats in the pattern you were clapping (one accented beat and one unaccented beat), and this meter is called *duple meter.*

Clap the following pattern:

figure 3.2

etc.

This meter is called *triple meter.*

Clap this pattern:

figure 3.3

 etc.

This is *quadruple meter.*

Bar Line

Meter is notated in music using a vertical line, called a *bar line,* across the staff:

figure 3.4

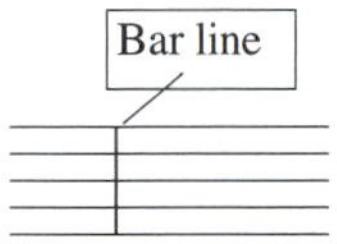

Bar lines are drawn between each group of beats in a meter:

figure 3.5

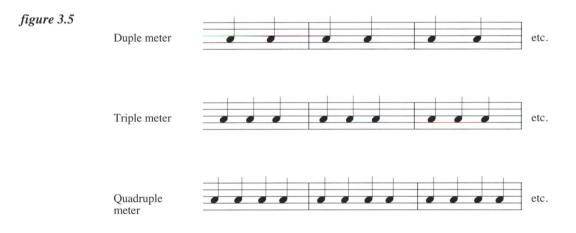

Duple meter   etc.

Triple meter   etc.

Quadruple meter   etc.

Measure

The music between two bar lines is called a *measure.*

figure 3.6

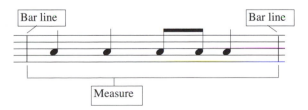

Bar lines identify the end of each measure. They are also points of reference that will help you locate specific places in the music.

Meter Signature

Meter is also indicated by a *meter signature* (or *time signature*), consisting of two numbers placed at the beginning of a piece of music:

figure 3.7

The lower number indicates a note value: 2 = half note, 4 = quarter note, 8 = eighth note, and so on. The upper number indicates the number of those note values in a measure. Study the examples in figure 3.8.

figure 3.8

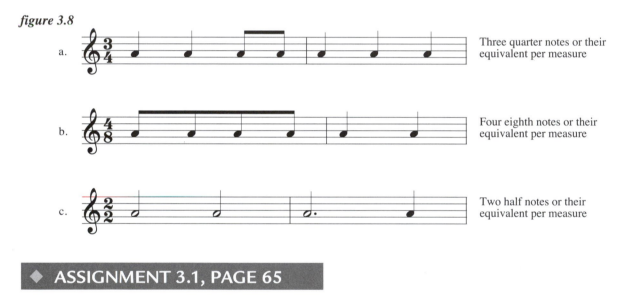

a. Three quarter notes or their equivalent per measure

b. Four eighth notes or their equivalent per measure

c. Two half notes or their equivalent per measure

◆ **ASSIGNMENT 3.1, PAGE 65**

Simple Meter

Thus far we have chosen to indicate the beat with notes without dots. As you will recall from Chapter 2, the division of these notes is in two parts, which we called simple division. Meters in which the beat is divided into two parts are called *simple meters*. In this chapter we will deal only with simple meters. You will learn about compound meters (division of the beat in three parts) in Chapter 4. The complete designation of the meters in figure 3.8 is:

  a. Triple-simple meter

  b. Quadruple-simple meter

  c. Duple-simple meter

figure 3.9

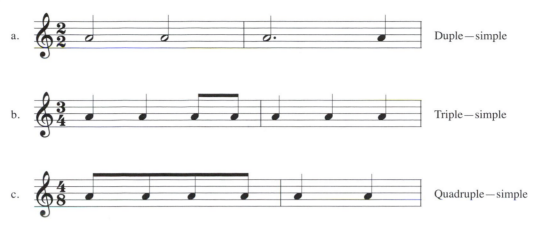

You will often see two other meter signatures: **C** to indicate $\frac{4}{4}$ meter and **¢** to indicate $\frac{2}{2}$ meter. These meter signatures are often called *common time* (**C**) and *cut time* (**¢**), but the **C** is not an abbreviation of the word "common," as is often supposed. Instead it is a holdover from a rhythmic notation system called *mensural notation,* which was in use from 1260 until 1600.

Quick Check

1. Look through the songbook and list three examples of each of the meters below:

   Duple-simple meter:

   a. _____

   b. _____

   c. _____

   Triple-simple meter:

   a. _____

   b. _____

   c. _____

   Quadruple-simple meter:

   a. _____

   b. _____

   c. _____

2. Practice some rhythms in duple-simple meter. We will choose $\frac{2}{4}$ meter since it is the most common duple-simple time. To get a feel for the stress pattern in duple-simple meter, count the beats as follows:

figure 3.10

Count: 1   (&)   2   (&)   1   &   2   &

Play example 3 and tap, play, or sing the rhythms while counting aloud.

3. Listen for the beat, then the voice saying: **"one, two, ready, go,"** and begin on the next beat.

a. 2/4

1 (&) 2   &   1   &   2   &   1   &   2 (&)   1 (&) 2 (&)

1 (&) (2) &

b. 2/4

1 (&) (2) &   1   (&) (2) &

c. 2/4

d. 2/4

(For additional practice, see Using What You Have Learned, p. 59.)
Do Ear-Training Exercises I, II, and III (p. 26) using the patterns above.

2/2 Meter

In 2/2 meter (we often say 2/2 *time*), the beat is written as a half note. Figure 3.11 shows two notations for the same rhythm, one in 2/4 meter and the other in 2/2 meter.

figure 3.11

1   (&)   2   &   1   (&)   (2)   &

1   (&)   2   &   1   (&)   (2)   &

These two rhythms will sound exactly the same in performance. Notice that half a note in $\frac{2}{2}$ time is the same duration as a quarter note in $\frac{2}{4}$ time. That relationship is constant for other note values as well. For example, quarter and eighth notes in $\frac{2}{2}$ time are the same duration as eighths and sixteenths in $\frac{2}{4}$, respectively.

Quick Check

1. Write the counting under each of the following rhythms in $\frac{2}{2}$ time, then tap, sing, or clap them, using example 3. Remember to wait for the voice counting. Now perform them again without the musical background.

(For additional practice, see Using What You Have Learned, p. 59.)
Do Ear-Training Exercises I, II, and III (p. 26) using the patterns above.

2. The following rhythms in triple-simple time are notated in $\frac{3}{4}$, the most common triple-simple meter signature. Write the counting under each rhythm and then perform them as you have the previous examples using example 4. Listen for the beat followed by the voice saying: **"One, two, three, now, ready, go,"** and begin on the next beat.

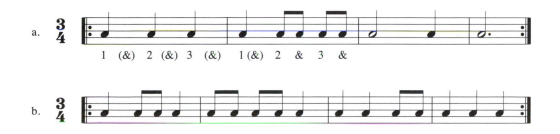

Try the patterns above without the musical background.
(For additional practice, see Using What You Have Learned, p. 59.)
Do Ear-Training Exercises I, II, and III (p. 26) using the patterns above.

 Go to the Online Learning Center and click on Chapter 3. Activity 3.2, Tapping in Triple-Simple Meter, will give you the opportunity to experience triple-simple meter. Be sure to use the number keys for this exercise.

3. Perform the following rhythms in quadruple-simple time, using example 5. These rhythms are notated in $\frac{4}{4}$ time, the most common meter signature. Listen for the beat followed by the voice saying: **"One, two, three, four, one, two, ready, go,"** and begin on the next beat. Perform the rhythms again without the musical background.

(For additional practice, see Using What You Have Learned, p. 59.)
Do Ear-Training Exercises I, II, and III (p. 26) using the patterns above.

 Go to the Online Learning Center and click on Chapter 3. Activity 3.3, Tapping in Quadruple-Simple Meter, will give you the opportunity to experience quadruple-simple meter. Be sure to use the number keys for this exercise.

The Upbeat

Rhythms do not necessarily begin on the first beat of a measure. Often you will see one or more notes before the first full measure. Such notes are referred to as an *upbeat* or *anacrusis*.

figure 3.12

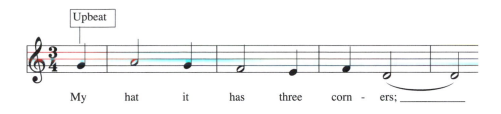

If a melody begins on an upbeat, you are likely to find similar patterns elsewhere in the melody. Usually, the final measure will be shortened by the rhythmic value of the upbeat. This allows for repetition of the melody without breaking the regularity of the meter.

figure 3.13

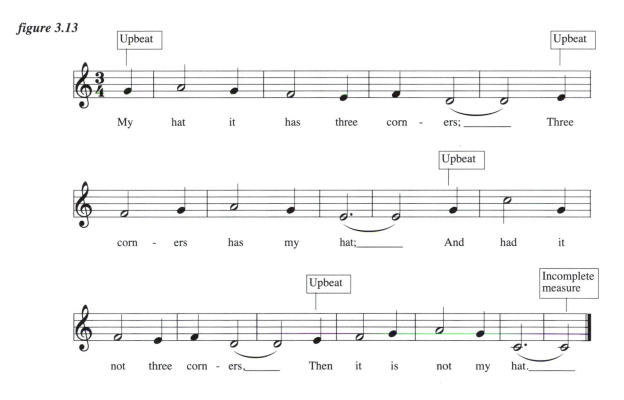

Look through the songbook to find three examples of songs that begin with upbeats.

1. _____

2. _____

3. _____

Subdivision of the Beat

Play example 6 and count with the beat as follows:

figure 3.14

Beat:

Count: 1(e & a) 2 (e & a) 3 (e & a) 4 (e & a)

You are counting the *subdivision of the beat.* The subdivision of a quarter note into four parts is notated with *sixteenth notes:*

figure 3.15

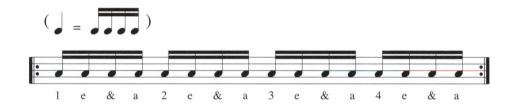

1   e   &   a   2   e   &   a   3   e   &   a   4   e   &   a

As you can see from the example above, two beams are used in groups of sixteenth notes. When they appear alone they are written with two flags:

figure 3.16

1. Write the counts below each of the following duple-simple rhythms, then tap, clap, or speak them using example 3. Remember to wait for the voice before beginning.

(For additional practice, see Using What You Have Learned, p. 59.)
Do Ear-Training Exercises I, II, and III (p. 26) using the patterns above.

The Dotted Eighth Note

The *dotted eighth note* works in much the same way as the dotted quarter note. It is equal to an eighth note tied to a sixteenth, or three sixteenth notes. Two common rhythmic patterns involving the dotted eighth are:

figure 3.17

These figures are counted:

figure 3.18

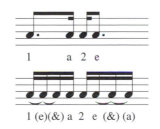

1. The following are several common rhythmic patterns involving subdivision of the beat. Practice each of these patterns using example 6. First count them and then clap or tap the rhythms.

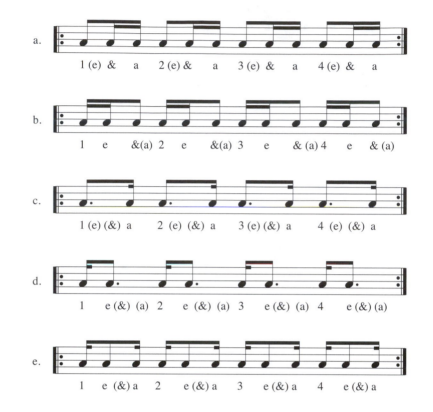

a.
1 (e) & a   2 (e) & a   3 (e) & a   4 (e) & a

b.
1   e   &(a) 2   e   &(a) 3   e   & (a) 4   e   & (a)

c.
1 (e) (&) a   2 (e) (&) a   3 (e) (&) a   4 (e) (&) a

d.
1   e (&) (a) 2   e (&) (a) 3   e (&) (a) 4   e (&) (a)

e.
1   e (&) a   2   e (&) a   3   e (&) a   4   e (&) a

2. Write the counting under each of the following triple-simple rhythms, then speak, clap, or tap them using example 4. Remember to wait for the voice before beginning.

a.
1(e)(&) a   2(e)(&)(a)3   e   &   a

b.

c.

d.

Perform these patterns again without the musical background.
Do Ear-Training Exercises I, II, and III (p. 26) using the patterns on page 56.

◆ **ASSIGNMENT 3.3, PAGE 69**

Triplets

You have learned that the beat can be divided into two parts (simple division), or into three parts (compound division). Occasionally compound divisions will occur in songs in simple meter. A compound division in simple meter is called *a triplet,* which is shown by adding the number "3" to the notated rhythm:

figure 3.19

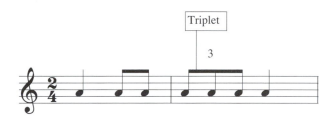

Look at "The Linden Tree" and "Lonesome Valley" in the songbook for examples of triplets. You can perform triplets easily if you remember that they are only one beat of compound time and if you count them as you would a compound division.

figure 3.20

KEY TERMS

Define the following terms in your own words:

Accent _____

Meter _____

Bar line _____

Measure _____

Meter signature _____

Duple-simple meter _____

Triple-simple meter _____

Quadruple-simple meter _____

Common time _____

Cut time _____

Upbeat _____

Subdivision _____

Sixteenth note _____

Dotted eighth note _____

Triplet _____

LISTENING

The following songs are all in simple meters. Listen to some of them and try to identify if they are duple-simple, triple-simple, or quadruple-simple. Check your perceptions by looking in the songbook. (It is often difficult to distinguish duple from quadruple, but you should work to be able to hear the distinctive difference of triple meter.)

"America the Beautiful" (p. 266, CD track 10, or the Web site)
"Barbara Ellen" (p. 268, CD track 14, or the Web site)
"Bendemeer's Stream" (p. 270, CD track 16, or the Web site)
Cantemus Hymnum (p. 272, CD track 19, or the Web site)
Dona Nobis Pacem (p. 276, CD track 22, or the Web site)
"Goodby, Old Paint" (p. 279, CD track 27, or the Web site)
"Morning Has Broken" (p. 290, CD track 40, or the Web site)
"My Bonnie" (p. 290, CD track 41, or the Web site)
"Oh, What a Beautiful Mornin' " (p. 292, CD track 43, or the Web site)
"Pat-a-Pan" (p. 295, CD track 46, or the Web site)
"Scarborough Fair" (p. 301, CD track 53, or the Web site)
"Skip to My Lou" (p. 305, CD track 62, or the Web site)
"Sweet Betsy from Pike" (p. 305, CD track 63, or the Web site)
Tumbalalaika (p. 308, CD track 68, or the Web site)
"We Shall Overcome" (p. 311, CD track 71, or the Web site)

USING WHAT YOU HAVE LEARNED

1. Practice the following examples in duple-simple meter with example 3:

2. Practice the following examples in triple-simple meter with example 4:

3. Practice the following examples in quadruple-simple meter with example 5.

4. Practice the following rhythms with sixteenth notes in duple-simple meter using example 3.

5. Look at the following songs in the songbook. Count the rhythm until you feel comfortable with it, then play the notes on a keyboard instrument, and, finally, sing the melody.

"The First Noël" (p. 278)

"Scarborough Fair" (p. 301)

"Sweet Betsy from Pike" (p. 305)

"Twinkle, Twinkle Little Star" (p. 309)

6. Write rhythms to go with examples 3, 4, and 5. Write the counting under each rhythm and speak, tap, or clap it with the appropriate exercise.

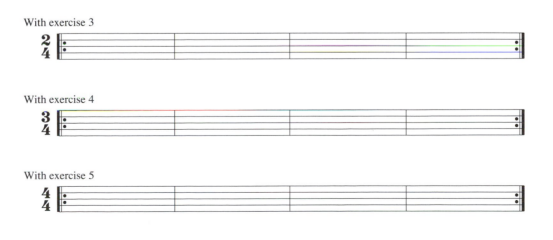

7. Copy the following excerpt from "Do-Re-Mi" by Rodgers and Hammerstein, moving the melody up one octave.

8. Copy the first four measures of "Children's Prayer" in the bass clef. You should write the melody one octave below the original.

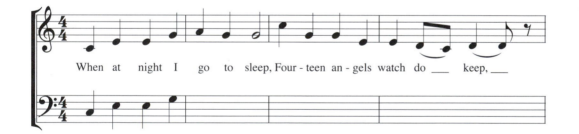

9. Copy the following excerpt from "Morning Has Broken" in the treble clef. Write the melody one octave above the original.

10. Given the rhythm on the first line, write a second rhythm that fills in all divisions of the beat. Your rhythm should have a rest for (or at least at the beginning of) each note in the original rhythm and then notes that represent each division of the beat. For example:

Represent each eighth-note division by a note on either the upper or lower staff, but not on both.

11. Play, sing, or tap the original rhythm while a friend performs the "fill-in" pattern. The result should be that the two performers never clap or tap at the same time and every division is filled. This exercise is particularly good when the original pattern has long notes or rests that often are rushed in performance.

12. Listen to several favorite pieces of music (on the radio or TV, or from your personal collection of recordings). Identify if the divisions of the beat are simple or compound. (You may use pieces you have already identified in Chapter 1 here.) Choose works in simple meter and try to identify if they are duple-simple, triple-simple, or quadruple-simple. To do this try counting "one-two," "one-two-three," and "one-two-three-four" along with the music. One of these patterns should seem more comfortable than the others. Please note that it is often difficult to distinguish duple and quadruple meters by sound. If your instructor asks, bring an example of duple, triple, and quadruple to share with the class.

 Go to the Online Learning Center and click on Chapter 3. Activity 3.4, Simple Meter Identification Activity, will test your ability to identify the meters of several recorded examples.

CHAPTER 3 — ASSIGNMENT 3.1
Counting in Simple Meter

Name _____

Section _____

Date _____

Draw the bar lines in the proper places in the following rhythms as indicated by the meter signature. Count the number of measures and write this number on the blank at the right. (See example.)

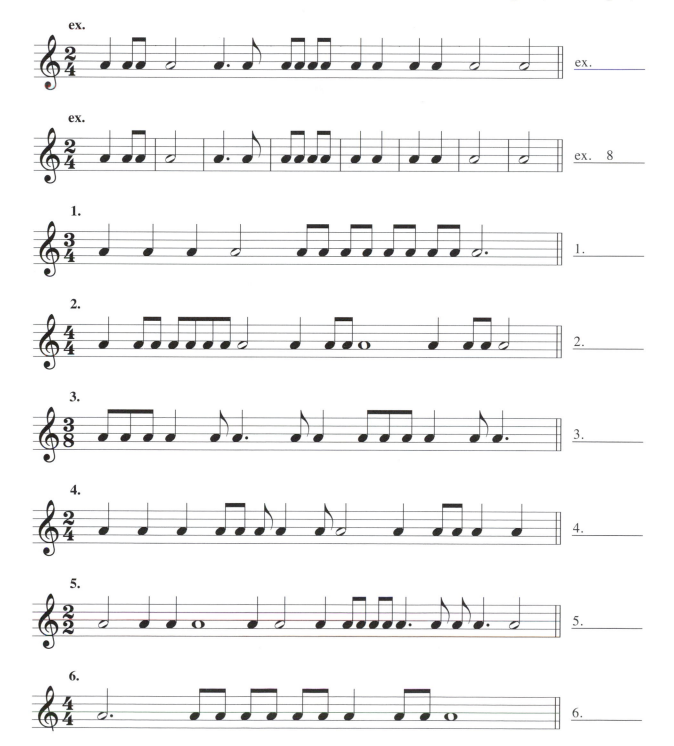

CHAPTER 3 — ASSIGNMENT 3.2a
Equivalent Notation in Simple Meters

Name _____

Section _____

Date _____

Rewrite the following rhythms in the time signatures indicated so that they will sound exactly the same as the original rhythms. (See example.)

Write rhythms in each of the following meters. Check each measure to see if it has the correct number of beats. Write the counting beneath each rhythm. (See example.)

Name _____

Section _____

Date _____

Write the correct meter signature for each of the following rhythms. There may be more than one correct answer. If so, write both meter signatures. (See example.)

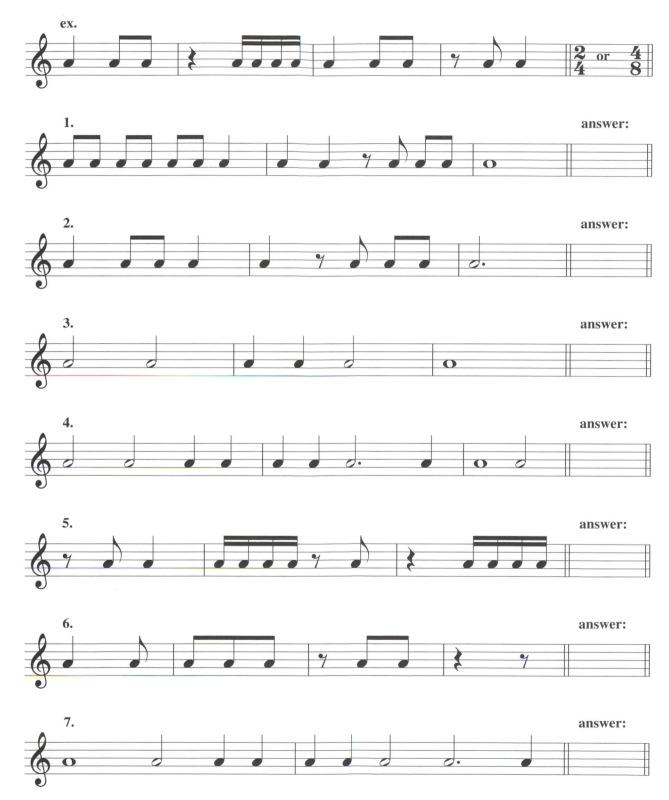

ASSIGNMENT

8.   answer:

9.   answer:

10.   answer:

CHAPTER FOUR
Compound Meter

In Chapter 2 you learned about simple and compound division of beats. In Chapter 3 we concentrated on the simple meters—meters in which the beats are divided into two parts. In this chapter you will learn about *compound meters*—meters in which the beats are divided into three parts. Compound meters have meter signatures with 6, 9, or 12 as the upper number. Examples of compound meters are: $\frac{6}{8}$, $\frac{9}{8}$, $\frac{12}{8}$, $\frac{6}{4}$, $\frac{9}{4}$, $\frac{12}{4}$, and so on. If the tempo is slow, you can count rhythms in these meters just as you learned to do in Chapter 3:

figure 4.1

In figure 4.1 the eighth note has the beat, and there are six eighth notes per measure. The song "Silent Night" is a good example of $\frac{6}{8}$ meter in a slow tempo. Listen to it and count along with the recording.

figure 4.2 "Silent Night"

As the tempo increases, we begin to sense the eighth notes as divisions of a beat that is represented by a dotted quarter note:

figure 4.3

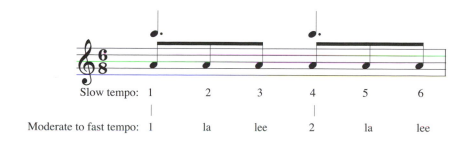

CHAPTER FOUR
Compound Meter

In Chapter 2 you learned about simple and compound division of beats. In Chapter 3 we concentrated on the simple meters—meters in which the beats are divided into two parts. In this chapter you will learn about *compound meters*—meters in which the beats are divided into three parts. Compound meters have meter signatures with 6, 9, or 12 as the upper number. Examples of compound meters are: $\frac{6}{8}$, $\frac{9}{8}$, $\frac{12}{8}$, $\frac{6}{4}$, $\frac{9}{4}$, $\frac{12}{4}$, and so on. If the tempo is slow, you can count rhythms in these meters just as you learned to do in Chapter 3:

figure 4.1

In figure 4.1 the eighth note has the beat, and there are six eighth notes per measure. The song "Silent Night" is a good example of $\frac{6}{8}$ meter in a slow tempo. Listen to it and count along with the recording.

figure 4.2 "Silent Night"

As the tempo increases, we begin to sense the eighth notes as divisions of a beat that is represented by a dotted quarter note:

figure 4.3

71

Duple-Compound Meter

Play example 7 and count the following *duple-compound* pattern, repeating it until you feel comfortable with the division of the beat.

figure 4.4

Notice that each measure has two beats (duple) and that the beat is divided into three parts (compound).

Meter signatures with 6 as the upper number indicate duple-compound meter.

The most common duple-compound meter signatures are:

figure 4.5

The $\frac{6}{8}$ meter signature is sometimes written as $\overset{2}{\raisebox{-0.5ex}{\scriptsize $\bullet$}}\!\cdot$ to show more clearly that two beats per measure are intended (figure 4.6).

figure 4.6

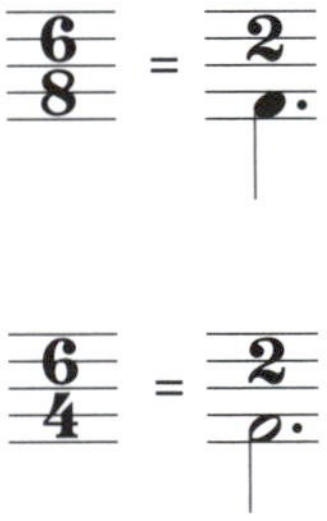

$$\frac{6}{8} = \frac{2}{\text{♩.}}$$

$$\frac{6}{4} = \frac{2}{\text{♩.}}$$

Now practice some rhythms in duple-compound time. The following patterns present a mixture of the two common duple-compound meter signatures shown in figure 4.5. Remember to count the divisions of the beat as follows:

figure 4.7

Play example 7 and tap, sing, or play the rhythms while counting aloud. Listen for the beats, then the voice saying: **"one, two, one-la-lee, two-la-lee,"** and begin on the next beat.

(For additional practice, see Using What You Have Learned, p. 79.)
Do Ear-Training Exercises I and III (p. 26) using the patterns above.

◆ ASSIGNMENT 4.1, PAGES 85–86

Triple-Compound Meter

Play example 8 and count the following *triple-compound* pattern, repeating it until you feel comfortable with the division of the beat:

figure 4.8

You can easily determine the meter signature for figure 4.8 now that you understand that it is the division of the beat that is referred to:

figure 4.9

= 9 eighth notes per measure

Meter signatures with 9 as the upper number indicate triple-compound meter.

The most common triple-compound meter signatures are:

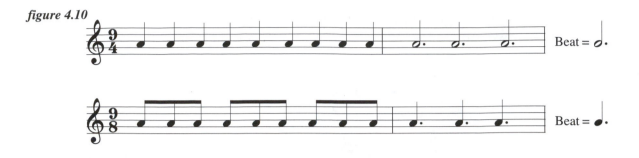

figure 4.10

Triple-compound meters are sometimes notated as in figure 4.11 to show the number of beats per measure more clearly.

figure 4.11

Now practice some rhythms in triple-compound time. The following patterns present a mixture of the two common triple-compound meter signatures shown in figure 4.10. Remember to count the divisions of the beat as follows:

figure 4.12

Quick Check

Play example 8 and tap, sing, or play the rhythms while counting aloud. Listen for the beats, then the voice saying: **"one, two, three, one-la-lee, two-la-lee, three-la-lee,"** and begin on the next beat.

(For additional practice, see Using What You Have Learned, p. 79.)
Do Ear-Training Exercises I and III (p. 26) using the patterns above.

 Go to the Online Learning Center and click on Chapter 4. Activity 4.1, Tapping in Triple-Compound Meter, will give you the opportunity to experience triple-compound meter. Be sure to use the number keys for this exercise.

◆ **ASSIGNMENT 4.2, PAGES 87–88**

Quadruple-Compound Meter

Play example 9 and count the following *quadruple-compound* pattern, repeating it until you feel comfortable with the division of the beat:

figure 4.13

It should come as no surprise that the meter signature for the pattern in figure 4.13 will have the number 12 as the upper number in the signature:

figure 4.14

= 12 eighth notes per measure

Meter signatures with 12 as the upper number indicate quadruple-compound meter.

The most common *quadruple-compound* meter signatures are:

figure 4.15

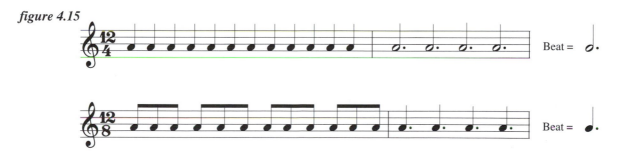

Quadruple-compound meters are sometimes notated as in figure 4.16 to show the number of beats per measure more clearly.

figure 4.16

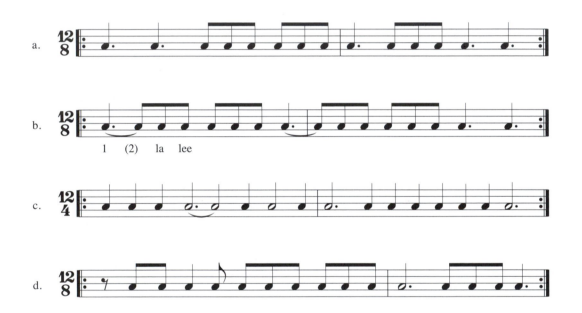

Quick Check

1. Now practice some rhythms in quadruple-compound time. Play example 9 and sing, tap, or play the rhythms while counting aloud. Listen for the beats, then the voice saying: **"one, two, three, four, one-la-lee, two-la-lee, three-la-lee, four-la-lee,"** and begin on the next beat.

a.

b.

1 (2) la lee

c.

d.

(For additional practice, see Using What You Have Learned, p. 79.)
Do Ear-Training Exercises I and III (p. 26) using the patterns above.

  Go to the Online Learning Center and click on Chapter 4. Activity 4.2, *Tapping in Quadruple-Compound Meter,* will give you the opportunity to experience quadruple-compound meter. Be sure to use the number keys for this exercise.

◆ ASSIGNMENT 4.3, PAGES 89–90

2. The most common compound meter is duple-compound time. Look through the songbook and list four examples of duple-compound meter and two of triple-compound meter in the spaces below:

Duple-compound meter:

_____

_____

_____

_____

Triple-compound meter:

_____

_____

Listen to these songs and count along with the recording.

Beaming in Simple and Compound Meters

In Chapter 2 you learned that eighth notes are beamed together within a beat (see figure 2.5, p. 23). To compare the beaming in simple and compound meters, look at figure 4.17, in which the same durations are notated in both $\frac{3}{4}$ and $\frac{6}{8}$ time.

figure 4.17

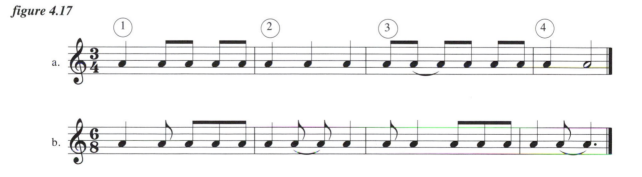

In measure 1 the four quarter notes are beamed in pairs in $\frac{3}{4}$ time to show the position of the second and third beats. They are split into a group of one and a group of three in $\frac{6}{8}$ time to show the position of the second beat of the measure (figure 4.18).

figure 4.18

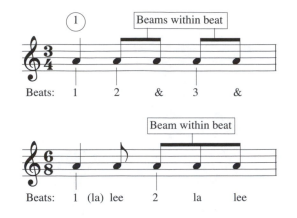

In the second measure of figure 4.17, the quarter note on the second beat in $\frac{3}{4}$ time is shown as two eighth notes tied together in $\frac{6}{8}$ because the second beat in $\frac{6}{8}$ occurs on the second eighth note, as shown in figure 4.19.

figure 4.19

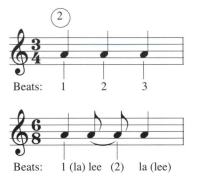

In measures 3 and 4 the changes in notation are made for the same reasons:

figure 4.20

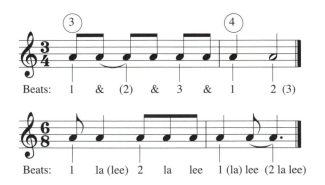

Since beaming helps the performer to keep track of the beat, it is important that you observe proper beaming when you write music.

KEY TERMS

Define the following terms in your own words:

Duple-compound meter _____

Triple-compound meter _____

Quadruple-compound meter _____

LISTENING

The following songs are all in compound meters. Listen to them and try to identify if they are duple-compound or triple-compound. Check your perceptions by looking in the songbook.

Auprès de ma Blonde (p. 267, CD track 12, or the Web site)

"Down in the Valley" (p. 277, CD track 24, or the Web site)

"I Saw Three Ships" (p. 282, CD track 31, or the Web site)

"I've Got to Know" (p. 283, CD track 33, or the Web site)

"Lavender's Blue" (p. 285, CD track 35, or the Web site)

"Over the River and Through the Wood" (p. 294, CD track 45, or the Web site)

"Row, Row, Row Your Boat" (p. 298, CD track 50, or the Web site)

"Three Blind Mice" (p. 306, CD track 64, or the Web site)

USING WHAT YOU HAVE LEARNED

1. Practice these rhythms in duple-compound time. Use example 7.

   (You can also use these rhythms for ear training.)

2. Practice these rhythms in triple-compound time. Use example 8.

3. Practice these rhythms in quadruple-compound time. Use example 9.

4. Write a rhythm to be clapped, tapped, or played on rhythm instruments along with example 7. Use $\frac{6}{8}$, $\frac{6}{4}$, or $\frac{6}{16}$ meter and make sure that your rhythm is **exactly four complete measures** in length. Perform your rhythm in class, accompanied by example 7.

5. Write a rhythm to be clapped, tapped, or played on rhythm instruments along with example 8. Use $\frac{9}{8}$, $\frac{9}{4}$, or $\frac{9}{16}$ meter and make sure that your rhythm is **exactly four complete measures** in length. Perform your rhythm in class, accompanied by example 8.

6. Write a rhythm to be clapped, tapped, or played on rhythm instruments along with example 9. Use $\frac{12}{8}$, $\frac{12}{4}$, or $\frac{12}{16}$ meter and make sure that your rhythm is **exactly four complete measures** in length. Perform your rhythm in class, accompanied by example 9.

7. Write the given notes in all octaves on the grand staff. (See example.) You should have at least four notes for each problem.

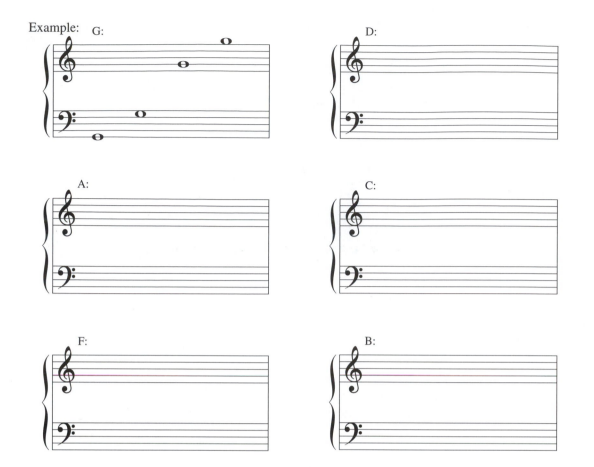

8. Copy the following excerpt from "Over the River and Through the Wood" in the treble clef. The melody should be one octave higher than shown.

Over the River and Through the Wood

9. Listen to several favorite pieces of music (on the radio or TV, or from your personal collection of recordings). Identify whether the divisions of the beat are simple or compound. (You may use pieces you have already identified in Chapter 1 here.) Choose works in compound meter and try to identify whether they are duple-simple, triple-simple, or quadruple-simple. (You may find fewer pieces in compound meter. This is generally true of most styles of Western music, particularly popular music.) To do this try counting "one-two," "one-two-three," and "one-two-three-four" along with the music. One of these patterns should seem more comfortable than the others. Please note that it is often difficult to distinguish duple and quadruple meters by sound. If your instructor asks, bring examples of duple, triple, and quadruple to share with the class.

 Go to the Online Learning Center and click on Chapter 4. Activity 4.3, Meter Identification Activity, will test your ability to identify simple and compound meters with several recorded examples

CHAPTER 4 — ASSIGNMENT 4.1a
Counting Compound Meters

Name _____

Section _____

Date _____

Draw bar lines in the correct places in the following rhythmic patterns. Count the number of measures and place the number in the blank to the right. (See example.)

Compound Meter   85

CHAPTER 4 — ASSIGNMENT 4.1b
Supply the Missing Note

Each measure in the following rhythm patterns is missing one note. Complete each measure by adding a single note. (See example.)

CHAPTER 4 — ASSIGNMENT 4.2a
Meter Classification of Songs

Name _____

Section _____

Date _____

Look at each of the following songs in the songbook. Write the meter signature, the meter classification (duple-simple, triple-compound, etc.), the note value receiving one beat, and the normal division of the beat. (See example.)

Song	Meter signature	Meter classification	Beat	Division
Auprès de ma Blonde (p. 267)	6/8	Duple - compound	♩.	♪♪♪
"Aura Lee" (p. 268)	_____	_____ - _____	_____	_____
"Barbara Ellen" (p. 268)	_____	_____ - _____	_____	_____
"Billy Boy" (p. 270)	_____	_____ - _____	_____	_____
"The Caisson Song" (p. 271)	_____	_____ - _____	_____	_____
"Down in the Valley" (p. 277)	_____	_____ - _____	_____	_____
Six Rounds in Major Keys 006 (p. 304)	_____	_____ - _____	_____	_____
Three Rounds in Minor Keys 003 (p. 307)	_____	_____ - _____	_____	_____
"When the Saints Go Marching In" (p. 311)	_____	_____ - _____	_____	_____

CHAPTER 4 — ASSIGNMENT 4.2b
Counting Compound Meters

Draw bar lines in the correct places in the following rhythm patterns. Count the number of measures and place the number in the blank to the right. (See example.)

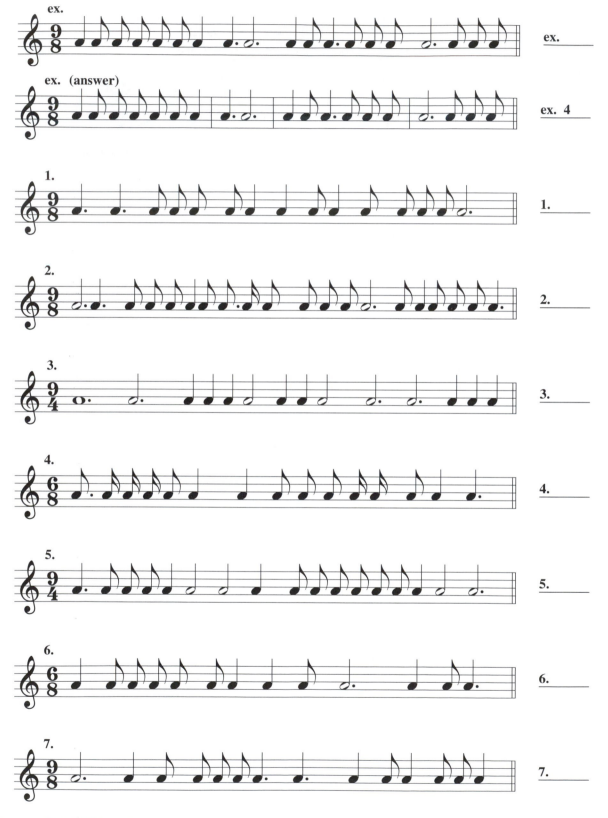

CHAPTER 4 — ASSIGNMENT 4.3a
Supply the Missing Note

Name _____

Section _____

Date _____

Each measure in the following rhythm patterns is missing one note. Complete each measure by adding a single note. (See example.)

CHAPTER 4 — ASSIGNMENT 4.3b
Meter Classification

For each of the following meter signatures list the meter classification (duple-compound, triple-simple, etc.), the note value that receives one beat, and the normal division of the beat. (See example.)

	Meter signature	Meter classification	Beat	Division
1. (ex.)	$\frac{6}{8}$	Duple - compound		
2.	$\frac{4}{2}$	_____ - _____	_____	_____
3.	$\frac{3}{8}$	_____ - _____	_____	_____
4.	$\frac{12}{8}$	_____ - _____	_____	_____
5.	$\frac{9}{4}$	_____ - _____	_____	_____
6.	$\frac{6}{2}$	_____ - _____	_____	_____
7.	$\frac{2}{8}$	_____ - _____	_____	_____
8.	$\frac{3}{2}$	_____ - _____	_____	_____
9.	$\frac{6}{4}$	_____ - _____	_____	_____

Music should never be harmless.

—*Robbie Robertson, 1943– (guitarist and songwriter)*

Pop music is ultimately a show, a circus. You've got to hit the audience with it. Punch them in the stomach, and kick them on the floor. Pop music will cease to be of any interest if it becomes too interested in musical or lyrical obscurity, because when it comes down to it, its purpose and its value is in the creation of an immediate and overwhelming excitement.

—*Peter Townshend, 1945– (composer, guitarist, and playwright)*

I think music in itself is healing. It's an explosive expression of humanity. It's something we are all touched by. No matter what culture we're from, everyone loves music.

—*Billy Joel, 1949– (pianist and songwriter)*

Musical innovation is full of danger to the State, for when modes of music change, the laws of the State always change with them. . . . The introduction of novel fashions in music is a thing to beware of as endangering the whole of society, whose most important conventions are unsettled by any revolution in that quarter.

—*Plato, 427–347 B.C.E. (Greek philosopher)*

Music is the greatest communication in the world. Even if people don't understand the language that you're singing in, they still know good music when they hear it.

—*Lou Rawls, 1933–2006 (singer)*

In what ways would Robbie Robertson and Plato agree about the power of music? In what ways would they disagree? How does music influence and shape our society? What is the effect of the "immediate and overwhelming excitement" that Townshend sees as the primary purpose of music? Would you agree with Plato that music is such a powerful force that it must be regulated for the good of society? Why or why not? Do we underestimate the power of music?

CHAPTER FIVE
The Keyboard

Look at a piano or other keyboard instrument, or at the Piano Keyboard Chart in the pocket inside the back cover of this book. Notice that there are black keys between each of the white keys except from **B** to **C** and **E** to **F**.

The Half Step

The smallest difference in pitch on the keyboard is called a *half step*. **B** to **C** and **E** to **F** are half steps, but all other half steps involve a black key.

figure 5.1

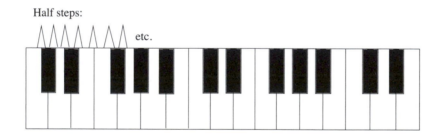

Play a number of half steps on the keyboard to become accustomed to their sound.

The Whole Step

Two half steps can be combined to form a *whole step*.

figure 5.2

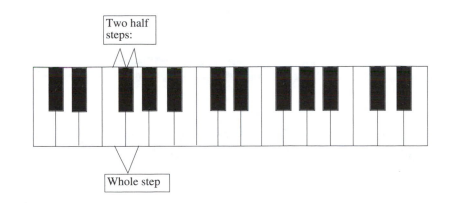

Play a number of whole steps on the keyboard to become accustomed to their sound.

The black keys are usually named for the white keys that are nearest to them, with special symbols. The three most common such symbols are the sharp sign: ♯, the flat sign: ♭, and the natural sign: ♮.

The Sharp Sign

You can notate the black key immediately to the *right* of a given white key by adding a *sharp sign* in front of the note.

figure 5.3

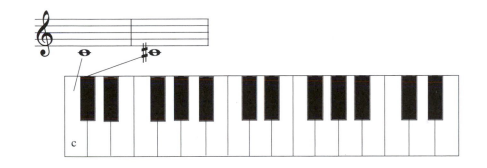

(We say "**C-sharp**" when referring to this key, but the symbol is always written to the left of the note.) **C** to **C-sharp** is a half step, so we can say that **the sharp sign raises the pitch of a note by a half step**.

A part of the melody "Do-Re-Mi" (songbook p. 276) is shown in figure 5.4.

figure 5.4

From THE SOUND OF MUSIC. Lyrics by Oscar Hammerstein II. Music by Richard Rodgers. Copyright © 1959 by Richard Rodgers and Oscar Hammerstein II. Copyright Renewed. WILLIAMSON MUSIC owner of publication and allied rights throughout the world. International Copyright Secured. All Rights Reserved.

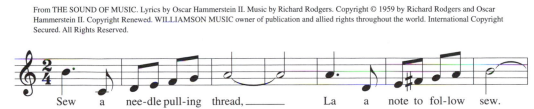

Notice the sharp sign in the sixth measure. You would play the passage this way:

figure 5.5

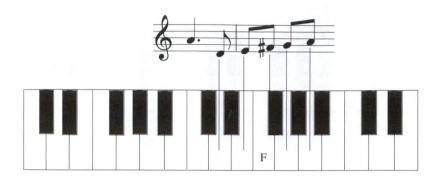

Try playing figure 5.4 on a keyboard.

The Flat Sign

You can notate the black key immediately to the *left* of a given white key by adding a *flat sign* in front of the note.

figure 5.6

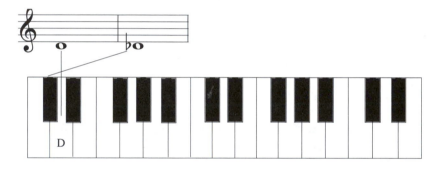

This note is named "**D-flat,**" but again, the symbol is always drawn to the left of the note. **The flat sign lowers the pitch of a note by one half step.**

A part of the Italian melody *O Sole Mio* (songbook p. 293) is shown in figure 5.7.

figure 5.7

Notice the flat sign before the **A** in the second measure. You would play this passage this way:

figure 5.8

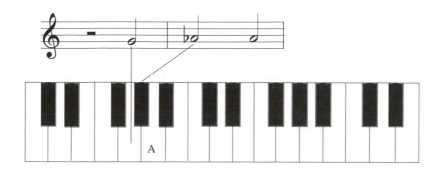

Listen to *O Sole Mio* (p. 293, CD track 44, or the Web site), and pay particular attention to the A-flats.

The Natural Sign

The *natural sign* is the symbol used to cancel the effect of a sharp or a flat.

figure 5.9

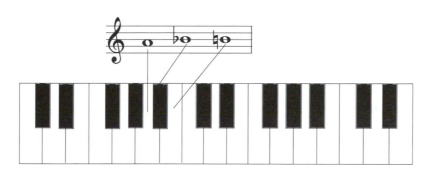

The natural sign returns a note to its original meaning. This sign is necessary because sharps, flats, and naturals apply to all notes of a given pitch that appear after them in a given measure.

figure 5.10

Thus it is necessary to cancel sharps and flats with naturals if the sharps and flats do not apply to succeeding notes in a measure.

figure 5.11

The following is a part of the famous Neapolitan boating song *Santa Lucia* (songbook p. 299).

figure 5.12

Now 'neath the sil-ver moon,   o - cean is glow- ing,   O'er the calm bil - low,

Notice the need to cancel the **F-sharp** in the sixth measure. You would play this passage thus:

figure 5.13

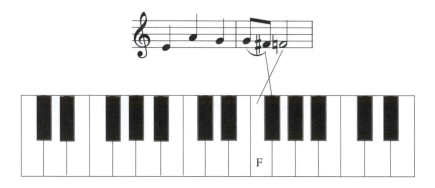

Listen to *Santa Lucia* (p. 299, CD track 51, or the Web site).

Enharmonic Equivalents

The same black key can be given two different names (**G-sharp** and **A-flat,** for example), depending on the way it is notated. Two notes that sound the same but are notated differently are said to be *enharmonic equivalents.*

figure 5.14

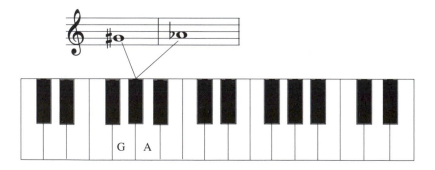

Go to the Online Learning Center and click on Chapter 5. Activity 5.1, Keyboard Note Reading, will help you to play notes accurately on the keyboard. Both white and black keys are included in this exercise.

◆ **ASSIGNMENT 5.1, PAGE 105**

Writing Sharps, Flats, and Naturals

Sharps, flats, and naturals are written immediately to the left of the note to which they apply and on the same line or space as the note itself.

figure 5.15

On the staff, sharps and naturals cover approximately three lines or spaces: the one they are centered on and those above and below.

figure 5.16

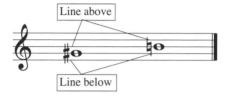

For practice, write sharp signs in front of the first four notes and natural signs in front of the last four notes. (Be sure to make them large enough; study the examples carefully.)

Flats cover the line or space above, but not the line or space below.

figure 5.17

Practice writing flat signs in front of the notes given below.

Writing Half Steps and Whole Steps

You can write half steps either as two notes of the same name or as two notes with adjacent names:

figure 5.18

Whole steps are always written as two notes of adjacent names:

figure 5.19

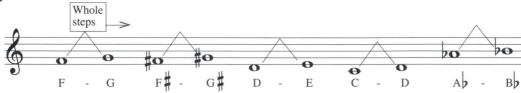

See figure 5.20. **B** to **D-flat** would not be a correctly written whole step; you would have to write the second note as **C-sharp**.

figure 5.20

◆ **ASSIGNMENT 5.2, PAGES 107–108**

The Key Signature

A *key signature* consists of one or more sharps or flats written at the beginning of each staff and which apply to all notes of a given letter name. This makes the music easier to read because the symbols do not have to be written in front of each individual note. The key signature also gives us other information about a piece, as you will learn in Chapter 6.

figure 5.21

Natural signs are used when the sharps or flats in the key signature are canceled.

figure 5.22

Sharps, flats, or naturals that cancel notes in the key signature are called *accidentals*.

It is important that you understand the following distinction: **Sharps, flats, and naturals written within a measure apply only to one pitch and not to pitches of the same name in other octaves, whereas the sharps and flats in a key signature apply to all notes of that letter name, regardless of octave.**

figure 5.23

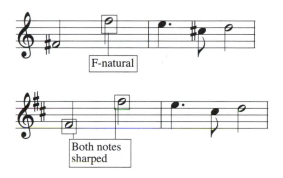

A part of the melody *Dona Nobis Pacem* (Give Us Peace) (songbook p. 276) is shown in figure 5.24.

figure 5.24

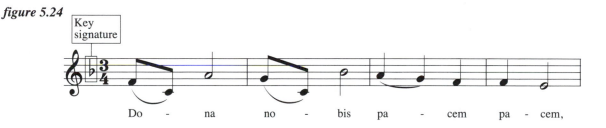

Notice the key signature of one flat on the **B** line. In the second and all other measures with **B**s in them you must remember to play or sing **B-flats**.

figure 5.25

Turn to *Dona Nobis Pacem* in the songbook, listen to the recording (p. 276, CD track 22, or the Web site), and then learn to play or sing it. This song has eight **B-flats**. Try to play them correctly on your first performance. Remembering the key signature is one of the most important skills you must learn as a musician. Playing along with the recording is excellent practice.

Quick Check

Try singing the following songs along with the recording. Next, play the notes on a keyboard, taking careful note of the accidentals in the key signature. Count out the rhythms, and when you feel confident with them, try playing the notes with the correct rhythm. Eventually, work toward singing and playing at the same time.

"Aura Lee" (p. 268, CD track 13, or the Web site)

"Wayfaring Stranger" (p. 310, CD track 70, or the Web site)

Cielito Lindo (p. 275, CD track 21, or the Web site) (Remember the **F-sharps, C-sharps,** and **G-sharps**.)

"America the Beautiful" (p. 266, CD track 10, or the Web site)

 Go to the Online Learning Center and click on Chapter 5. Activity 5.2, Pitch Pattern Matching, will test your ability to recognize pitch patterns accurately.

The Double Sharp

The *double sharp* (𝄪) is a less-common symbol that raises the pitch of a note two half steps:

figure 5.26

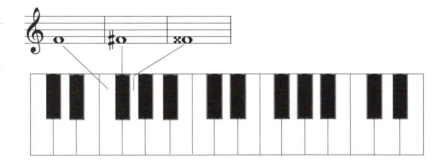

The Double Flat

Another less-common symbol is the *double flat* (𝄫), which, as you might expect, lowers the pitch of a note by two half steps:

figure 5.27

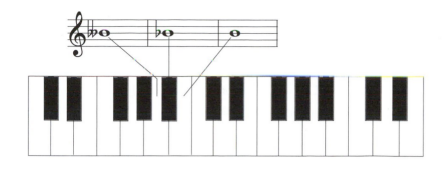

A single natural sign will cancel a double flat or double sharp just as it cancels a flat or a sharp.

The double sharp and double flat are not used in your songbook and we will not emphasize them here. This material is presented for reference only, and in case you should encounter these symbols in other music.

Quick Check

Listen to the following songs, which contain accidentals. Follow along in the songbook and sing or play the melody along with the recording.

"Greensleeves" (p. 280, CD track 28, or the Web site)

"It Came Upon the Midnight Clear" (p. 282, CD track 32, or the Web site)

KEY TERMS

Define the following terms in your own words:

Half step _____

Whole step _____

Sharp sign _____

Flat sign _____

Natural sign _____

Enharmonic equivalent _____

Accidental _____

LISTENING

Look at the following songs in the songbook. These songs include both simple and compound meters and may involve accidentals and key signatures. Play the recording and then sing the melody.

Count the rhythm until you feel comfortable with it, then put the rhythm with the pitches. As you improve, try to play the song on a keyboard and sing at the same time.

Auprès de ma Blonde (p. 267, CD track 12, or the Web site)
"Down in the Valley" (p. 277, CD track 24, or the Web site)
"Greensleeves" (p. 280, CD track 28, or the Web site)
"I Saw Three Ships" (p. 282, CD track 31, or the Web site)
"It Came Upon the Midnight Clear" (p. 282, CD track 32, or the Web site)
"Oh, What a Beautiful Mornin'" (p. 292, CD track 43, or the Web site)
"Over the River and Through the Wood" (p. 294, CD track 45, or the Web site)
"Silent Night" (p. 302, CD track 54, or the Web site)

USING WHAT YOU HAVE LEARNED

1. Perform the following rhythms with the recorded examples. (The relevant example is indicated with each rhythm.) After you have performed them with the CD, try performing without the CD. Feel the beat internally by imagining the sound of the recording as you perform the rhythms. (You can also use these rhythms for ear training.)

2. Write enharmonic equivalents for each of the following notes. The first example is completed as an example.

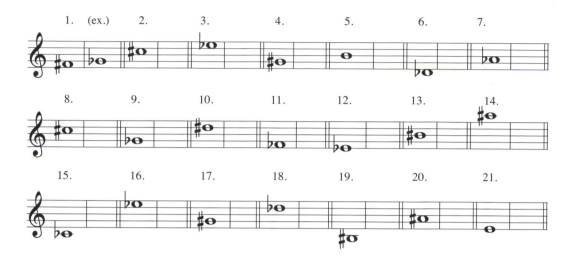

 Go to the Online Learning Center and click on Chapter 5. There are two creative activities here that you will find enjoyable and instructive. Activity 5.3, Blues Improv—Blueberry Jam, is a fun activity that allows you to apply your new knowledge of pitch patterns in a blues-jazz musical context. Activity 5.4, Funky Black Key Improv—Blackberry Jam, is an improvisation activity in which you use the black keys to improvise against a funk accompaniment.

CHAPTER 5 — ASSIGNMENT 5.1
Enharmonic Notation

Name _____

Section _____

Date _____

Write each of the indicated black keys, first as a sharp and then as a flat. (See example.)

ex.

1.

2.

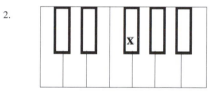 

3.

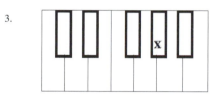 

4.

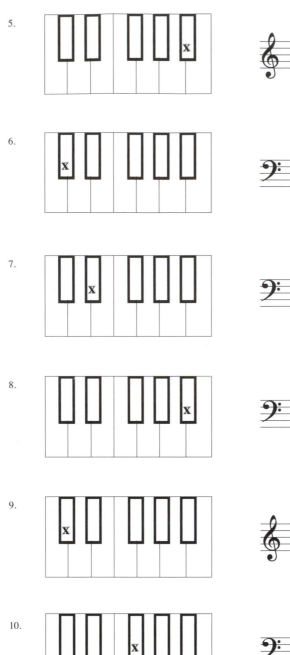

5.

6.

7.

8.

9.

10.

CHAPTER 5—ASSIGNMENT 5.2a
Writing Whole and Half Steps Above

Name _____

Section _____

Date _____

Write whole or half steps as requested above each of the following notes. There may be more than one correct answer.

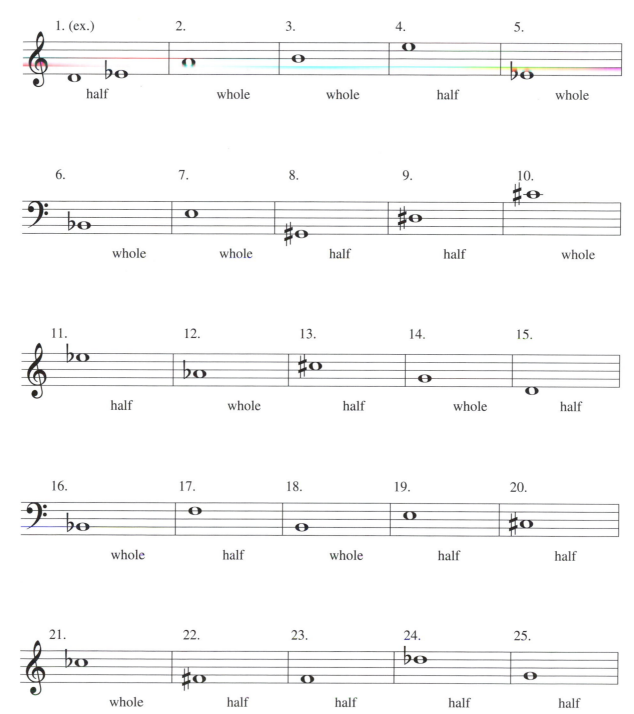

CHAPTER 5 — ASSIGNMENT 5.2b
Writing Whole and Half Steps Below

Write whole or half steps as requested below each of the following notes. There may be more than one correct answer.

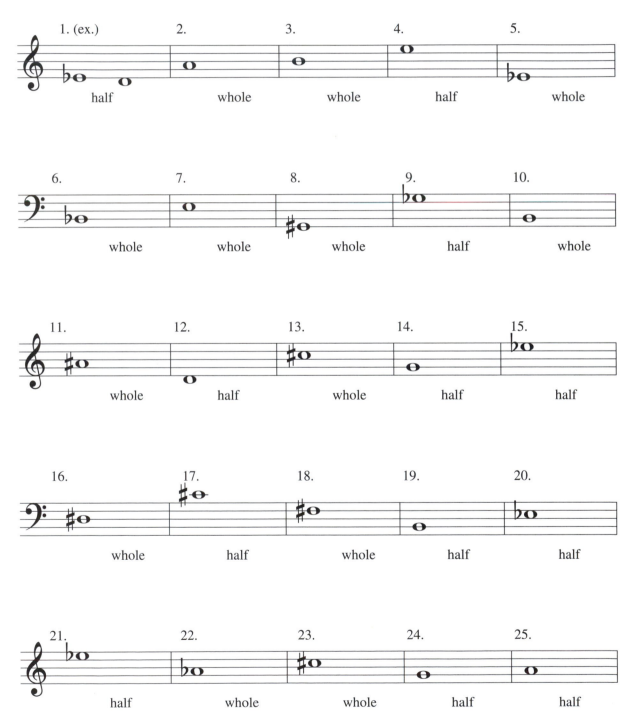

CHAPTER SIX
Major Scales/ Major Keys

"For we hold that the voice follows a natural law in its motion, and does not place the intervals at random."

—*Aristoxenus,* Harmonic Elements, *ca. 330 B.C.E.*

Major Scales

To understand how pitches are organized in music, you must understand scales. A *scale* is a collection of pitches arranged in order from lowest to highest (or from highest to lowest) pitch. The most common scale in Western music is the *major scale,* which you can hear by playing the white keys beginning and ending with **C**.

figure 6.1

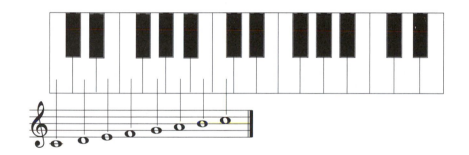

To see how the major scale is used in music, examine "Three Blind Mice" on page 306 of the songbook. Refresh your memory by playing the recording (CD track 64, or the Web site).

You can think of a scale as a summary of the pitch material of a piece of music, arranged in order from the lowest to the highest pitches. To find the scale, first list all the pitches in "Three Blind Mice," starting with the last pitch.

figure 6.2

The last pitch is middle **C**. Place middle C on a staff and continue listing the pitches in order, moving up. It is not necessary to list pitches more than once. Figure 6.3 shows the resulting list of pitches, or the pitch collection for "Three Blind Mice."

figure 6.3

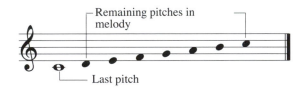

As you can see, the pitch collection is the major scale (compare figures 6.1 and 6.3), and we say that "Three Blind Mice" is in the key of C major.

The Tonic

The beginning (and ending) point of a scale is the *tonic* or *keynote*. The tonic is the resting point in the scale and will generally be found as the final note of a melody. The tonic of "Three Blind Mice" is **C** (the final note).

Half Steps and Whole Steps in the Major Scale

Observe the pattern of half and whole steps in the major scale:

figure 6.4

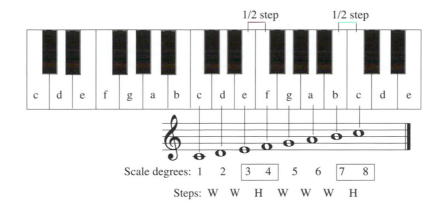

Scale degrees: 1   2   [3   4]   5   6   [7   8]

Steps: W   W   H   W   W   W   H

The major scale has half steps between the third and fourth and the seventh and eighth scale degrees and whole steps between the other scale degrees.

Diatonic Scales

Notice in figure 6.4 that the scale contains one note of each letter name. The major scale is one of the *diatonic scales,* which have *one and only one* note with each letter name. (The eighth scale degree, which duplicates the first scale degree, is the beginning of the next octave of the scale.)

The diatonic scales are a family of scales consisting of whole steps and half steps arranged in the order of the piano's white keys.

Turn to "Simple Gifts" and play the recording of this traditional melody (p. 302, CD track 55, or the Web site). Follow the same procedure for forming the scale as we did with "Three Blind Mice." Notice the last pitch of the song, shown in figure 6.5.

figure 6.5

Below is the pitch collection for this song.

figure 6.6

Because the tonic is **F** (the last note of the melody), start the scale on **F** and list the other pitches in order above it. Notice that **E** and the upper **F** will be written an octave above their position in the melody, and the pitch **D** is added in spite of the fact that it never appears in the melody.

figure 6.7

missing from
melody

A melody may or may not contain all the tones of the scale, and tones may have to be moved up or down octaves to form the scale. An analysis of the whole and half steps reveals that the pattern is the same as in "Three Blind Mice" (half steps between 3-4 and 7-8). "Simple Gifts" is based on the F major scale, and we say that the melody is *in the key of F major.*

figure 6.8

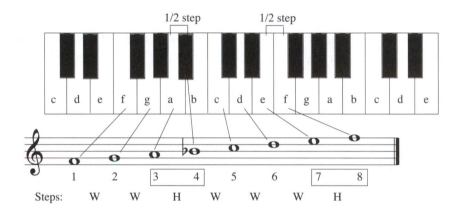

Other Major Scales

Musicians use different major scales to place songs in comfortable singing ranges and to provide tonal variety. You can form the major scale pattern on any pitch by observing the pattern of half and whole steps. In the example below, the D major scale is formed by adding two sharps to form the half steps between 3-4 and 7-8.

figure 6.9

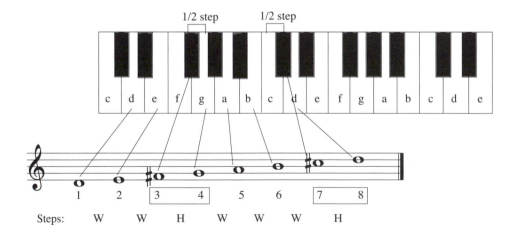

◆ **ASSIGNMENT 6.1, PAGES 123–124**

Key Signatures for Major Scales

To avoid writing the sharps or flats each time they occur in a composition, musicians write them as a *key signature*. (See Chapter 5, p. 98.)

figure 6.10

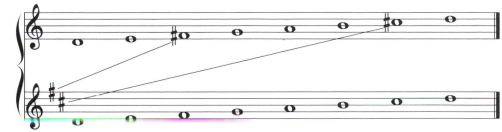

The sharps and flats in key signatures are always written in the same order on the staff:

Sharps: F♯ C♯ G♯ D♯ A♯ E♯ B♯

Flats: B♭ E♭ A♭ D♭ G♭ C♭ F♭

Thus, if a key signature has four sharps, they will be **F, C, G,** and **D**. If a key signature has three flats, they will be **B, E,** and **A**. Notice that the order of flats is exactly the reverse of the order of the sharps.

Each major scale has its own key signature. Figure 6.11 shows all the major scales and their key signatures. The standard keyboard fingerings are included on each scale, assuming the right hand is playing in the treble clef and the left hand is playing in the bass clef.

figure 6.11

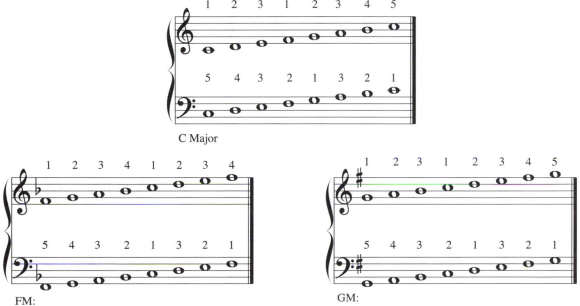

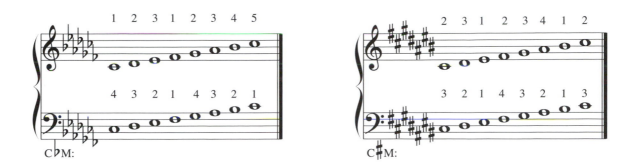

The Circle of Fifths

The *circle of fifths,* shown in figure 6.12, is a convenient device for memorizing the key signatures of the major scales. The chart is organized with C major at the top and the sharp keys in order moving clockwise. The flat keys appear in order moving counterclockwise. Notice that near the bottom of the circle, three keys are enharmonic with each other. This chart is complete for the major scales. In Chapter 8 we will add the minor scales to the circle.

figure 6.12

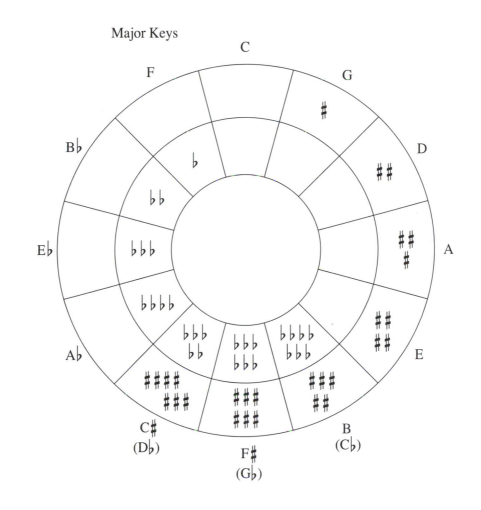

◆ **ASSIGNMENT 6.2, PAGES 125–128**

Determining the Key from a Key Signature

Here is an easy way to determine the major scale implied by a given key signature:

1. In key signatures with sharps, the tonic of the scale is located a half step above the last sharp to the right. (The last sharp is the seventh scale degree.)

figure 6.13

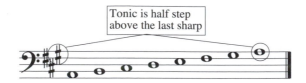

Tonic is half step above the last sharp

2. In key signatures with flats, the tonic is the next to last flat in the key signature. (The last flat is the fourth scale degree.)

figure 6.14

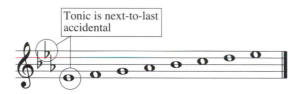

Tonic is next-to-last accidental

3. All flat keys have tonics with flats (e.g., **B-flat, E-flat,** etc.), *except* the key of **F**. Since F major has only one flat in its key signature, there is no "next to last flat," so you will need to remember this exception to 2 above. (**B-flat** *is* the fourth scale degree of F major.)

 Go to the Online Learning Center and click on Chapter 6. Activity 6.1, Key Signature Identification Activity—Major Keys, asks you to construct a circle-of-fifths graphic to demonstrate your knowledge of the major scales.

The Dominant

There are forty-eight notes in the song "Three Blind Mice" (page 306 in the songbook). The list below shows the number of times each tone occurs in the melody.

figure 6.15

	C	D	E	F	G	A	B	
Number of occurrences:	13	3	5	5	13	3	6	= 48 notes

The fifth scale degree (**G**) is as common as the tonic in the song. The fifth scale degree is usually very important even if it occurs less often than other scale degrees. For that reason, it is called the *dominant.* The tonic and the dominant are the two foundation tones of music based on major scales. These two pitches will guide you as you improve your skills in reading music.

Solfeggio

The solfeggio syllables (Do–Sol = tonic to dominant) are a convenient system for keeping the tonic and dominant in mind when singing. These names for the tones of the scale were invented perhaps as early as the eleventh century and have served musicians well for nearly 800 years. Figure 6.16 shows the names for the tones in the C major scale.

figure 6.16

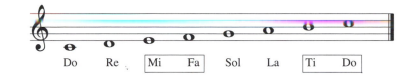

An alternative system for keeping the tonic and dominant in mind uses scale degree numbers (1–5 = tonic to dominant). If you are working in a class, your instructor may have a preference for one system or the other.

figure 6.17

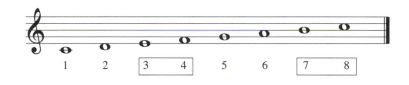

Before singing any melody based on a major scale, you will find it helpful to sing the scale on solfeggio syllables or numbers followed by the tonic and dominant tones. Then sing the melody, using the syllables or numbers. Singers, in particular, find that these reference points help them to keep the pitch relationships of the scale in mind. Pitch is a rather abstract thing to remember, and the labels (syllables or numbers) make the relationships more concrete. Instrumentalists have fewer difficulties because the instruments themselves provide a frame of reference. Sing "Three Blind Mice" several times, using solfeggio syllables or numbers until you feel comfortable with them. Now sing "Morning Has Broken" on page 290 using solfeggio syllables or numbers. (This melody is also in C major.)

Quick Check

1. Sing the following melodies in C major using solfeggio syllables or numbers. Sing the major scale and the tonic and dominant as a warm-up.

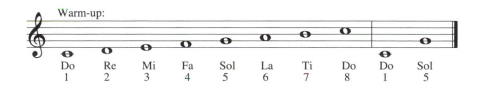

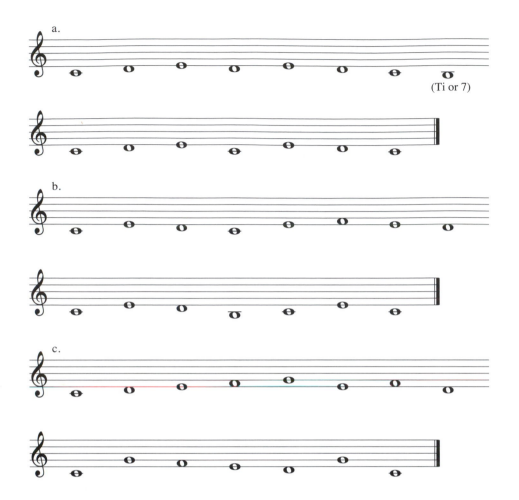

(Ti or 7)

a.

b.

c.

2. Play example 1. Sing the following melodies using the solfeggio syllables or numbers. Example 1 has the complete major scale in each sixteen-beat group:

| Do | Do | Re | Re | Mi | Mi | Fa | Fa | Sol | Sol | La | La | Ti | Ti | Do | Do |
| 1 | 1 | 2 | 2 | 3 | 3 | 4 | 4 | 5 | 5 | 6 | 6 | 7 | 7 | 8 | 8 |

Wait for the beginning of the pattern before singing.

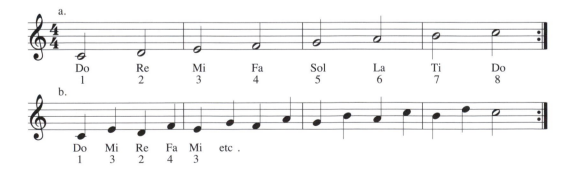

a.

| Do | Re | Mi | Fa | Sol | La | Ti | Do |
| 1 | 2 | 3 | 4 | 5 | 6 | 7 | 8 |

b.

| Do | Mi | Re | Fa | Mi | etc. |
| 1 | 3 | 2 | 4 | 3 | |

3. Play example 2. This example in duple-compound meter has the major scale in reverse order, starting with the upper tonic and descending:

Do	Do	Ti	Ti	La	La	Sol	Sol	Fa	Fa	Mi	Mi	Re	Re	Do
8	8	7	7	6	6	5	5	4	4	3	3	2	2	1

Listen for the beginning of a pattern and sing the following melodies:

KEY TERMS

Define the following terms and concepts in your own words:

Scale _____

Major scale _____

Tonic/Keynote _____

Diatonic scale _____

Key signature _____

Circle of fifths _____

Dominant _____

Solfeggio _____

LISTENING

Listen to the following songs. All of these songs are in major keys. Follow along in the songbook and play or sing the melody with the recording.

"Battle Hymn of the Republic" (p. 269, CD track 15, or the Web site)

Cielito Lindo (p. 275, CD track 21, or the Web site)

"The First Noël" (p. 278, CD track 25, or the Web site)

"I Never Will Marry" (p. 281, CD track 30, or the Web site)

"The Linden Tree" (p. 286, CD track 36, or the Web site)

"Lonesome Valley" (p. 288, CD track 37, or the Web site)

"The Riddle Song" (p. 298, CD track 49, or the Web site)

Santa Lucia (p. 299, CD track 51, or the Web site)

"Saturday Night" (p. 300, CD track 52, or the Web site)

"Silent Night" (p. 302, CD track 54, or the Web site)

USING WHAT YOU HAVE LEARNED

1. Below are more rhythms in simple and compound meters for you to perform. Try performing these rhythms without the recorded support, but if you are unsure of the beat, use the recording. Remember to count several measures to establish the tempo before you begin. The relevant example is indicated in each case. (You can also use these rhythms for ear training.)

a. (example 3)

b. (example 5)

c. (example 7)

d. (example 8)

e. (example 3)

f. (example 7)

g. (example 9)

2. Thus far we have been singing only one melody at a time. In music you will often hear several melodies (or *parts*) at the same time. A good way to practice singing in more than one part is to sing rounds. (For this activity you will need to recruit several classmates or friends.)

Turn to "Three Blind Mice" on page 306 of the songbook. First determine the key (C major in this case) and practice singing the scale with solfeggio or numbers. Sing the song together using syllables or numbers. Now divide into two groups. One group begins singing "Three Blind Mice" using either words, solfeggio, or numbers. When the first group reaches number 2 in the fifth measure, the next group begins singing at the beginning. When a group reaches the end of the song, they may start again at the beginning.

When you can sing the round in two parts comfortably, you can sing a four-part version by dividing into four groups and having each new group enter when the previous group reaches number 2. This will create quite a full choral sound if each group can maintain good pitches and rhythms.

Other rounds in major keys include: "Are You Sleeping" on page 266, *Dona Nobis Pacem* on page 276, "Row, Row, Row Your Boat" on page 298, "Six Rounds in Major Keys" on page 303, and "White Coral Bells" on page 312. Sing these rounds in the manner described above.

Try to find favorite pieces that are in major keys. To do this, first identify the tonic. It is often the final note in a melody or the tone that "sticks in your head" after the piece is over. When you have identified the tonic, see if you can sing a major scale from that tone. Do the scale tones seem to fit most of the music? If so, the piece is likely in a major key. If your instructor asks, bring an example of music in a major key to class to share with other class members.

 Go to the Online Learning Center and click on Chapter 6. Activity 6.2, Scale-Building Activity—Major Keys, assists you in building major scales in all the keys.

Determining the Major Key and Scale

Name _____

Section _____

Date _____

Determine the key for each of the following songs by first forming the scale as described on page 110.

1. "Aura Lee":

Pitch collection:

Scale:

Key: _____

2. "I Never Will Marry":

Pitch collection:

Scale:

Key: _____

3. Cielito Lindo:

Pitch collection:

Scale:

Key: _____

CHAPTER 6 — ASSIGNMENT 6.1b
Determining the Major Key and Scale

Determine the key for each of the following songs by first forming the scale as described on page 110.

1. "Barbara Ellen":

Pitch collection:

Scale:

Key: _____

2. "Billy Boy":

Pitch collection:

Scale:

Key: _____

3. "The Caisson Song":

Pitch collection:

Scale:

Key: _____

CHAPTER 6 — ASSIGNMENT 6.2a
Major Scales on the Keyboard

Name _____

Section _____

Date _____

1. Mark the tones of a major scale on the keyboard, starting on the key marked with an "X."

2. Write the scale on the staff provided, using accidentals. (Remember that there must be only one of each letter name in the scale.)

3. Write the proper key signature for the scale on the second staff. (See example.)

(For reference, the key signatures of seven sharps and seven flats are shown in both treble and bass staves.)

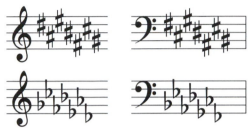

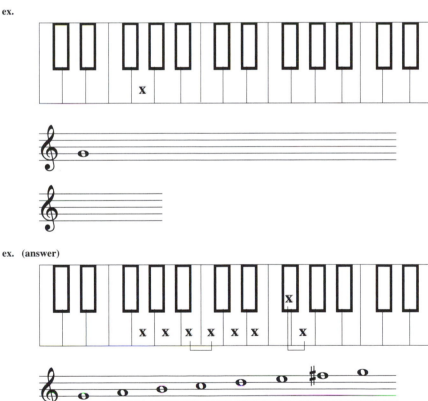

ex.

ex. (answer)

1.

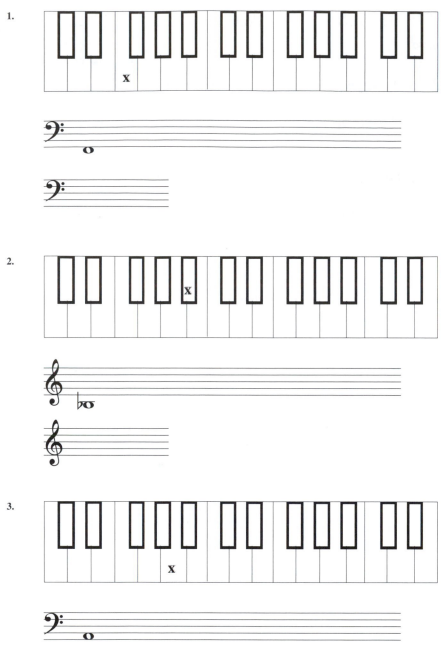

2.

3.

ASSIGNMENT 6.2a (continued)

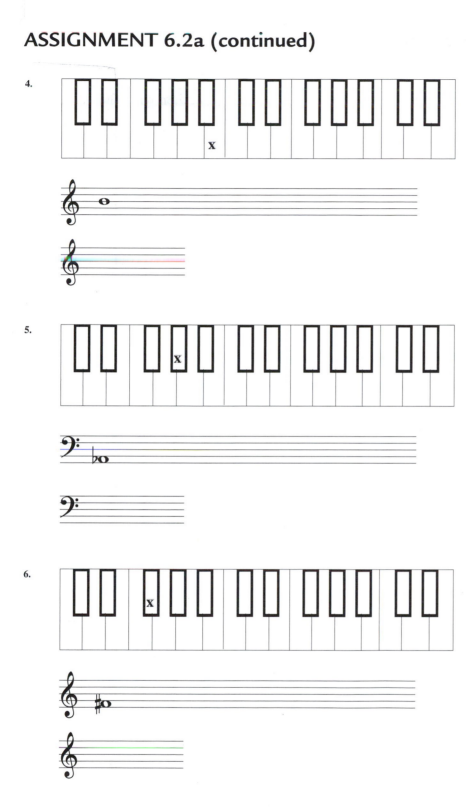

Major Scales on the Keyboard

Write the proper key signature for each of the following major scales, and then write the scale. (See example.)

1. (ex.) E major

2. D♭ major

3. C♯ major

4. E♭ major

5. B♭ major

6. D major

7. D♭ major

8. A♭ major

9. G♭ major

CHAPTER 6 — ASSIGNMENT 6.3a
Major Key Signatures—Tonic and Dominant

Name _____

Section _____

Date _____

Name the major key for each of the following key signatures and write the tonic and dominant on the staff. (See example.)

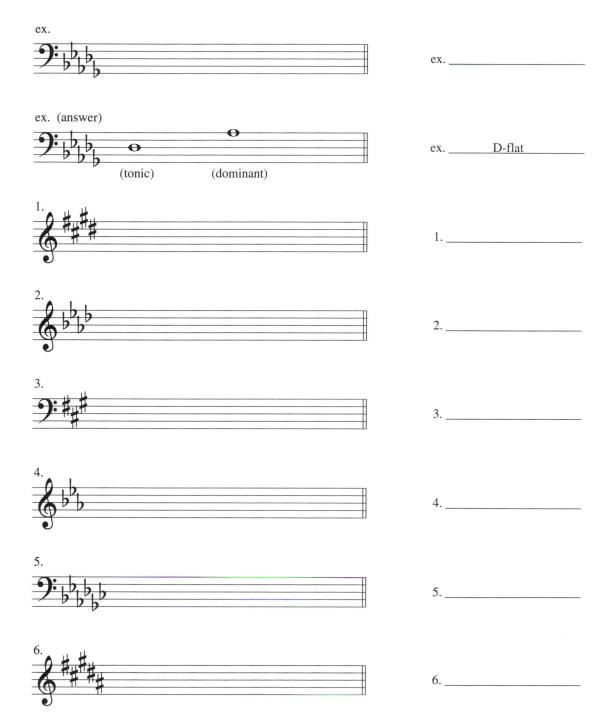

ex. _____

ex. (answer)

(tonic)   (dominant)

ex. _____ D-flat _____

1. _____

2. _____

3. _____

4. _____

5. _____

6. _____

CHAPTER 6 — ASSIGNMENT 6.3b
Writing Key Signatures for Major Keys

Write the key signature for each of the following major scales. (See example.)

ex.
G major

1.
E-flat major

9.
F major

2.
F-sharp major

10.
D major

3.
G-flat major

11.
E major

4.
C-sharp major

12.
A major

5.
A-flat major

13.
B major

6.
D-flat major

14.
G major

7.
C-flat major

15.
C major

8.
B-flat major

16.
A major

Music is the universal language of mankind.

—*Henry Wadsworth Longfellow, 1807–1882 (poet)*

The language of tones belongs equally to all mankind, and melody is the absolute language in which the musician speaks to every heart.

—*Richard Wagner, 1813–1883 (German composer)*

Music is forever; music should grow and mature with you, following you right on up until you die.

—*Paul Simon, 1941– (singer and songwriter)*

Meaning and communication cannot be separated from the cultural context in which they arise. Apart from the social situation there can be neither meaning nor communication. An understanding of the cultural and stylistic presupposition of a piece of music is absolutely essential to the analysis of its meaning.

—*Leonard B. Meyer, 1918– (American music psychologist)*

There are more love songs than anything else. If songs could make you do something we'd all love one another.

—*Frank Zappa, 1940–1993 (composer)*

Do you agree with Longfellow that music is a "universal language"? How would you respond to Leonard B. Meyer's claim that all meaning arises within a given cultural context? Is Wagner's "melody" an "absolute language that speaks to every heart"? Imagine a conversation between Paul Simon and Frank Zappa.

CHAPTER SEVEN
Intervals

The distance (or relationship) between any two tones is called an *interval.* Intervals are named for the number of diatonic notes (notes with *different* letter names) that can be contained within them. For example, the whole step **G** to **A** contains only two diatonic notes (**G** and **A**) and hence is called a *second.*

figure 7.1

The following chart shows all the interval numbers within an octave:

figure 7.2

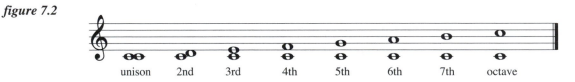

Intervals and Scale Degrees

Notice in figure 7.2 that the interval numbers correspond to the scale degree numbers for the major scale. The interval consisting of two notes of the same pitch is often called the *unison* (see figure 7.2). The other interval names are second, third, fourth, and so on up to octave. Remember that the term *octave* refers to the number 8 (its interval number).

figure 7.3

Quick Check

Below is a part of the melody *Dona Nobis Pacem*. Name the interval numbers between each of the notes in this melody. To do this, look at groups of two notes and count from the lower note up to the higher note regardless of their order in the melody. Notice, for example, that the first interval in *Dona Nobis Pacem* is identified as a fourth, which you find by counting all the notes from middle **C** up to **F**: **C, D, E, F.**

Dona Nobis Pacem

Specific Qualities of Intervals

Intervals are given a second, more specific, name depending on their quality. There are two basic qualities of intervals: *perfect intervals* and *major intervals*.

Perfect Intervals

The intervals from the tonic (keynote) up to the fourth and fifth scale degrees of a major scale are called *perfect*.

figure 7.4

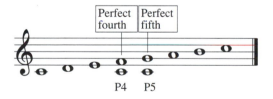

In addition, the unison and the octave are called *perfect*.

figure 7.5

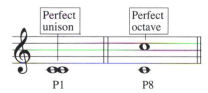

Notice the standard abbreviation for the intervals in figures 7.4 and 7.5. P1 = perfect unison; P4 = perfect fourth; P5 = perfect fifth; and P8 = perfect octave. To write a perfect interval above any note, consider that note to be the tonic of a major scale and write the correct scale degree (1, 4, 5, or 8) above that note.

figure 7.6

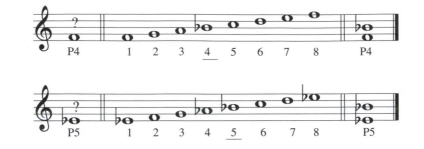

Major Intervals

The intervals from the tonic (keynote) up to the second, third, sixth, and seventh scale degrees of a major scale are called *major.*

figure 7.7

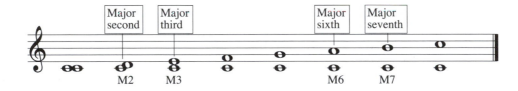

Notice the standard abbreviation for the major intervals: M2 = major second; M3 = major third; M6 = major sixth; M7 = major seventh. To write a major interval above any note, consider that note to be the tonic of a major scale and write the correct scale degree (2, 3, 6, or 7) above that note.

figure 7.8

◆ ASSIGNMENT 7.1, PAGES 143–144

Minor Intervals

When a major interval is made one half step smaller, it becomes a minor. This can be done by either raising the bottom tone or lowering the top tone:

figure 7.9

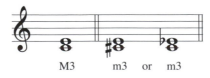

Only major intervals can become minor.

Identify the given intervals as perfect, major, or minor:

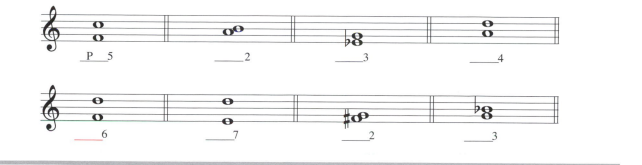

Writing Intervals Below a Given Note

You can write an interval below a given note in several ways. One possibility is to consider the given note as the proper scale degree of some major scale and write the tonic of that scale. For example, to write a major third below **G,** consider **G** to be the third scale degree of a major scale and write the tonic of the scale:

figure 7.10

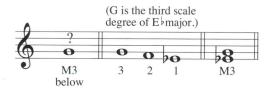

For another way of writing intervals below a given note, go to Appendix 1, page 243.

1. Write the indicated intervals below the given note.

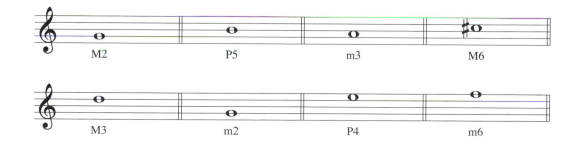

2. Below is the same excerpt from *Dona Nobis Pacem* as on page 133, with the proper interval numbers given for each interval. (This will be a good opportunity to check the accuracy of your previous work in identifying the interval numbers.) Now add the proper designation ("M," "m," or "P") to indicate the precise size of each interval. (The first three intervals are completed as an example.)

Dona Nobis Pacem

The Augmented Fourth and Diminished Fifth

We now have a specific interval name for all interval relationships but one. This is the interval that lies between the perfect fourth and the perfect fifth.

figure 7.11

This interval is called either an *augmented fourth* or a *diminished fifth,* depending on its notation (see figure 7.12). The term *augmented* means "made larger," while *diminished* means "made smaller." (Augmented is abbreviated: "A"; and diminished is abbreviated: "d.")

figure 7.12

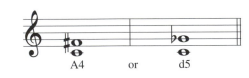

This interval divides the octave into two equal parts:

figure 7.13

The augmented fourth and diminished fifth are both usually called the *tritone* because each contains three whole steps.

figure 7.14

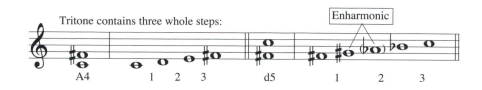

Summary of Common Intervals

Figure 7.15 summarizes the common intervals in this chapter. The chart shows the number of half steps contained in each interval.

figure 7.15

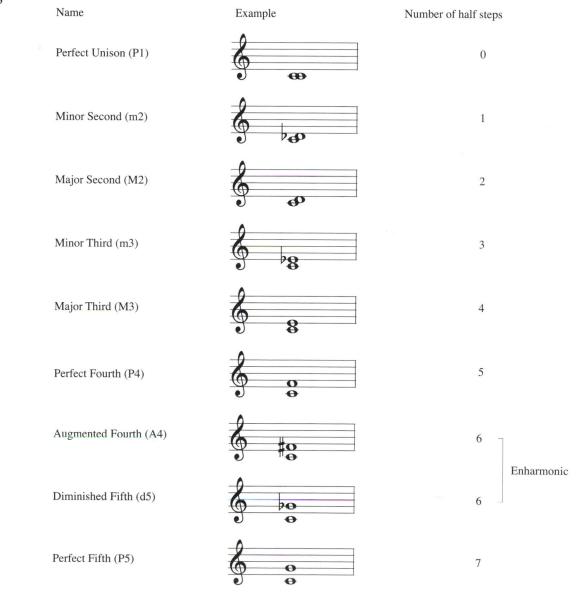

Name	Example	Number of half steps
Perfect Unison (P1)		0
Minor Second (m2)		1
Major Second (M2)		2
Minor Third (m3)		3
Major Third (M3)		4
Perfect Fourth (P4)		5
Augmented Fourth (A4)		6
Diminished Fifth (d5)		6
Perfect Fifth (P5)		7

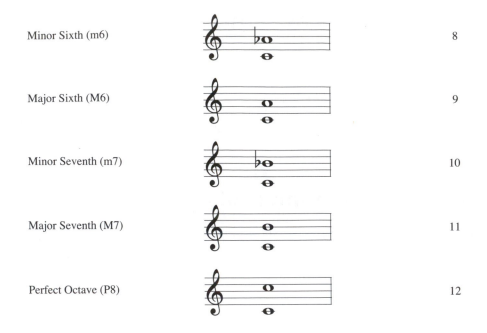

Minor Sixth (m6)		8
Major Sixth (M6)		9
Minor Seventh (m7)		10
Major Seventh (M7)		11
Perfect Octave (P8)		12

 Go to the Online Learning Center and click on Chapter 7. Two activities will help you in writing and identifying the sound of the intervals. Activity 7.1, Alien Interval Aural Identification, will assist you in learning the sound of the intervals. 7.2, Alien Interval Written Identification, will assist you in writing intervals. Make good use of both of these activities because skill with intervals will be important in all the later chapters.

Other Intervals

Intervals can be written in other ways, but they are enharmonic; that is, they sound the same as the intervals previously discussed.

figure 7.16

You can name each of these *enharmonic* intervals if you understand the following system for labeling intervals:

figure 7.17

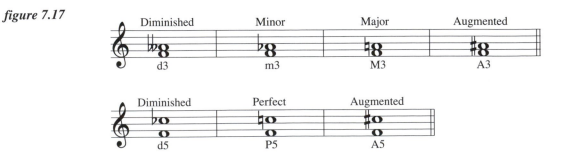

KEY TERMS

Define the following terms in your own words:

Interval _____

Unison _____

Octave _____

Perfect interval _____

Major interval _____

Minor interval _____

Augmented interval _____

Diminished interval _____

Enharmonic interval _____

LISTENING

The following songs are organized according to the first interval that occurs in the melody. Listen to these songs and concentrate your attention on the opening interval in the melody. (In some cases the first tone is repeated before the listed interval occurs.) Sing the melody, paying particular attention to the quality of the opening interval.

Auprès de ma Blonde (minor second) (p. 267, CD track 12, or the Web site)

"Wondrous Love" (major second down) (p. 313, CD track 74, or the Web site)

"Lullaby" (minor third) (p. 289, CD track 39, or the Web site)

Cielito Lindo (minor third down) (p. 275, CD track 21, or the Web site)

"Morning Has Broken" (major third) (p. 290, CD track 40, or the Web site)

"Skip to My Lou" (minor third down) (p. 305, CD track 62, or the Web site)

"Simple Gifts" (perfect fourth) (p. 302, CD track 55, or the Web site)

"Twinkle, Twinkle Little Star" (perfect fifth) (p. 309, CD track 69, or the Web site)

"Go Down Moses" (minor sixth) (p. 278, CD track 26, or the Web site)

USING WHAT YOU HAVE LEARNED

1. Sing the following melodies in C major, using solfeggio syllables or numbers. Sing the major scale and the tonic and dominant for warm-up.

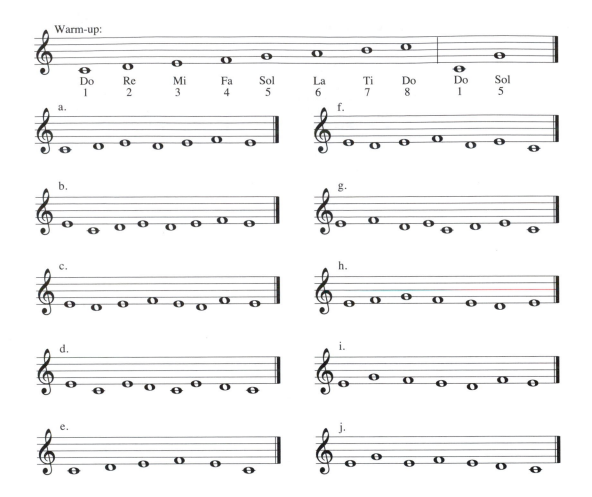

Do Ear-Training Exercises I, II, and III (p. 26), using these melodies.

2. Consider each of the following notes a given scale degree in a major scale. Find the major scale in each case. (See example.)

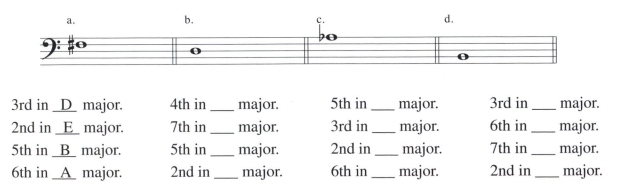

3rd in __D__ major.	4th in ___ major.	5th in ___ major.	3rd in ___ major.
2nd in __E__ major.	7th in ___ major.	3rd in ___ major.	6th in ___ major.
5th in __B__ major.	5th in ___ major.	2nd in ___ major.	7th in ___ major.
6th in __A__ major.	2nd in ___ major.	6th in ___ major.	2nd in ___ major.

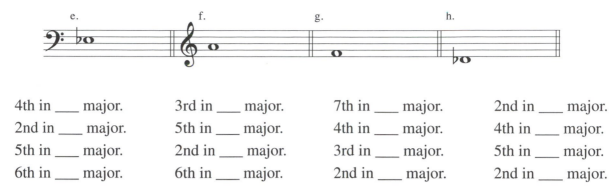

4th in ___ major.	3rd in ___ major.	7th in ___ major.	2nd in ___ major.
2nd in ___ major.	5th in ___ major.	4th in ___ major.	4th in ___ major.
5th in ___ major.	2nd in ___ major.	3rd in ___ major.	5th in ___ major.
6th in ___ major.	6th in ___ major.	2nd in ___ major.	2nd in ___ major.

3. Play and sing some of the intervals in assignments 7.1 and 7.2 on pages 143 and 145. Play each tone separately, then play the two tones together. Sing the interval and then sing its name. (See example below.)

4. Make up a song in a major key. Use a favorite poem or write the words yourself. Recite the poem aloud several times and listen carefully to the rhythm of your speech. This will suggest the rhythms of the song. (Recording your recitation may be helpful here.) Also listen for the natural rise and fall of your voice as you speak the text. This will suggest the rise and fall of the melody. Write out your song, paying particular attention to correct rhythmic notation. See the songbook for examples of the proper way to write the text under the melody. Perform your song in class, either as a solo or as a group effort.

5. Some songs can be combined with others and sung by two groups of singers at the same time. These so-called *partner songs* are fun to sing and will help you to develop your ability to sing in parts. Sing each of the following pairs of songs alone until you feel comfortable with them and then join with a friend (your instructor may divide the class in half) and sing them at the same time. Now switch parts and sing them again.

"Row, Row, Row Your Boat" (p. 298)   at the same time as   "Three Blind Mice" (p. 306)

"Skip to My Lou" (p. 305)   at the same time as   "Pawpaw Patch" (p. 295)

6. Sing or play a melody you know well. Isolate the first two notes of the melody and identify the interval between these two notes. That song may help you to remember the sound of that interval. Can you find melodies for other intervals? Perhaps your class will want to form a list of "Interval Melodies You Like to Sing" to help you identify the sounds of each of the intervals. You will find that certain intervals are much more common than others as beginning intervals of songs.

Write the specific name of each interval (M3, P4, etc.) in the blank below. (See example.)

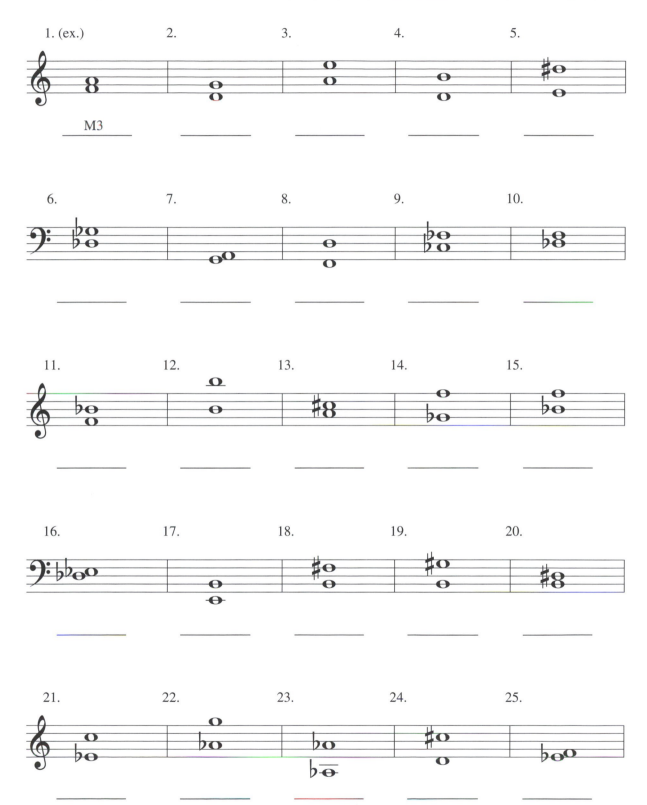

1. (ex.)   M3
2.
3.
4.
5.

6.
7.
8.
9.
10.

11.
12.
13.
14.
15.

16.
17.
18.
19.
20.

21.
22.
23.
24.
25.

CHAPTER 7 — ASSIGNMENT 7.1b
Interval Identification

In the blanks below, write the names of the intervals (M3, P4, etc.) in the following melody.
(See example.)

CHAPTER 7 — ASSIGNMENT 7.2a
Intervals in a Melody

Name _____

Section _____

Date _____

Write the name of each interval in "White Coral Bells" in the blanks below the melody. (See example.)

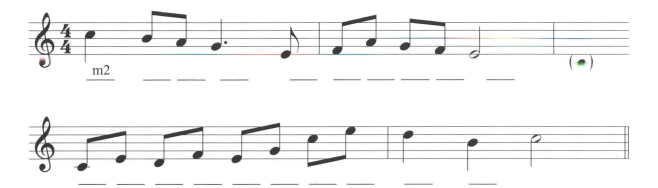

CHAPTER 7 — ASSIGNMENT 7.2b
Intervals in a Melody

Write the names of all the intervals in "Scarborough Fair" in the blanks below the melody. (See example.)

Writing Intervals Above and Below

Name _____

Section _____

Date _____

Write the requested intervals both above and below the given notes. (See example.)

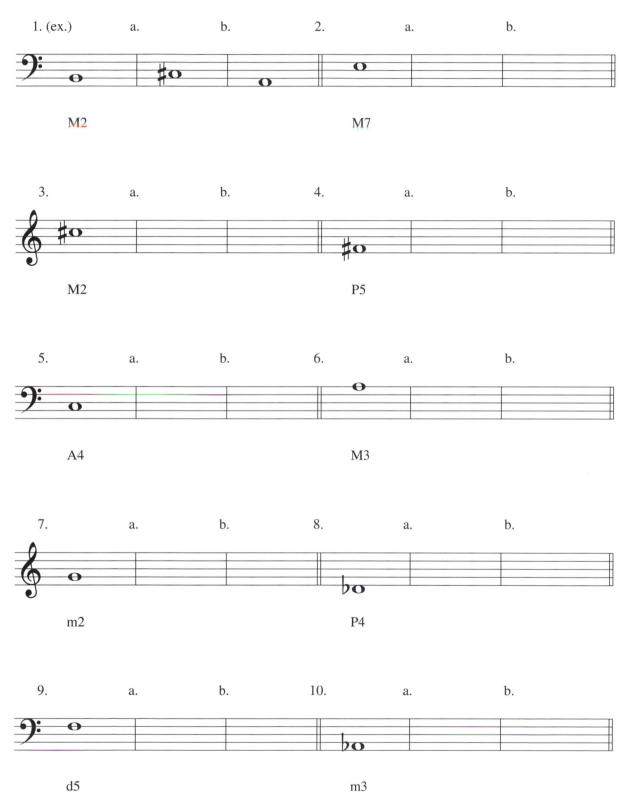

1. (ex.)   a.   b.   2.   a.   b.

M2   M7

3.   a.   b.   4.   a.   b.

M2   P5

5.   a.   b.   6.   a.   b.

A4   M3

7.   a.   b.   8.   a.   b.

m2   P4

9.   a.   b.   10.   a.   b.

d5   m3

Same instructions as 7.3a.

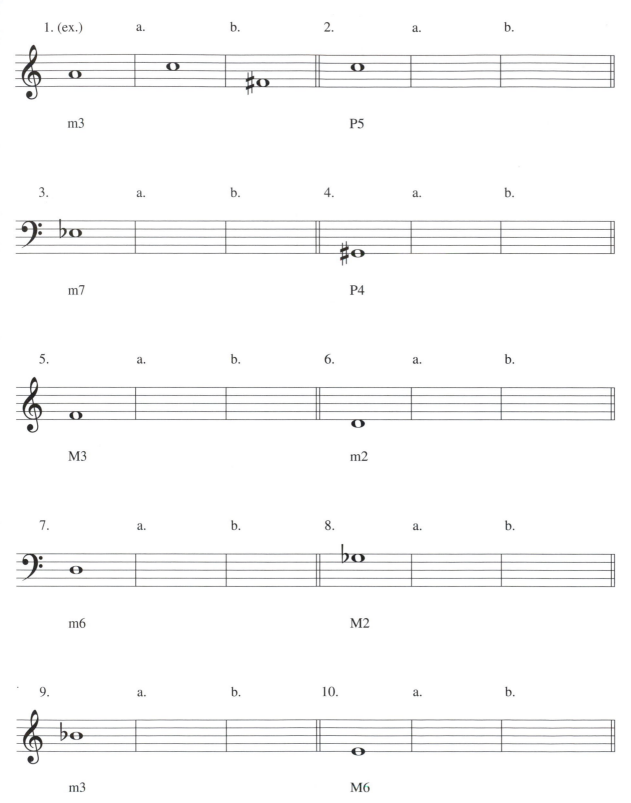

CHAPTER EIGHT
Minor Scales/ Minor Keys

The Natural Minor Scale

The minor scale is the second most common scale in Western music. It is a *diatonic scale* (one and only one note with each letter name) and, in its *natural* or *pure* form, has half steps from the second to the third and the fifth to the sixth scale degrees. You can hear the *natural minor* scale by playing the white keys beginning and ending on **A**:

figure 8.1

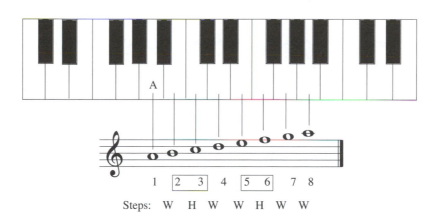

Several songs in the songbook are based on minor scales, for example, "Wayfaring Stranger" in the songbook (page 310) and below.

figure 8.2

Wayfaring Stranger

Play the recording of this song to familiarize yourself with it (p. 310, CD track 70, or the Web site). Figure 8.3 shows the pitch content of the melody, listed in scale order:

figure 8.3

List of pitches:

The tonic (or keynote) of "Wayfaring Stranger" is **D**—the final note of the song and the tone that feels like a point of rest, where the song should conclude. If the pitches in figure 8.3 are listed with **D** as the beginning and ending pitches, the following scale emerges:

figure 8.4

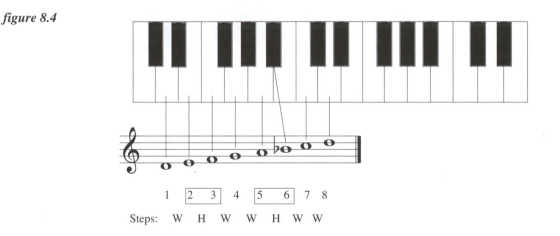

Notice that the missing pitch, **E,** is filled in. Melodies don't always contain all scale degrees.

If you compare the pattern of half and whole steps in figure 8.4 with those in figure 8.1, you will see that they are the same. "Wayfaring Stranger" is based on the *natural minor* scale.

The Harmonic Minor Scale

More often than not, melodies in minor will have some tones that lie outside the key signature and appear as accidentals on certain notes. Play the recording of "Three Rounds in Minor Keys," no. 3 (p. 307, CD track 67, or the Web site).

figure 8.5

Ah, Poor Bird

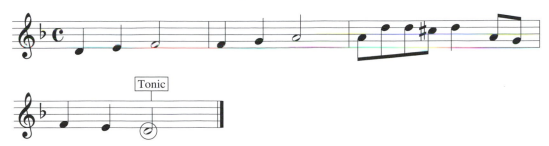

The tonic is clearly **D** (the last note). If it were not for the **C-sharps** the scale would follow the pattern of the natural minor scale (half steps from 2-3 and 5-6).

figure 8.6

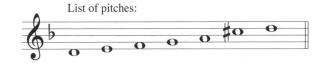

List of pitches:

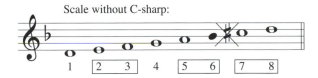

Scale without C-sharp:

The accidental on the seventh scale degree is the most common accidental found in minor, and this form of the minor scale is generally referred to as the *harmonic minor scale*.

figure 8.7

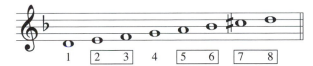

The harmonic minor scale has half steps from the second to the third, the fifth to the sixth, and the seventh to the eighth scale degrees. Notice that the alteration causes an augmented second between the sixth and seventh scale degrees.

figure 8.8

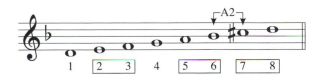

The Melodic Minor Scale

Because the augmented second is not particularly easy to sing, it is usually avoided in melodies. "Three Rounds in Minor Keys," no. 3 avoids **B-flat** entirely. Another way of avoiding the augmented second is to raise the sixth scale degree as well, creating a form that is commonly called the *melodic minor scale.*

Observe the melody "Greensleeves" in the key of **E** minor (play the recording of this song) (p. 280, CD track 28, or the Web site), which has accidentals on both the sixth and seventh scale degrees (**C-sharp** and **D-sharp**).

figure 8.9

Greensleeves

Figure 8.10 shows the list of pitches and the scale:

figure 8.10

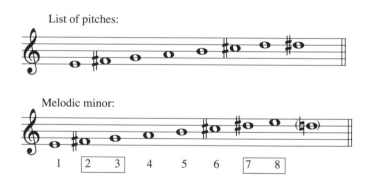

Notice that the sixth scale degree is always raised. The seventh scale degree appears both in its natural form (in measures 2, 3, 4, etc.) and its raised form (in measures 7 and 15). In these measures you will see the raised sixth scale degree used to avoid an augmented second.

figure 8.11

The melodic minor scale is usually written both ascending and descending, with the natural minor in the descending section. This scale indicates the common tendency in minor to raise the sixth and seventh scale degrees when they move upward to the tonic (eighth scale degree), and to use the natural form when the sixth and seventh scale degrees move downward to the dominant (fifth scale degree). From the discussion above, you can see that the minor scale is somewhat more complicated than the major scale. It is actually a family of scale forms, consisting of one pure form and two with altered tones. Figure 8.12 summarizes the interval patterns in all three forms of the minor scale:

figure 8.12

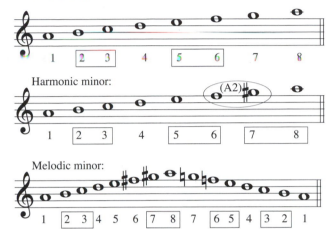

Natural minor:

Harmonic minor:

Melodic minor:

◆ **ASSIGNMENT 8.1, PAGE 163**

Key Signatures for Minor Scales

The minor scales use the same set of key signatures as the major scales. This means that each key signature implies either a major or a minor key. Only the music can tell you which scale is in use. Notice the key signature of one flat in the song "Wayfaring Stranger." The key signature of one flat implies either **F** major or **D** minor.

figure 8.13

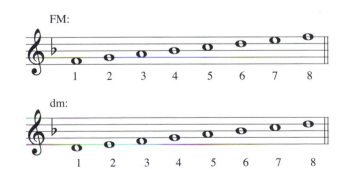

FM:

dm:

The key signature of "Go Down Moses" contains no sharps or flats. This key signature implies either **C** major or **A** minor.

figure 8.14

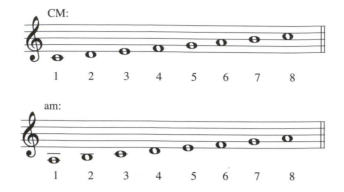

The key signature of "Greensleeves" is one sharp. This key signature implies either **G** major or **E** minor.

figure 8.15

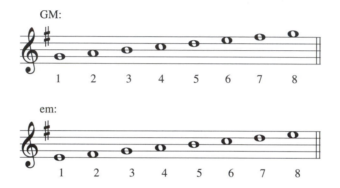

Remember that the raised forms of the sixth and seventh scale degrees in the harmonic and melodic forms of the minor scale are added with accidentals in the music and do not appear as a part of the key signature.

 Go to the Online Learning Center and click on Chapter 8. Go to 8.2, Scale-Building Activity—Minor Keys, which assists you in building minor scales in all the keys.

Relative Major and Minor Scales

The two scales (one major and one minor) that share the same key signature are called *relative scales*. We say that **F** major is the *relative major* of **D** minor, and that **D** minor is the *relative minor* of **F** major. Study figures 8.13, 8.14, and 8.15 for a moment, and observe that the interval between the tonic of the minor scale and the tonic of its relative major is always a *minor third*. **To write the key signature of any minor scale, write the key signature of the major scale a minor third higher.** Another way of thinking of this relationship is to observe that the tonic of the minor scale is the sixth scale degree of its relative major.

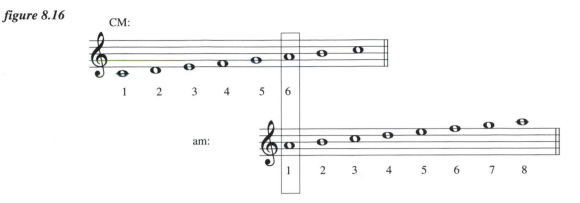

figure 8.16

The following circle of fifths shows both the major keys and their relative minors.

figure 8.17

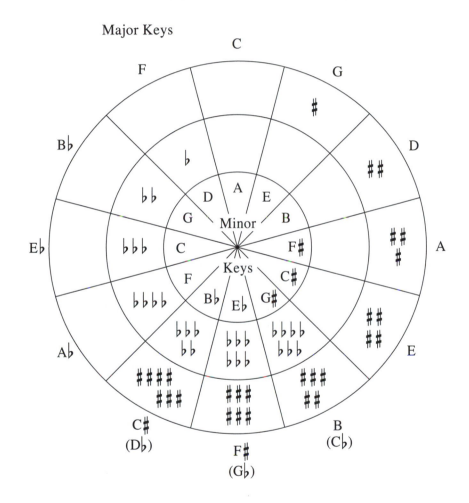

Tonic (Parallel) Major and Minor Scales

The two scales (one major and one minor) that share the same keynote or tonic (**A** minor and **A** major, for example) are said to be in *tonic* (or *parallel*) *relationship*. We say that **A** minor is the *tonic minor* (or *parallel minor*) of **A** major. Observe that the tonic major and minor scales (**A** minor and **A** major, for example) are three positions apart on the circle.

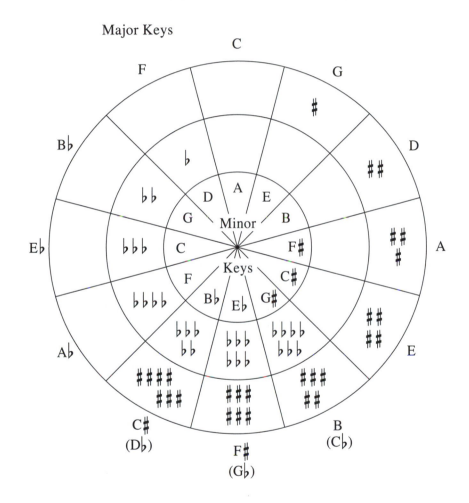

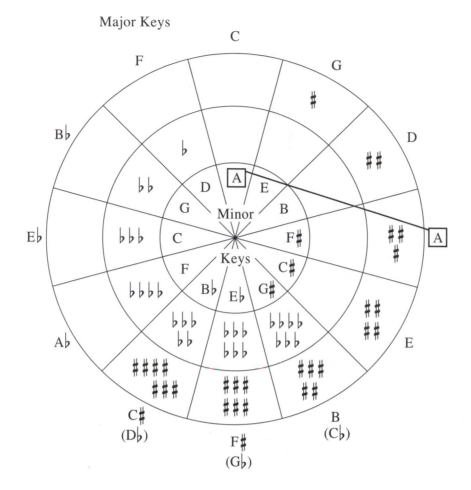

figure 8.18

Major Keys

This means that a minor key signature has three fewer sharps or three more flats than its tonic major. This gives us another method for writing the key signature for minor scales: **To write the key signature of a minor scale, think of the key signature of its tonic major and subtract three sharps or add three flats.** If there are fewer than three sharps, you can simply subtract the number of sharps from three and add that number of flats. For example, **G** major has only one sharp. To form the key signature of **G** minor, subtract one from three (leaving two) and add two flats. The key signature of **G** minor has two flats.

figure 8.19

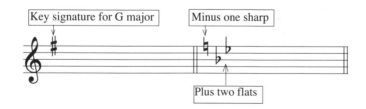

◆ **ASSIGNMENT 8.2, PAGES 165–167**

Go to the Online Learning Center and click on Chapter 8. Go to 8.1, Key Signature Identification Activity—Minor Keys, which asks you to construct the circle of fifths in minor keys. This will help you to memorize the pattern of minor keys on the circle of fifths.

The Dominant in Minor

The fifth scale degree of the minor scale is called the *dominant,* just as it is in major. To see why, look again at the song "Wayfaring Stranger." There are sixty-eight notes in this melody, and the chart below shows the number of times each tone occurs:

figure 8.20

Scale degrees:	1	2	3	4	5	6	7	
Names:	D	E	F	G	A	B	C	
Number of occurrences:	22	0	7	9	19	2	9	= 68

The tonic (**D**) and the dominant (**A**) emerge as the most emphasized pitches in this melody. The tonic-dominant relationship will provide as clear a framework in minor keys as it does in major keys.

Solfeggio and Numbers

If you have been using solfeggio or numbers in singing songs in the major keys, you may wonder how to deal with the minor keys. There are a number of systems in use for the minor scales, but we will suggest only two here. Your instructor may prefer another system, which she or he will explain to you.

Because the minor scale in its natural form is also the major scale beginning and ending with the sixth scale degree, we can keep the same solfeggio syllables for the minor scale:

figure 8.21

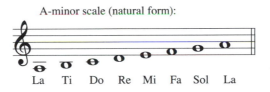

A-minor scale (natural form):

La Ti Do Re Mi Fa Sol La

To indicate the raised seventh scale degree in the harmonic form, substitute "Si" for "Sol":

figure 8.22

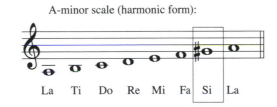

A-minor scale (harmonic form):

La Ti Do Re Mi Fa Si La

The raised sixth scale degree in melodic minor is sung as "Fi" instead of "Fa":

figure 8.23

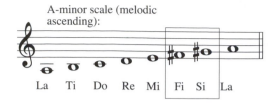

If you have been using numbers, you may continue as you have before with the tonic as "1" and the dominant as "5."

figure 8.24

Quick Check

1. Sing the following melodies in **A** minor using solfeggio syllables or numbers. Sing the minor scale and the tonic and dominant for warm-up.

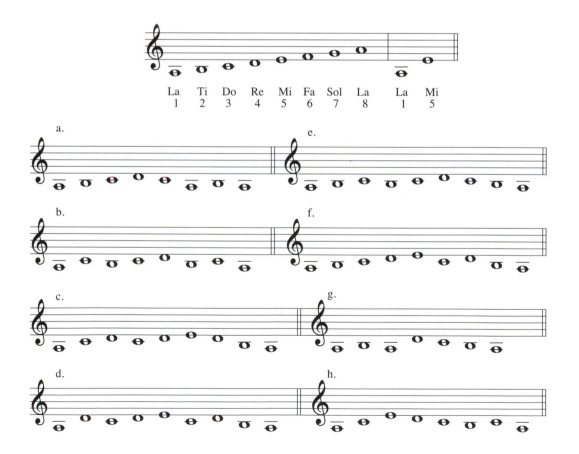

Do Ear-Training Exercises I, II, and III on page 26 using these melodies.

Transposition

Transposition is the process of rewriting a piece of music so that it sounds higher or lower in pitch. Your knowledge of scales and intervals will serve you well when you need to transpose a piece from one key to another. To transpose a melody, write the same interval above or below each tone of the melody. For example, the following melody in **G** minor is transposed to the key of **F** minor by lowering each tone a major second.

figure 8.25

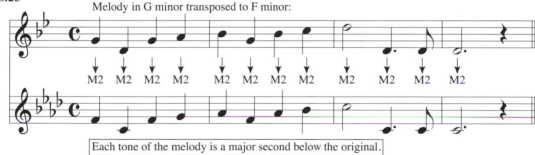

Notice that the key signature for **F** minor is also used. If you write the proper key signature, the pitches are easier to find, since they will naturally be in the scale of the new key.

figure 8.26

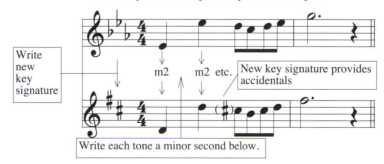

1. Transpose the first line of "America the Beautiful" from **B-flat** major to **C** major (a major second above):

O beau - ti - ful for spa - cious skies, For am - ber waves of grain,

2. Transpose "Wayfaring Stranger" from **D** minor to **C** minor (a major second below).

◆ **ASSIGNMENT 8.3, PAGES 169–170**

KEY TERMS

Define the following terms in your own words:

Natural minor _____

Harmonic minor _____

Melodic minor _____

Relative major _____

Relative minor _____

Tonic (parallel) minor _____

Tonic major _____

Circle of fifths _____

LISTENING

The following songs illustrate the three forms of the minor scale. Listen to the songs, paying particular attention to the effect of the minor scale in its various forms. Follow along in the songbook and sing or play the song with the recording. Note that accidentals are used in the harmonic and melodic forms of the minor scale.

"Go Down Moses" (harmonic form) (p. 278, CD track 26, or the Web site)

"Greensleeves" (melodic form) (p. 280, CD track 28, or the Web site)

"Hey, Ho, Anybody Home" (natural form) (p. 281, CD track 29, or the Web site)

"Pat-a-Pan" (harmonic form) (p. 295, CD track 46, or the Web site)

Tumbalalaika (melodic form) (p. 308, CD track 68, or the Web site)

"Three Rounds in Minor Keys" (p. 307, CD track 65–67, or the Web site)

    1. (natural form)

    2. (harmonic form)

    3. (harmonic form)

"Wayfaring Stranger" (natural form) (p. 310, CD track 70, or the Web site)

USING WHAT YOU HAVE LEARNED

1. Sing the following songs in minor keys:

   "Hey, Ho, Anybody Home" (p. 281, CD track 29, or the Web site)
   "Pat-a-Pan" (p. 295, CD track 46, or the Web site)
   "Go Down Moses" (p. 278, CD track 26, or the Web site)
   "Greensleeves" (p. 280, CD track 28, or the Web site)

2. Sing the "Three Rounds in Minor Keys" (p. 307, CD track 65–67, or the Web site). First sing each song together in unison, then sing the song in parts.

3. Identify each interval in "Go Down Moses":

Go Down Moses

4. Try to find favorite pieces that are in minor keys. To do this, first identify the tonic. It is often the final note in a melody or the tone that "sticks in your head" after the piece is over. When you have identified the tonic, see if you can sing a minor scale from that tone. Do the scale tones seem to fit

most of the pitches? If so, the piece is likely in a minor key. If your instructor asks, bring an example of music in a minor key to class to share with other class members. You will find that melodies in minor keys are less common than those in major keys. You may need to try several melodies before you find one in minor.

 Go to the Online Learning Center and click on Chapter 8. Go to 8.3, Major-minor Identification, which will help you to be able to identify music in major and minor by ear.

CHAPTER 8 — ASSIGNMENT 8.1
Determining Minor Keys and Scales

Name _____

Section _____

Date _____

Determine the minor scale in each of the following songs by first making a pitch collection as described on page 110. Fill in the tonic and the probable form of the scale for each in the blanks below the staves. (In some cases you will not be able to tell for sure, because some scale degrees are missing.)

1. **"Tumbalalaika" (p. 308):**

   Pitch collection:

   Scale:

   Tonic: _____   Form of scale: _____

2. **"Pat-a-Pan" (p. 295):**

   Pitch collection:

   Scale:

   Tonic: _____   Form of scale: _____

3. **Three Rounds in Minor Keys #1 (p. 307):**

   Pitch collection:

   Scale:

   Tonic: _____   Form of scale: _____

4. **Three Rounds in Minor Keys #3 (p. 307):**

   Pitch collection:

   Scale:

   Tonic: _____   Form of scale: _____

CHAPTER 8 — ASSIGNMENT 8.2a
Minor Scales on the Keyboard

Name _____

Section _____

Date _____

1. Mark the tones of the given form of each minor scale on the keyboard, starting on the key marked with an "X."

2. Write the scale on the staff provided, using accidentals. (Remember that there must be only one of each letter name in the scale.)

3. Write the proper key signature for the scale on the second staff. (See example for assignment 6.2a, p. 125.)

(For reference, the key signatures of 7 sharps and 7 flats are shown in both treble and bass staves.

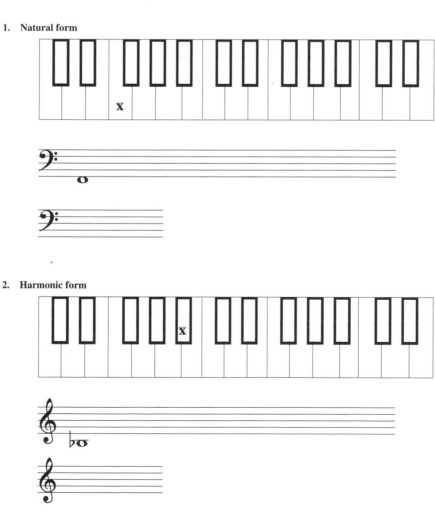

1. **Natural form**

2. **Harmonic form**

3. Melodic (ascending)

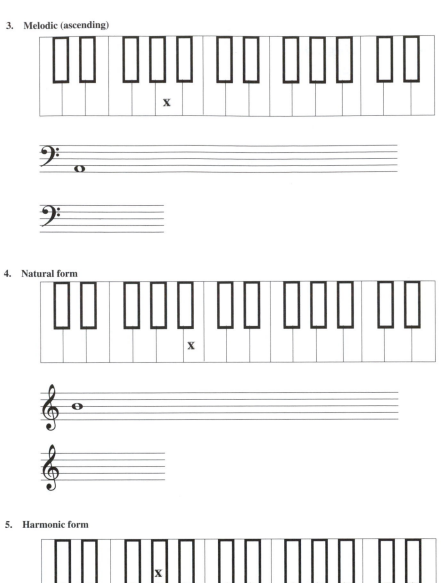

4. Natural form

5. Harmonic form

CHAPTER 8 — ASSIGNMENT 8.2b
Minor Scales on the Keyboard

Name _____

Section _____

Date _____

Write the proper key signature for each of the following minor scales. Then write the scale in the form indicated. (See example.)

1. (ex.) E minor
   (Harmonic)

2. C♯ minor:
   (Natural)

3. E♭ minor:
   (Melodic)

4. B♭ minor:
   (Melodic)

5. D minor:
   (Harmonic)

6. C♯ minor:
   (Harmonic)

CHAPTER 8 — ASSIGNMENT 8.3a
Transposition

Name _____

Section _____

Date _____

Transpose the following round by Haydn (Three Rounds in Minor Keys, no. 2), from F-sharp minor to G minor.

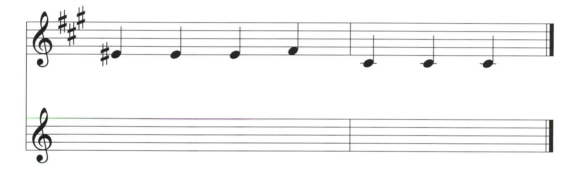

Transpose the following round by Webbe (Six Rounds in Major Keys, no. 4), from F major to A major.

CHAPTER 8 — ASSIGNMENT 8.3b
Naming Major and Minor Keys

Write the major and the minor keys for each of the following key signatures. (See example.)

ex.

_____**D**_____ major

_____**B**_____ minor

1.

_____ major

_____ minor

2.

_____ major

_____ minor

3.

_____ major

_____ minor

4.

_____ major

_____ minor

5.

_____ major

_____ minor

There is two kinds of music, the good and the bad. I play the good kind.

Louis Armstrong, 1901–1971 (jazz musician)

(Of Debussy's music) Better not listen to it; you risk getting used to it, and then you would end up by liking it.

Nikolay Rimsky-Korsakov, 1844–1908 (Russian composer)

Man, I can't LISTEN that fast!

Unnamed jazz musician on hearing Charlie Parker's and Dizzy Gillespie's "Shaw Nuff"

Music was originally discreet, seemly, simple, masculine, and of good morals. Have not the moderns rendered it lascivious beyond measure?

Jacob of Liège, ca. 1425 (music theorist)

Music is now so foolish that I am amazed. Everything that is wrong is permitted, and no attention is paid to what the old generation wrote as composition.

Samuel Scheidt, 1587–1654 (German composer)

What distinguishes dissonances from consonances is not a greater or lesser degree of beauty, but a greater or lesser degree of comprehensibility.

Arnold Schoenberg, 1874–1951 (Austrian composer)

One good thing about music, when it hits you, you feel no pain.

Bob Marley, 1945–1981 (reggae composer)

————————————————

Throughout history (at least judging from the quotes from Jacob of Liège and Samuel Scheidt above), people have disagreed about tastes in music. Why do people like or dislike particular kinds of music? Examine your own musical taste and try to determine how it was formed. Why do you dislike some kinds of music? Is there a danger that if you begin to listen to music you dislike that "you risk getting used to it, and then you would end up by liking it"?

CHAPTER NINE
Chords—Looking at the Musical Background

"If only the whole world could feel the power of harmony."
— WOLFGANG AMADEUS MOZART

Harmony

Our study up to this point has concentrated on melody and rhythm. We are now ready to introduce another important aspect of music: *harmony,* which is the study of tones sounding together.

Chords

The smallest unit of harmony is the *chord,* which consists of three or more tones sounded together.

figure 9.1

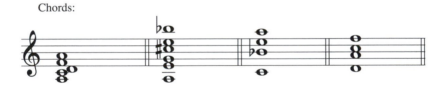

Chords:

(Two tones sounded together can *imply* harmony, but a chord must have at least three tones.)

Triads

Although any combination of three or more tones can be a chord, the *triad* is a specific three-tone chord built in thirds:

figure 9.2

Triads:

Thirds

Each tone in the triad has a name:

figure 9.3

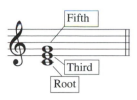

Because the *root* is considered the most important tone in a triad, all triads are named for their roots:

figure 9.4

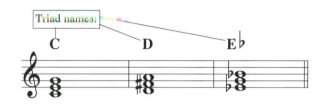

The most common triads have a perfect fifth between the root and the fifth, but the interval between the root and the third may be either major or minor, and the triad is more specifically identified by this interval as either a *major triad* or a *minor triad.*

figure 9.5

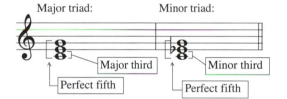

Quick Check

Identify the following triads as major or minor. The interval between the root and the fifth is a P5 in all these chords, so concentrate on the root-third relationship.

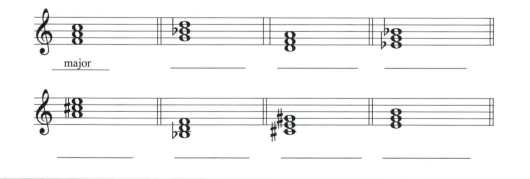

Popular-Music Chord Symbols

In jazz, folk, and popular music, chords are generally indicated above the melody by standard chord symbols:

figure 9.6

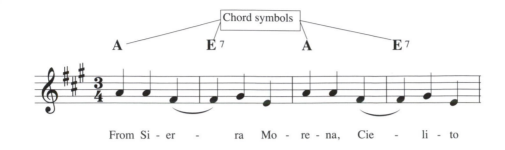

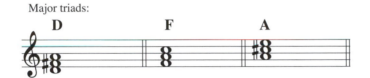

A major triad is indicated by a capital letter designating its root:

figure 9.7

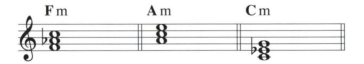

A minor triad is indicated by adding "m" to the previous symbol:

figure 9.8

Quick Check

1. Write popular music chord symbols above the eight chords you identified on page 173.

2. Look at "Morning Has Broken," shown below. Spell or write (from the lowest note up) each of the triads required to accompany this song on the staff below. (See the first four measures.) Play these chords on a keyboard along with the recording (CD track 40, or the Web site).

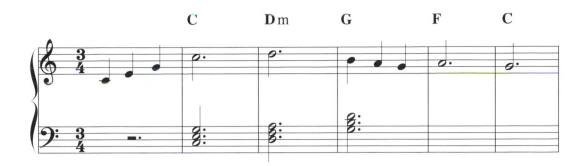

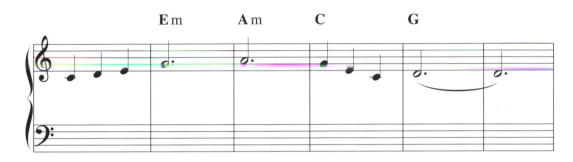

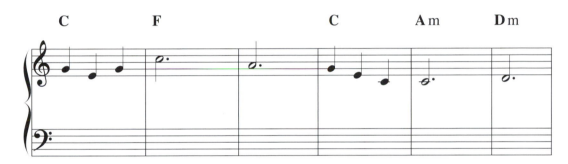

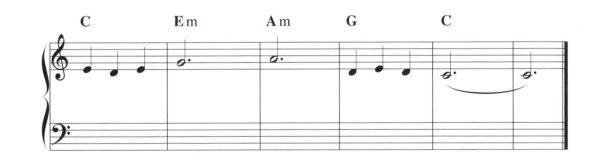

◆ **ASSIGNMENT 9.1, PAGES 185–186**

Diminished and Augmented Triads

Although major and minor triads account for the vast majority of triads you will find in music, you will also see two other triad qualities from time to time: the *diminished triad* with a diminished fifth (and a minor third) and the *augmented triad* with an augmented fifth (and a major third).

Chords—Looking at the Musical Background   175

figure 9.9

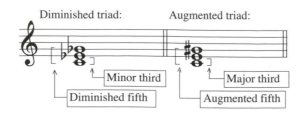

Diminished chords are indicated in popular music symbols by the addition of "dim" to the root name:

figure 9.10

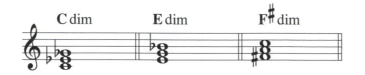

Augmented triads are indicated by the addition of "aug" to the root name:

figure 9.11

◆ **ASSIGNMENT 9.2, PAGES 187–188**

Quick Check

1. Identify these chords using popular-music chord symbols. These chords may be major, minor, augmented, or diminished, so examine both the root-third and the root-fifth relationships.

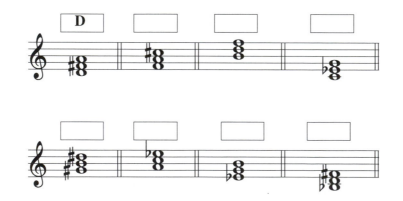

2. It is important that you begin to be able to recognize the sound of the various chord qualities. Sing the triads in assignments 9.1a and 9.2a as follows:

a. Play the triad on a keyboard.

b. Sing the intervals, starting with the root-third relationship "one, three, major third," followed by the root-fifth relationship "one, five, perfect fifth," and then the whole chord "one, three, five, three, one."

| 1 | 3 | Maj - or | third | 1 | 5 | Per - fect | fifth | 1 | 3 | 5 | 3 | 1 |

Repeated practice in this manner will help you to hear the various chord qualities and improve your music reading as well. Since many melodies contain chord outlines, recognizing these outlines will improve your skills.

Go to the Online Learning Center and click on Chapter 9. Go to 9.1, Chord Quality Identification Activity. In this activity you will learn to identify the four triads (major, minor, augmented, and diminished) by ear. You can listen to each chord melodically (one note at a time) or harmonically (all notes played together) before you identify the quality.

Simple and Expanded Positions of Triads

Thus far we have written triads in their *simple position,* with the root at the bottom and the third and fifth in order. It is important that you recognize that chords seldom appear in music in their simple position; instead they are *expanded* by doubling (duplicating tones in other octaves) and by spreading the chord tones over a wider range. It would be impossible to list all the many variations you are likely to encounter in music, but the following illustration will give you an idea of the variety of expanded positions you will find.

figure 9.12

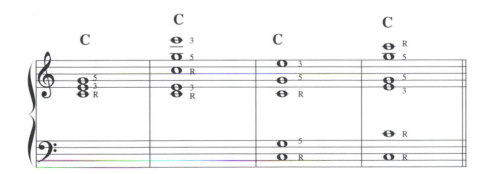

Inversion of Triads

In all the examples in figure 9.12 the root remains as the lowest chord tone, but other members of the chord can also be used as the lowest part (or *bass*). When a tone other than the root appears in the bass, the chord is said to be *inverted*. If the root is in the bass we say that the chord is in *root position;* if the third of the triad is in the bass, the chord is in *first inversion;* and if the fifth is in the bass, the chord is in *second inversion.*

(For a discussion of inversion of intervals, see Appendix I on page 243.)

figure 9.13

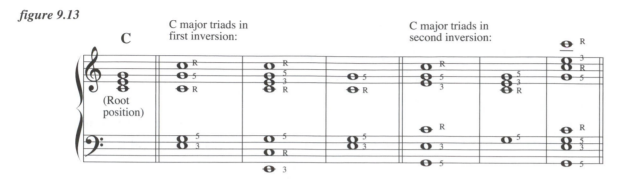

Quick Check

Play the following chords in root position and inversions on the keyboard.

Block Chords versus Arpeggiated Chords

A further variation in the way chords occur in music comes from *arpeggiation,* which is a successive presentation of chord tones in contrast with the simultaneous presentation (called *block style*) we have seen in the examples above.

figure 9.14

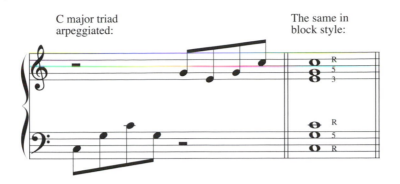

Examining piano music will show you many possibilities for mixing arpeggiation and block styles. In the following example by Bach, an extended violin melody is created entirely out of triad arpeggiation:

figure 9.15

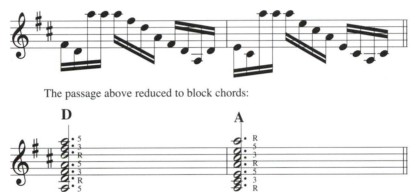

It is important that you be able to recognize chords whether they are presented in expansion, inversion, or arpeggiation.

Seventh Chords

We can form *seventh chords* by adding another third to a triad:

figure 9.16

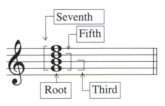

Although a number of different seventh-chord qualities occur in music, we will concentrate our attention on two types: the major triad with an added minor seventh and the minor triad with an added minor seventh. These chords are by far the most common seventh chords. (For further information on seventh chords and more complex chords, see Appendix 1.)

Chords—Looking at the Musical Background   179

The Dominant Seventh Chord

The *dominant* seventh chord is a major triad with an added minor seventh:

figure 9.17

This is the most common seventh chord in music, and it is indicated in popular-music chord symbols with a superscript "7" added to the name of the root:

figure 9.18

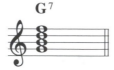

The Minor Seventh Chord

The *minor seventh chord* is formed by adding a minor seventh to a minor triad:

figure 9.19

The popular-music chord symbol for the minor seventh chord is a superscript "7" added to the symbol for the minor triad:

figure 9.20

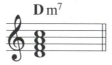

◆ ASSIGNMENTS 9.3 AND 9.4, PAGES 189 AND 191

1. Write popular-music chord symbols for the following minor seventh and major-minor seventh chords. Remember that the difference is in the root-third relationship.

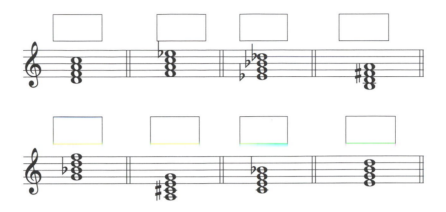

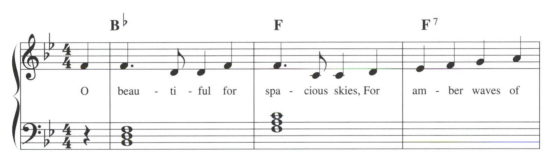

2. Look at "America the Beautiful," below. Spell or write each of the chords on the staff below and then play them on a keyboard along with the recording (CD track 10, or the Web site).

America the Beautiful

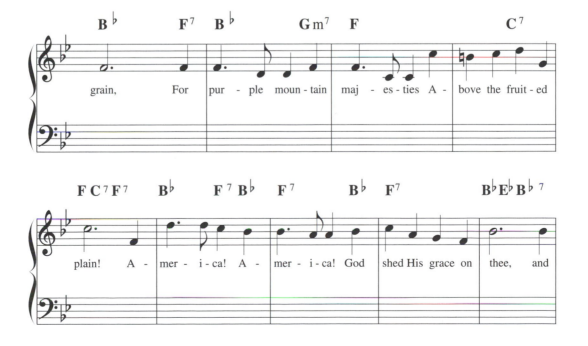

Chords—Looking at the Musical Background   181

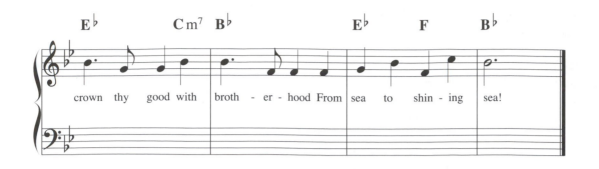

crown thy good with broth - er - hood From sea to shin - ing sea!

KEY TERMS

Define the following terms in your own words:

Harmony _____

Chord _____

Triad _____

Root _____

Major triad _____

Minor triad _____

Diminished triad _____

Augmented triad _____

Simple position _____

Expanded position _____

Inverted chords _____

Root position _____

First inversion _____

Second inversion _____

Block chord _____

Arpeggiated chord _____

Seventh chord _____

Dominant seventh chord _____

Minor seventh chord _____

LISTENING

The following songs outline various triads. The measures and chords involved are listed below. Listen to these songs, playing particular attention to the chord outlines. Follow along in the songbook and play or sing the melody with the recording.

"Barbara Ellen" (**D** in mm. 3 and 6, **G** in m. 5) (p. 268, CD track 14, or the Web site)

"Children's Prayer" (**C** in mm. 1 and 3, **F** in m. 13, **Gm** in m. 15, **Am** in m. 17) (p. 274, CD track 20, or the Web site)

Dona Nobis Pacem (**F** in m. 1, **C⁷** in m. 2. **C** in m. 23) (p. 276, CD track 22, or the Web site)

"Down in the Valley" (**G** in mm. 1 and 5, **D** in 2–3 and 6–7) (p. 277, CD track 24, or the Web site)

"I've Got to Know" (**E** in mm. 2, 4, 8, 10, and 12) (p. 283, CD track 33, or the Web site)

"Love Somebody" (**C** in mm. 1, 3, 5, 9–11, 13–14) (p. 288, CD track 38, or the Web site)

"Lullaby" (**C** in mm. 1–3, 10, and 14, **F** in m. 9 and 13) (p. 289, CD track 39, or the Web site)

"Morning Has Broken" (**C** in mm. 1–2, 10, and 16) (p. 290, CD track 40, or the Web site)

"Row, Row, Row Your Boat" (**C** in mm. 5–6) (p. 298, CD track 50, or the Web site)

"Skip to My Lou" (**F** in mm. 1–2, 5–6, 9–10, and 13–14. **E**dim in mm. 3–4 and 11–12) (p. 305, CD track 62, or the Web site)

USING WHAT YOU HAVE LEARNED

1. Look in the songbook for melodies that contain major and minor triad outlines. Be alert for arrangements that go beyond simple positions with root followed by third, followed by fifth.

2. List *all* the intervals that may occur among the root, third, and fifth of a major triad, a minor triad, a diminished triad, and an augmented triad. Consider various inversions and positions for each of the triads.

3. Look in music books that you may have available (books of popular or rock songs, hymnals, piano music, etc.) and find an example of each of the chords discussed in this chapter. Be alert for various inversions and spacings, as well as arpeggiated versus block-style chords.

Go to the Online Learning Center and click on Chapter 9. Activities 9.2 through 9.6 allow you to harmonize a given melody using the mouse or the keyboard. The first of these activities involves only three chords, but later activities have several different chords. You will probably find that it is easier to keep up with the melody if you use the computer keyboard.

CHAPTER 9 — ASSIGNMENT 9.1a
Popular-Music Chord Symbols

Name _____

Section _____

Date _____

Write the popular-music chord symbols for each of the following chords in the box above the chord.

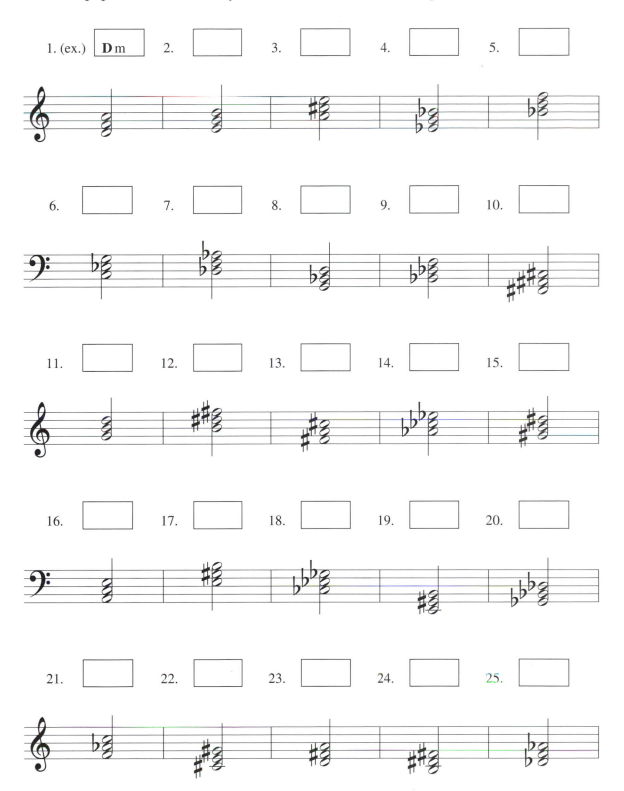

1. (ex.) **D m**   2. [ ]   3. [ ]   4. [ ]   5. [ ]

6. [ ]   7. [ ]   8. [ ]   9. [ ]   10. [ ]

11. [ ]   12. [ ]   13. [ ]   14. [ ]   15. [ ]

16. [ ]   17. [ ]   18. [ ]   19. [ ]   20. [ ]

21. [ ]   22. [ ]   23. [ ]   24. [ ]   25. [ ]

Chords—Looking at the Musical Background   185

Writing Major and Minor Triads

Write the major and minor triads requested below each popular-music chord symbol.

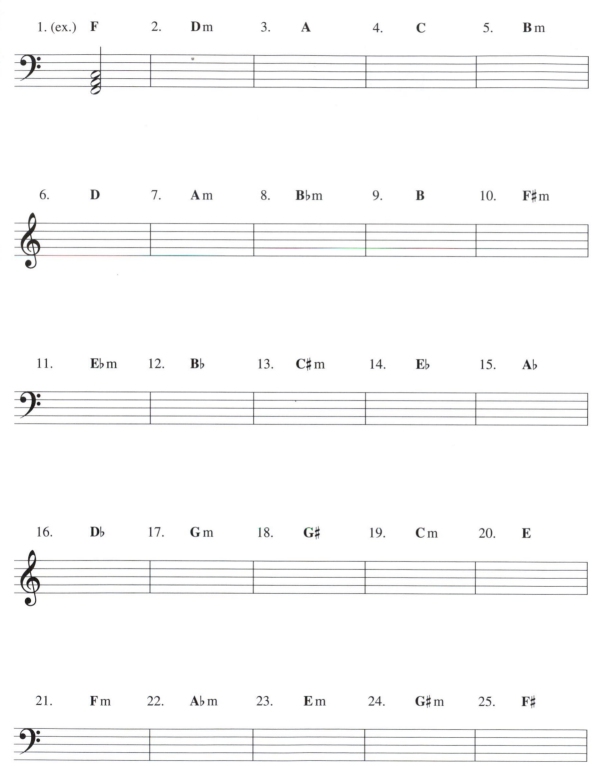

1. (ex.) **F**   2. **D**m   3. **A**   4. **C**   5. **B**m

6. **D**   7. **A**m   8. **B**♭m   9. **B**   10. **F**♯m

11. **E**♭m   12. **B**♭   13. **C**♯m   14. **E**♭   15. **A**♭

16. **D**♭   17. **G**m   18. **G**♯   19. **C**m   20. **E**

21. **F**m   22. **A**♭m   23. **E**m   24. **G**♯m   25. **F**♯

Name _____

Section _____

Date _____

Write the popular-music chord symbols for each of the following chords in the box above the chord.

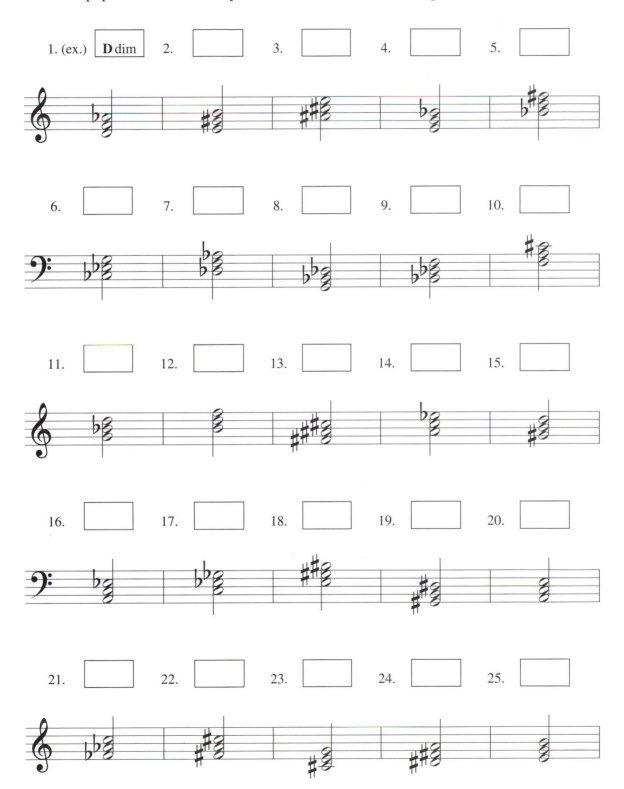

1. (ex.) **D** dim
2. [ ]
3. [ ]
4. [ ]
5. [ ]

6. [ ]
7. [ ]
8. [ ]
9. [ ]
10. [ ]

11. [ ]
12. [ ]
13. [ ]
14. [ ]
15. [ ]

16. [ ]
17. [ ]
18. [ ]
19. [ ]
20. [ ]

21. [ ]
22. [ ]
23. [ ]
24. [ ]
25. [ ]

CHAPTER 9 — ASSIGNMENT 9.2b
Writing Triads

Write the major, minor, augmented, or diminished triads requested below each popular-music chord symbol.

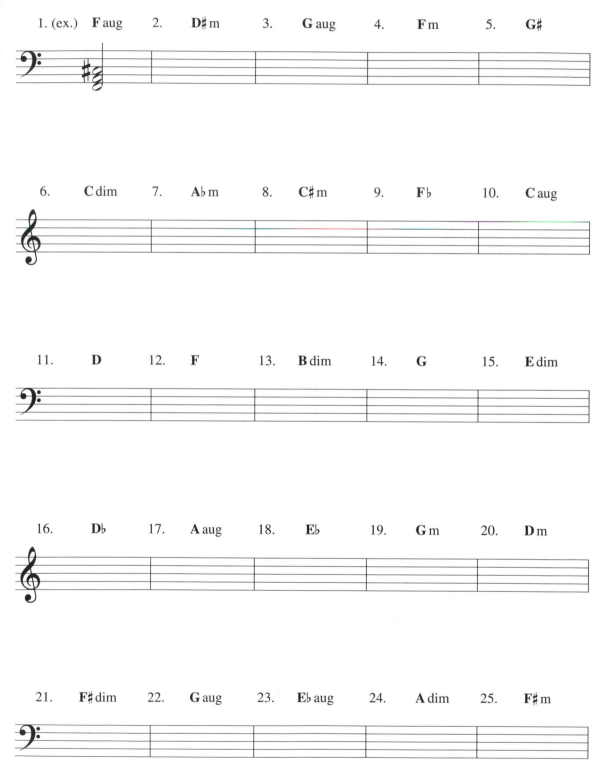

1. (ex.) **F** aug 2. **D♯** m 3. **G** aug 4. **F** m 5. **G♯**

6. **C** dim 7. **A♭** m 8. **C♯** m 9. **F♭** 10. **C** aug

11. **D** 12. **F** 13. **B** dim 14. **G** 15. **E** dim

16. **D♭** 17. **A** aug 18. **E♭** 19. **G** m 20. **D** m

21. **F♯** dim 22. **G** aug 23. **E♭** aug 24. **A** dim 25. **F♯** m

CHAPTER 9 —ASSIGNMENT 9.3a
Popular-Music Chord Symbols

Name _____

Section _____

Date _____

Write the chords indicated by the popular-music chord symbols on the bass staff below the melody "Aura Lee." Use whole notes for each chord.

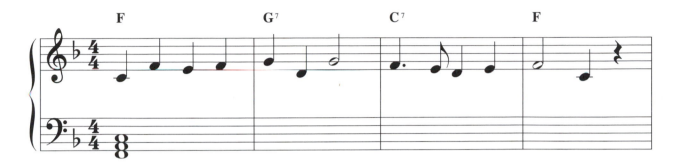

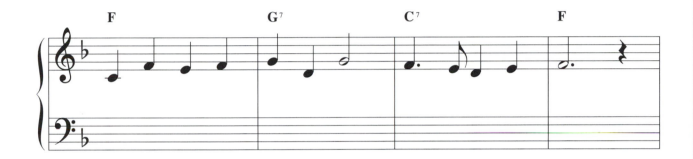

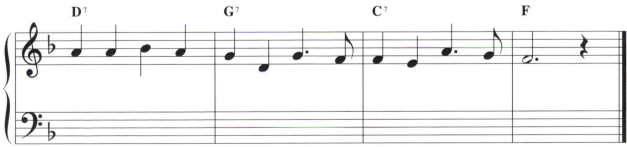

ASSIGNMENT

Write the chords indicated by the popular-music chord symbols on the bass staff below the melody "God of Our Fathers." Use proper note values for each chord as indicated. (Melody and chord note values may differ. Be sure the chords in each measure add up to four beats.)

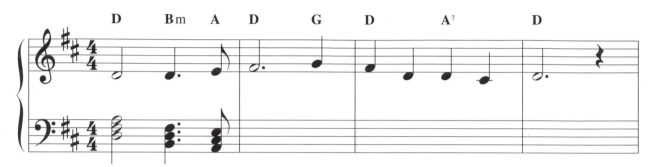

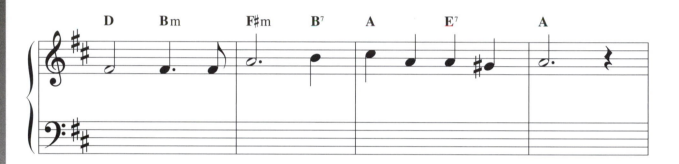

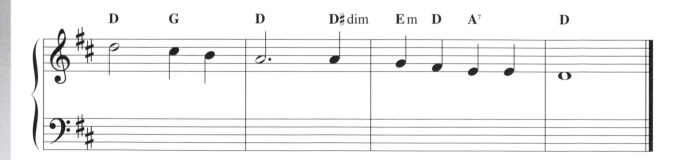

CHAPTER 9—ASSIGNMENT 9.4a
Finding Chords in Music Literature

Name _____

Section _____

Date _____

Sections of the following excerpts from music literature are in numbered boxes. Each box contains a single chord. Write the chord in simple position on the staff in the proper box below and provide a popular-music chord symbol for the chord. Be sure to look at the clefs and key signatures. (See example.)

ex.

Schubert: Sonata for Piano op. 122 (third movement, trio)

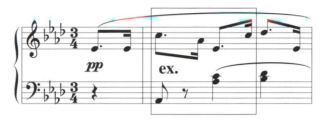

Mendelssohn: *Songs without Words* op. 30, no. 3

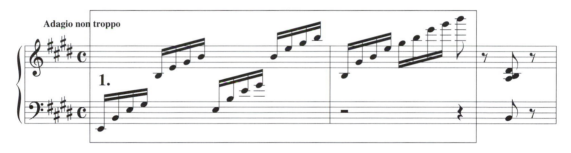

Haydn: Sonata no. 8 in A Major, Hob. XVI/5 (second movement)

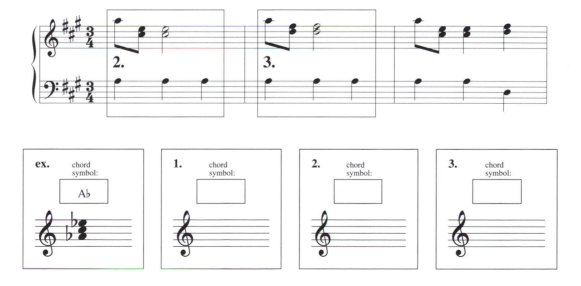

Chords—Looking at the Musical Background   **191**

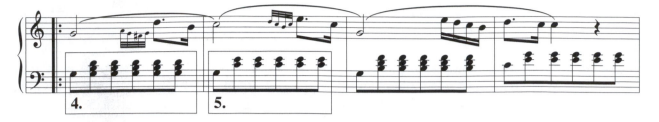

Weber: *Theme from Variations über ein Original Thema*, op. 2

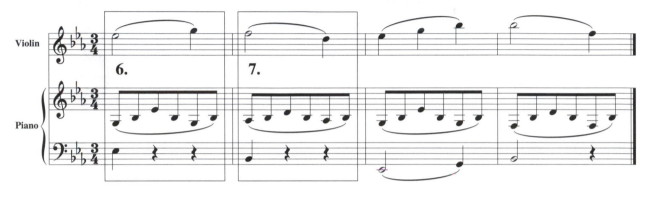

Schubert: Sonatina for Violin and Piano op. 137, no. 3, Menuetto (Allegro vivace)

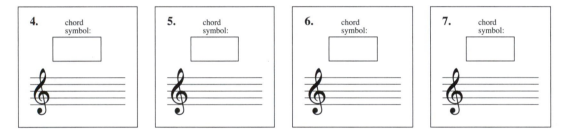

| 4. chord symbol: | 5. chord symbol: | 6. chord symbol: | 7. chord symbol: |

ASSIGNMENT 9.4a (continued)

Name _____

Section _____

Date _____

Beethoven: Sonata op. 79, third movement

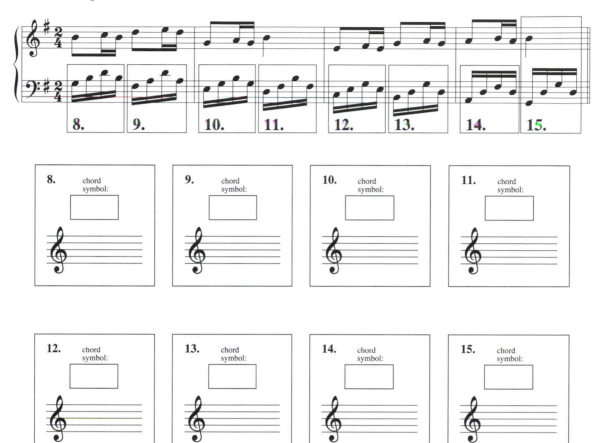

Schubert: *Wohin?* from *Die Schöne Müllerin,* op. 25, no. 2

Chopin: Mazurka in G Minor, op. 67, no. 2

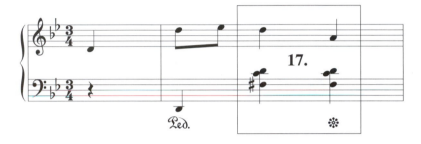

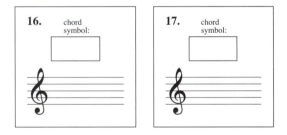

CHAPTER 9—ASSIGNMENT 9.4b
Finding Chords in Music Literature

Name _____

Section _____

Date _____

Sections of the following excerpts from music literature are in numbered boxes. Each box contains a single chord. Write the chord in simple position on the staff in the proper box below and provide a popular-music chord symbol for the chord. Be sure to look at the clefs and key signatures.

Chopin: Nocturne in C♯ Minor, op. Post.

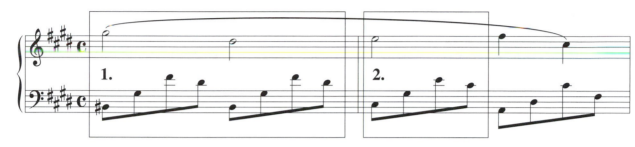

Bach: *The Well-Tempered Clavier* Book 1, BWV 846, Prelude I

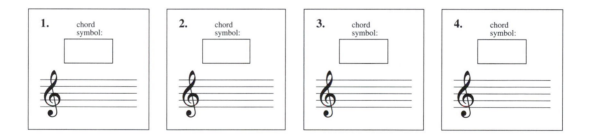

Schumann: *Ich grolle nicht, Dichterliebe, no. 7*

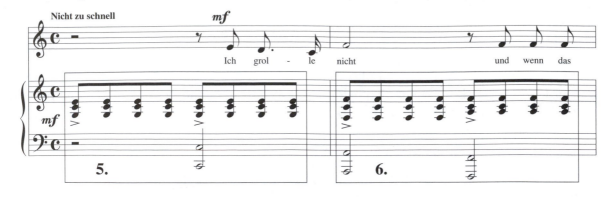

Mendelssohn: *Songs without Words* op. 30, no. 6

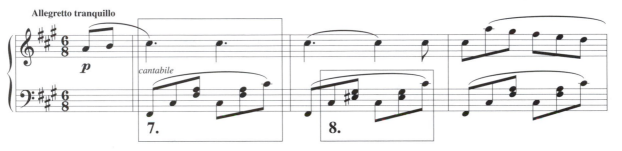

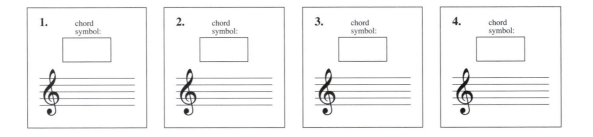

ASSIGNMENT 9.4b (continued)

Name _____

Section _____

Date _____

Brahms: *Wiegenlied,* op. 49, no. 4

Mozart: Theme with Variations, K. 284

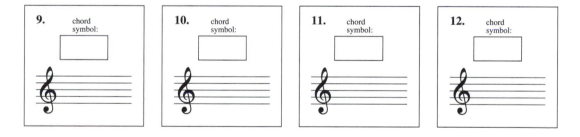

Chopin: Mazurka in B♭ Major, op. 7, no. 1

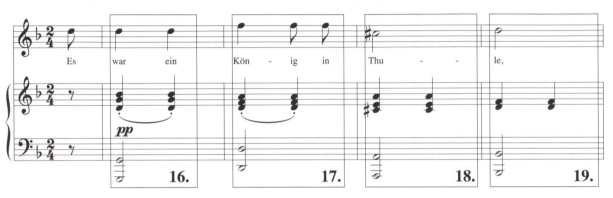

Schubert: *Der König in Thule,* D. 367

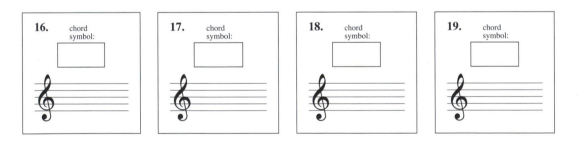

13. chord symbol:

14. chord symbol:

15. chord symbol:

16. chord symbol:

17. chord symbol:

18. chord symbol:

19. chord symbol:

CHAPTER TEN
The Harmonic System

"Country music is three chords and the truth."
— HARLAN HOWARD, 1927–2002
(country songwriter)

The Harmonic System in Major Keys

In this chapter you will learn how to choose chords to fit a melody. The logic in the harmonic system will help you in making your own chord choices. You can begin to see it by examining the chords for two songs contained in the songbook: "Down in the Valley" and "My Hat."

Examine the popular-music chord symbols above the melody in "Down in the Valley" (songbook p. 277). You will see that this song has only two chords: **G** and **D**^{7}.

figure 10.1

An examination of "My Hat" (songbook p. 291) shows that it also has only two chords: **C** and **G**^{7}.

figure 10.2

Listen to these songs (CD tracks 24 and 42, or the Web site).

At first glance it may not be easy to see the similarity between the chords for these two songs, but figure 10.3 clearly shows that the two chords are built on the tonic and the dominant (fifth scale degree) in both songs.

figure 10.3

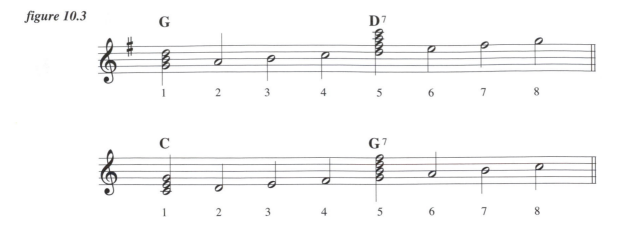

The chords on the tonic and dominant are the most common chords in music based on major and minor scales.

Roman-Numeral Analysis

Chords are labeled according to the scale degree of their roots. To make the distinction between the scale degree and the chord, use roman numerals for all chords: the tonic chord will be labeled **I**, and the dominant chord will be labeled **V**. The seventh chord will be labeled with a superscript "7" beside the roman numeral. The key will be indicated by its letter name followed by a colon. When chords are labeled with roman numerals, the result is called a *roman-numeral analysis*. This analysis will help you to understand the structure of harmony.

figure 10.4

Triads can be built on each scale degree, as shown in figure 10.5:

figure 10.5

Play each of these triads and note that three triad qualities are represented: major, minor, and diminished. The quality of triads is shown in roman numerals as follows:

> major triads uppercase roman numerals (**I**)
>
> minor triads lowercase roman numerals (**ii**)
>
> diminished triads lowercase roman numerals with a degree sign (**vii°**)

Figure 10.6 shows the roman-numeral analysis of each of the triads in C major:

figure 10.6

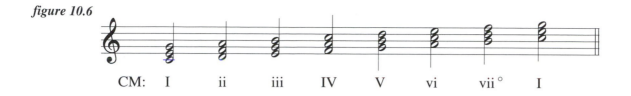

CM: I   ii   iii   IV   V   vi   vii°   I

Look at the chords suggested for "Lullaby" by Brahms in the songbook (p. 289, CD track 39, or the Web site). Do a roman-numeral analysis of these chords. You will see three different roman numerals in this song: **I, IV,** and **V⁷.** The **IV** chord is known as the *subdominant chord.* This name comes from the fact that fourth scale degree (subdominant) is a P5 below the tonic, whereas the dominant is a P5 above.

figure 10.7

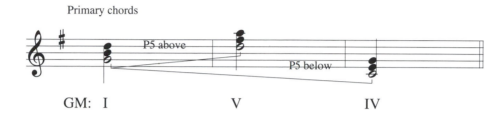

Primary chords

P5 above

P5 below

GM: I   V   IV

Primary Chords

The tonic, dominant, and subdominant chords are known as the *primary chords.* Most simple melodies can be harmonized with only these three chords. Listen to the recording and then do a roman-numeral analysis of "Silent Night" (p. 302, CD track 54, or the Web site) and *Cielito Lindo* (p. 275, CD track 21, or the Web site) in the songbook. In spite of the fact that these songs are in different keys with different chords, the roman numerals show that they are harmonized using the three primary chords. Roman-numeral analysis is a valuable method of showing the underlying similarity in chord choice in melodies in a variety of keys.

Go to the Online Learning Center and click on Chapter 10. Activities 10.1, 10.2, and 10.3 present opportunities to identify the primary chords in a musical setting. Follow the instructions and continue to try different answers until you get all the roman numerals correct. It may take several tries to accomplish this.

Secondary Chords

The chords on scale degrees other than the tonic, dominant, and subdominant are known as the *secondary chords.* They are used to provide color and variety in harmonization. Listen to the recording and then do a roman-numeral analysis of "Sweet Betsy from Pike" (p. 305, CD track 63, or the Web site) and "We Shall Overcome" (p. 311, CD track 71, or the Web site). These two songs are good illustrations of the use of secondary chords (**ii, iii, vi,** and **vii°**) to add interest and color to harmonization.

◆ **ASSIGNMENT 10.1, PAGES 211, 213**

Go to the Online Learning Center and click on Chapter 10. Activities 10.4, 10.5, and 10.6 present opportunities to identify the primary and secondary chords in a musical setting. These activities are arranged in a sequence of increasing difficulty, with few clues on the screen to help you. You must rely more and more on what you hear to identify the chords correctly.

Quick Check

1. Play each of the songs you have analyzed with the chords indicated. Play or sing the melody and have a friend play the chords. Then switch parts and play the chords while your friend plays or sings the melody. The important thing is that you hear the harmonic background along with the melody. "Silent Night" is written out in figure 10.8 to show you the pattern.

figure 10.8

Silent Night

* Move chords down an octave when they would conflict with melody notes.

2. If you own a guitar, you can play the chords for the preceding songs and sing the melodies. Appendix 3 lists fingerings for all common chords. Notice that both the Popular-Music Chord Symbols chart and the Guitar Chords chart (appendixes 2 and 3) list the chords so that the dominant and dominant seventh chords (**V** and **V⁷**) are directly above the tonic (**I**), and the subdominant chord (**IV**) is directly below the tonic.

The Harmonic System in Minor Keys

To understand the harmonic system in minor keys, look at "Pat-a-Pan" in the songbook (p. 295, CD track 46, or the Web site). Do a roman-numeral analysis of the chords in this song. Remember to use uppercase roman numerals for major triads and lowercase for minor triads. An analysis shows that only three chords occur in this song: Em = **i**, Am = **iv**, and B⁷ = **V⁷**. These are the *primary chords* in minor. These three chords contain all the tones of the E minor scale in harmonic form:

figure 10.9

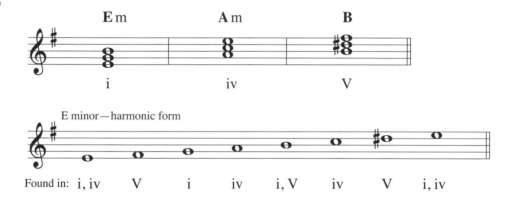

Most harmony in minor keys derives from the harmonic form of the scale (which accounts for the scale's name). Figure 10.10 shows the triads on each scale degree in the harmonic minor.

figure 10.10

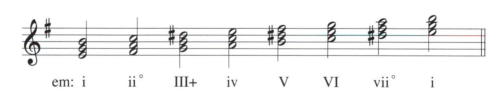

Listen to the recording and then do a roman-numeral analysis of "Go Down Moses" in the songbook (p. 278, CD track 26, or the Web site). Again, you will see that the primary chords are used exclusively.

figure 10.11

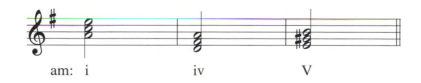

Although the primary chords in the harmonic form of minor appear more often than in other chords, some songs use the full harmonic resources of the minor scale. As you can see in figure 10.12, the minor scale in all its forms contains a wide variety of chords:

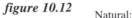

Do a roman-numeral analysis of "Greensleeves" and find the chords in figure 10.12 (p. 280, CD track 28, or the Web site). The chords for this song occur primarily in the natural and melodic forms of the scale, and the chords in "Greensleeves" are an excellent example of the colorful harmony that is possible in minor.

Quick Check

Perform "Go Down Moses, "Pat-a-Pan," and "Greensleeves" with friends or classmates. One person can play the chords on the piano while the others play or sing the melody, or you may like to use other instruments. Experiment with various combinations.

Circle Progressions

The strongest harmonic progressions in tonal music are those consisting of major and minor triads (and the seventh chords built on these triads) whose roots are a perfect fifth apart. The descending fifth (or ascending fourth) progressions are particularly strong and are known as *circle progressions* (or *circle of fifth progressions*). Figure 10.13 shows the circle for major keys. (Some progressions are written as ascending fourth progressions to keep the chords on the staff.)

figure 10.13

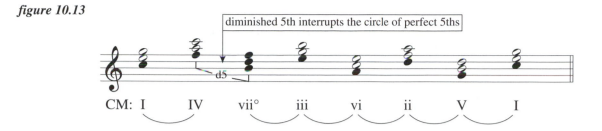

diminished 5th interrupts the circle of perfect 5ths

d5

CM:　I　　　IV　　vii°　　iii　　　vi　　　ii　　　V　　　I

Examine the harmonic progressions in "Morning Has Broken" in the songbook (p. 290, CD track 40, or the Web site). This song contains eighteen harmonic progressions. Seven of these are circle progressions (major and minor triads and related seventh chords in descending fifth or ascending fourth relationship). The circle progressions are marked with connecting lines in figure 10.14. Of the nineteen chords in this song, twelve are primary chords. Listen to the recording, paying particular attention to the circle progressions.

figure 10.14

Morning Has Broken

In general, good harmonization will result from an emphasis on the primary chords and circle progressions. The chart of Popular-Music Chord Symbols in Appendix 2, page 245, is arranged in a circle progression. Use it to help you make strong choices in harmonizing melodies.

The Harmonic Background of Rounds

In Chapter 6 you learned to sing in parts by singing rounds. With your understanding of harmony, you can now find out how rounds work. Figure 10.15 shows "Are You Sleeping?" (p. 266, CD track 11, or the Web site) with the four sections of the melody directly below each other. The fifth line shows the resulting chords.

figure 10.15

It is clear that the four parts of "Are You Sleeping?" fit together because they create the tonic and dominant seventh chords. This is the fundamental principle of all singing in harmony: the parts fit together to create or imply chords.

◆ **ASSIGNMENT 10.2, PAGES 215, 217**

Part Songs

Another way of singing in harmony is *part singing*. One or more melodic lines are added to the main melody to create the impression of harmony. Because chords are built in thirds, it is logical that the favorite interval in part songs is the third. To experience part singing, turn to "Saturday Night" in the songbook (p. 300, CD track 52, or the Web site). This song is harmonized entirely in thirds, making it very easy to sing. First sing each individual part until you are comfortable with it. Then divide into groups (or find a friend or two) and sing the song in parts along with the recording. Notice that the second measure contains a "triplet" figure (see p. 300). To complete the performance have someone play the chords on a keyboard or guitar.

Even with only two parts moving in thirds there is still considerable harmonic interest added to the melody. If other intervals are added, the harmony parts begin to be independent melodic lines creating additional musical interest.

Turn to *Tumbalalaika* (p. 308, CD track 68, or the Web site), which begins with a passage in thirds, as did "Saturday Night." Notice that in measures 8 and 9 of *Tumbalalaika*, the two parts are in unison (indicated by double stems), and in measures 10 and 11 the lower part remains on one note while the upper part moves. Similar patterns occur elsewhere in the song. Learn each part of this song separately and then sing them together with the recording. It may help to have someone play both parts on a keyboard when you first try putting the parts together. After you feel secure, add the chords on keyboard or guitar.

More Part Singing

The following two- and three-part songs will provide additional experience in part singing or playing. Be sure that you can perform each part alone before you attempt them in a group.

Two-part songs:
"Battle Hymn of the Republic" (p. 269, CD track 15, or the Web site)
Cantemus Hymnum (p. 272, CD track 19, or the Web site)

Three-part songs:
"Jacob's Ladder" (p. 284, CD track 34, or the Web site)
"The Linden Tree" (p. 286, CD track 36, or the Web site)
"Pick a Little, Talk a Little and Goodnight Ladies" (p. 296, CD track 48, or the Web site)

KEY TERMS

Define the following terms in your own words:

Roman-numeral analysis _____

Primary chords _____

Secondary chords _____

Circle progression _____

Part singing _____

LISTENING

The following songs are harmonized entirely with the primary chords (I, IV, V or V^7) in major keys. Listen to a number of these songs and follow along in the songbook. Play the primary chords on a keyboard along with the recording.

"Billy Boy" (p. 270, CD track 17, or the Web site)

Cielito Lindo (p. 275, CD track 21, or the Web site)

"Down in the Valley" (p. 277, CD track 24, or the Web site)

"Goodby, Old Paint" (p. 279, CD track 27, or the Web site)

"I Never Will Marry" (p. 281, CD track 30, or the Web site)

"I Saw Three Ships" (p. 282, CD track 31, or the Web site)

"I've Got to Know" (p. 283, CD track 33, or the Web site)

"Lavender's Blue" (p. 285, CD track 35, or the Web site)

"Lonesome Valley" (p. 288, CD track 37, or the Web site)

"Love Somebody" (p. 288, CD track 38, or the Web site)

"Lullaby" (p. 289, CD track 39, or the Web site)

"My Hat" (p. 291, CD track 42, or the Web site)

"Over the River and Through the Wood" (p. 294, CD track 45, or the Web site)

"Pawpaw Patch" (p. 295, CD track 47, or the Web site)

Santa Lucia (p. 299, CD track 51, or the Web site)

"Silent Night" (p. 302, CD track 54, or the Web site)

"Simple Gifts" (p. 302, CD track 55, or the Web site)

"Skip to My Lou" (p. 305, CD track 62, or the Web site)

"Twinkle, Twinkle Little Star" (p. 309, CD track 69, or the Web site)

USING WHAT YOU HAVE LEARNED

Make up melodies to go with the following chord progressions (shown both in popular-music chord symbols and in roman numerals). Play a chord progression until you are familiar with it and then add the melody. Write your melody on the staff provided. Join with a friend to perform your melody with the chords.

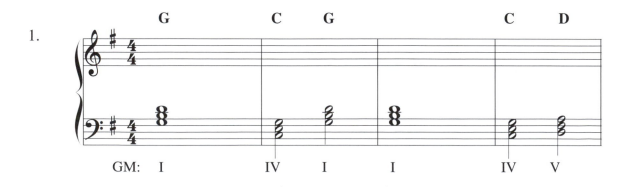

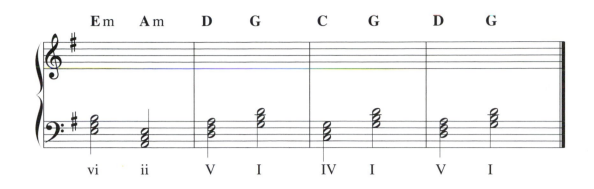

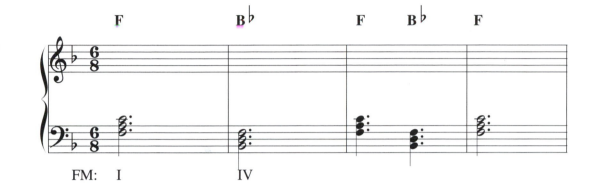

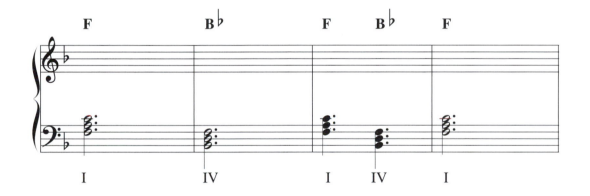

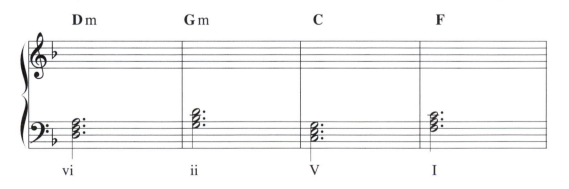

The Harmonic System   209

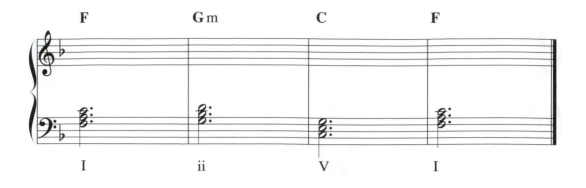

CHAPTER 10 — ASSIGNMENT 10.1a
Chord Analysis in Songs

Name _____

Section _____

Date _____

Write the chords for each of the following songs as called for by the popular-music chord symbols. Use the tones of the scale provided as the roots. If both a triad and a seventh chord occur on a single-scale degree, write the seventh chord. Write the key followed by a colon, followed by the correct roman numeral under each of the chords. Remember that uppercase roman numerals are used for major triads and that lowercase roman numerals indicate minor triads. (See the example.)

ex. **"Skip to My Lou" - F major (p. 305):**

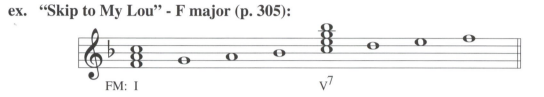

1. **"Love Somebody" - C major (p. 288):**

2. **"I've Got To Know" - E major (p. 283):**

3. **"Lavender's Blue" - D major (p. 285):**

4. **"Battle Hymn of the Republic" - B-flat major (p. 269):**

5. *Dona Nobis Pacem* - F major (p. 276):

6. "Barbara Ellen" - D major (p. 268):

7. "Sweet Betsy from Pike" - C major (p. 305):

8. "The First Noël" - C major (p. 278):

9. "Saturday Night" - D major (p. 300):

10. "We Shall Overcome" - C major (p. 311):

Name _____

Section _____

Date _____ _____

Write the primary triads (I, IV, V) in each of the following major keys. Remember to write the proper key signature in each case. Label each chord with the appropriate roman numeral. (See example.)

ex. F major:

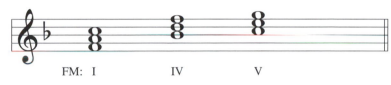

1. D major:

2. C major:

3. G major:

4. B-flat major:

5. A major:

6. **E-flat major:**

7. **A-flat major:**

8. **E major:**

9. **D-flat major:**

10. **B major:**

11. **G-flat major:**

12. **F-sharp major:**

CHAPTER 10 — ASSIGNMENT 10.2a
Primary Triads in Minor

Name _____

Section _____

Date _____

Write the primary triads (i, iv, V) in each of the following minor keys. Using the harmonic minor in each case, and remember to write the proper key signature. Label each chord with the appropriate roman numeral. (See example.)

ex. C minor:

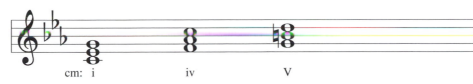

cm: i   iv   V

1. A minor:

2. B minor:

3. E minor:

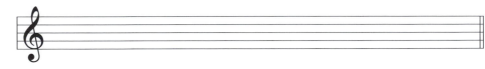

4. G minor:

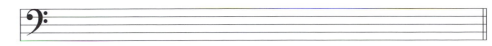

5. **F-sharp minor:**

6. **C-sharp minor:**

7. **F minor:**

8. **C minor:**

9. **B-flat minor:**

10. **E-flat minor:**

CHAPTER 10 — ASSIGNMENT 10.2b
Finding Chords in Rounds

Name _____

Section _____

Date _____

Copy the rounds indicated on the staves below. Examine each beat in all parts and write the harmonic background on the final stave. Nonharmonic tones are circled in the songbook, but you should ignore them. (See Chapter 11 for a discussion of these tones.) Do a roman-numeral analysis of the chords implied on each beat of the measures. (See figure 10.15, p. 206, for an example of the proper procedure.)

1. **Six Rounds in Major Keys, no. 4 - F major (p. 304):**

Harmonic Background:

2. Six Rounds in Major Keys, no. 2 - F major (p. 304):

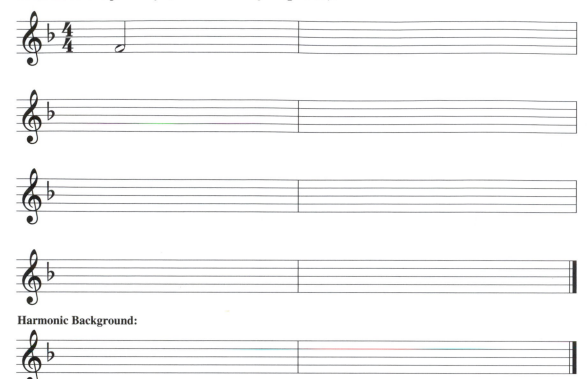

Harmonic Background:

3. "Row, Row, Row Your Boat" - C major (p. 298):

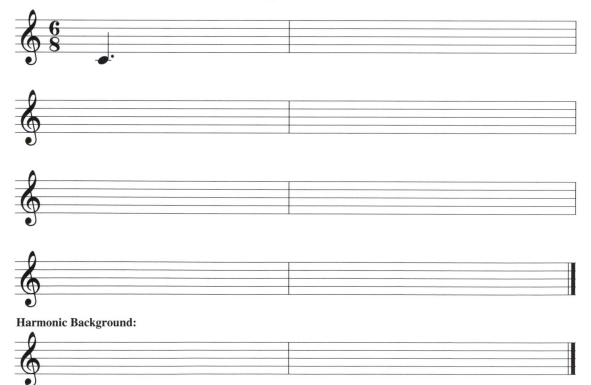

Harmonic Background:

ASSIGNMENT 10.2b (continued)

4. Three Rounds in Minor Keys, no. 3 ("Ah, Poor Bird") - D minor (p. 307):

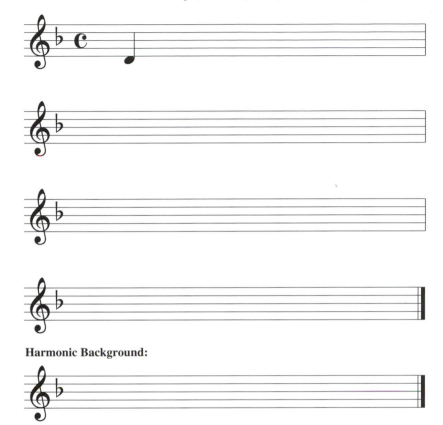

Harmonic Background:

Works of art are not created; they are there, waiting to be discovered.

—Edward Elgar, 1857–1934 (English composer)

You just pick up a chord, go twang, and you've got music.

—Sid Vicious, 1957–1979 (punk rock musician)

There's a basic rule that runs through all kinds of music,
kind of an unwritten rule. I don't know what it is, but I've got it.

—Ron Wood, 1947– (rock guitarist)

I didn't know composers had to take to the hills or the beach
and talk with the muses for a few months to get a show.

—Duke Ellington, 1899–1974 (American composer)

All the inspiration I ever needed was a phone call from a producer.

—Cole Porter, 1891–1964 (American composer)

Without craftsmanship, inspiration is a mere reed shaken in the wind.

—Johannes Brahms, 1833–1897 (German composer)

———————————————

Throughout history, people have studied and discussed the nature of artistic creativity. Do you agree with Elgar that the creative process involves tapping into forces outside normal experience? Do you think that musical principles are as mysterious as Ron Wood seems to imply? Is inspiration as simple as "a phone call from a producer"? What is the role of craftsmanship in creating music? Is musical creativity fundamentally different or similar to creativity in other areas?

CHAPTER ELEVEN
Introduction to Harmonizing and Composing

"It is better to make a piece of music than to perform one, better to perform one than to listen to one, better to listen to one than misuse it as a means of distraction, entertainment, or acquisition of 'culture.'"

—JOHN CAGE, 1912–1992 *(American composer)*

Learning to create music requires study and practice that goes beyond the limits of a fundamentals book. This chapter provides a brief introduction to the art of writing and harmonizing melodies to get you started. If you are interested in improving your composing skills, I urge you to seek a teacher who can give you further guidance.

Harmonizing Melodies

Selecting chords to accompany melodies requires careful examination of the whole melody to determine the best selection. Some melodies consist mostly of chord outlines, and these are easiest to deal with. For example, look at the first four measures of "Pawpaw Patch" in the songbook (p. 295, CD track 47, or the Web site). The first two measures outline an F-major triad and the third and fourth contain a C-major triad.

figure 11.1

In this case the chords are easy to select once you discover the chord outlines, and it would probably not be effective to harmonize these measures in any other way than with the tonic and dominant chords indicated in the songbook.

In other cases a chord is chosen to fit each tone of a melody. Examine "Twinkle, Twinkle Little Star" in the songbook (p. 309, CD track 69, or the Web site), where, except for the rising fifths (**C** to **G**), each note or repeated note group is given its own chord.

222

figure 11.2

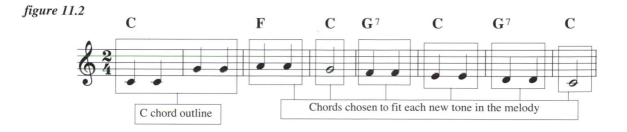

Listen to these songs and pay particular attention to the chords in the accompaniment.

Nonharmonic Tones

If you examine the melodies whose chords you analyzed in Chapter 10, you will find that not all tones in melodies are chord tones. So you can better understand the relationship between melody and harmony, all notes are circled that are not a part of the suggested chords in the song "My Bonnie."

figure 11.3

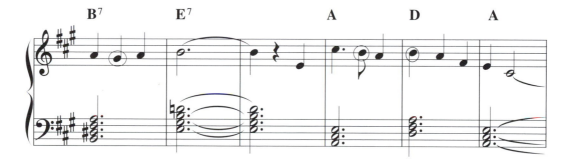

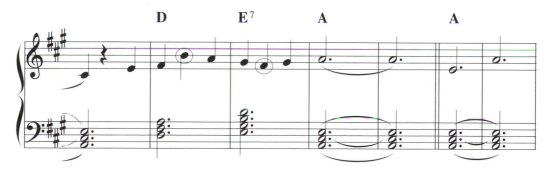

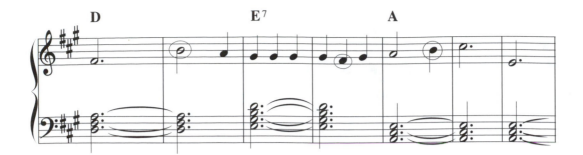

Listen to the song, paying attention to the nonharmonic tones.

The circled tones are called *nonharmonic tones* because they are not a part of the prevailing chord structure. As you can see, there are many more chord tones than nonharmonic tones in the melody. Notice in particular that most nonharmonic tones are smoothly connected with surrounding melody notes with steps both approaching and leaving the nonharmonic tone:

figure 11.4

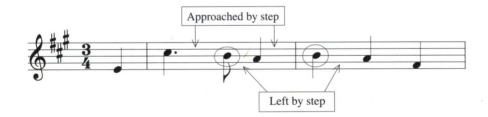

All the nonharmonic tones in "My Bonnie" are left by step, and in only three cases are there leaps to a nonharmonic tone, in contrast with the fact that nearly one third of the intervals in "My Bonnie" are leaps (nineteen leaps and thirty-three steps).

figure 11.5

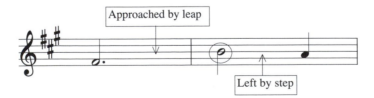

Nonharmonic tones are usually connected to chord tones by step motion.

Harmonic Rhythm

The change from one chord to another creates a rhythmic pattern referred to as the *harmonic rhythm* of a piece. This rhythm can actually be written out as shown in figure 11.6:

figure 11.6

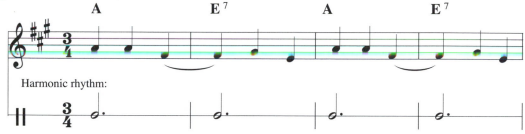

This rhythm is often quite regular, as in *Cielito Lindo* (p. 275, CD track 21, or the Web site) above, but sometimes it varies considerably throughout a phrase, as in "Children's Prayer" (p. 274, CD track 20, or the Web site):

figure 11.7

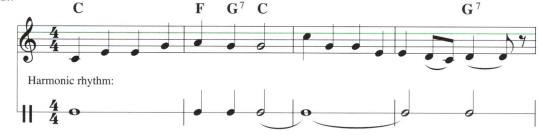

Listen to these songs to hear the effect of the harmonic rhythm.

Important harmonic changes tend to occur on the first beats of measures. A fairly regular harmonic rhythm with chords changing on first beats of measures will generally result in a better accompaniment. Chord patterns that emphasize the primary chords and contain circle progressions are generally stronger than those containing other progressions.

Playing Accompaniments on a Keyboard

After you choose chords, either by the methods described in Chapter 10 or by following the chords suggested in the songbook, you can begin to create accompaniments at the keyboard. In Chapter 9 the melodies were accompanied by block chords in root position. A disadvantage of this method of accompanying a melody is that chord changes force you to move your left hand around the keyboard. An alternative, which alleviates this problem and creates smoother-sounding accompaniments, involves inversions of chords. You can choose inversions that put the chord tones under the hand with little or no motion. The general principle that will usually produce good results is the *common tone* principle: **If the following chord has any tones in common with the present chord, keep the common tone in the same location and move the other tones to the nearest chord tone.** An accompaniment for the song "Lullaby" will demonstrate the common-tone principle. Note that "Lullaby" contains only the primary chords (**I, IV,** and **V^7**).

figure 11.8

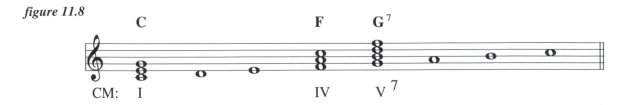

In moving to the **G^7** chord in measure 4, keep the common tone (**G**) and move to the nearest chord tones:

figure 11.9

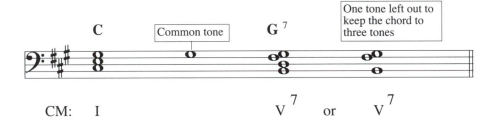

In moving to the **F** chord in measure 9, keep the common tone (**C**) and move to the nearest chord tones:

figure 11.10

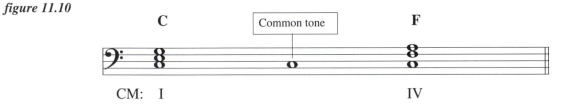

Figure 11.11 shows "Lullaby" (p. 289, CD track 39, or the Web site) with the chords as described above. (Nonharmonic tones in the melody are circled.)

figure 11.11

Lullaby

Johannes Brahms

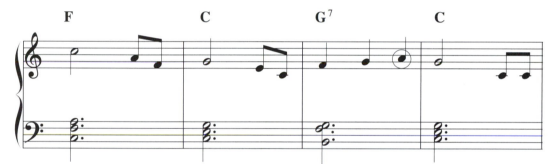

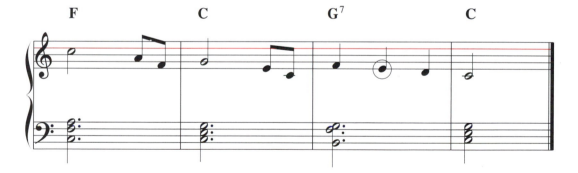

Play the chords in the bass clef along with the recording.

Adding Rhythm to Accompaniments

Accompaniments serve two important functions: they provide harmonic support and rhythmic support to a melody. The emphasis thus far has been on providing harmonic support. Now we will add rhythmic support. The simplest way to provide rhythmic support is just to repeat the chord on each beat.

Introduction to Harmonizing and Composing   227

figure 11.12

Play the melody of "Lullaby" (figure 11.11) while a friend plays the accompaniment. Repeat the chords on each beat as illustrated above.

Another form of rhythmic support is a repeating rhythmic pattern in each measure. Figure 11.13 shows a common rhythmic pattern in $\frac{3}{4}$ time.

figure 11.13

Play "Lullaby" (figure 11.11) with a friend, using the $\frac{3}{4}$ pattern in figure 11.13. Switch parts and play the piece again.

If you would like help in developing your skill in accompanying, you might consider private or class lessons on the keyboard. Many teachers are interested in helping adult beginners develop their keyboard proficiency.

Phrases in Music

Music is divided into phrases, much like the sentences of language. A *phrase* is the smallest complete musical thought. You can identify phrases by the pauses you sense in a melody. You will naturally take a breath at such points. If there is a text with a melody, the musical phrases normally coincide with punctuation marks in the text. "The First Noël" (p. 278, CD track 25, or the Web site) is reprinted in figure 11.14 with the phrases marked. Notice that most phrases have punctuation in the text and that each phrase ends with a longer note value.

figure 11.14

The First Noël

Most phrases are either two, four, or eight measures in length, with four measures being most common. Notice that all the phrases in "The First Noël" are four measures long.

Melodic Contour of Phrases

An examination of the first phrase of "The First Noël" reveals a shape that rises to the **C** in the third measure and falls from there to the **G** at the end of the phrase.

figure 11.15

This shape is the *melodic contour* of the phrase. Melodies can be seen as rising and falling patterns of pitch, and a study of many melodies reveals that a common contour is a rise to a high point somewhere within the phrase and a fall from that point to the end of the phrase. Examine each phrase in "The First Noël" to see the contours.

figure 11.16

Listen to "The First Noël," paying particular attention to the phrases and melodic contour.

This common pattern of a falling contour at the end of phrases corresponds to the falling pitch at the end of sentences in speech, and is called the *cadence*. The word *cadence* comes from the Latin word *cadere,* which means "to fall." Thus the cadence is a form of musical punctuation, similar to the period or comma in written language.

Harmonic Cadence

The ends of phrases are also marked by harmonic patterns that have the function of punctuation or cadence. An examination of the end of each phrase in "The First Noël" reveals that all phrases end with a tonic chord (**C**), and the chord just before is either the subdominant (**F**) or the dominant (**G**^{7}).

These harmonic patterns represent two common cadence patterns in tonal music. They are: the *authentic cadence* (**V - I**) and the *plagal cadence* (**IV - I**).

figure 11.17

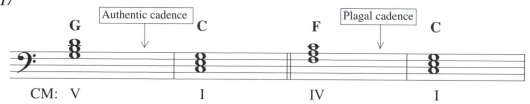

The first phrase of "Lullaby" demonstrates the other common cadence pattern: the *half cadence,* which is a cadence on the dominant chord.

figure 11.18

This cadence gets its name because it is "half" of an authentic cadence.

Form

A song is much more than a collection of phrases. An examination of "The First Noël" reveals that the first, third, and fifth phrases are very similar, as are the second, fourth, and sixth phrases. If we label the first phrase "A" and the second phrase "B," the following pattern of phrases emerges:

A   B   A   B   A'   B'

(The primes on the final **A** and **B** indicate that these phrases are similar to, but not exactly the same as, the previous statements of these phrases.) The pattern of repeated or similar phrases you observe in "The First Noël" creates a sense of unity that holds the melody together. This is referred to as the *form* of the song.

Observe the form of "My Bonnie," which we discussed at the beginning of the chapter. Each phrase in the song is four measures in length, with the following form:

A   A'   A   B   ‖   C   D   C   D'

Each four-measure phrase is labeled in figure 11.19 ("Bendemeer's Stream") (p. 270, CD track 16, or the Web site). Listen to this song and follow the form.

figure 11.19

Bendemeer's Stream

The following form emerges (taking the repeated section into account):

A   B   A   B   C   D   A'   B

The "**C**" and "**D**" phrases provide contrast, and the return to the "**A**" and "**B**" phrases give a sense of completion and closure to the melody. A satisfying musical form has repetition of material to provide unity and fresh musical ideas to provide variety. Achieving the proper balance of unity and variety is one of the most important skills the composer must learn. Listen to a number of songs in the songbook and analyze the form. Ask yourself what provides unity and what introduces variety in each song.

◆ **ASSIGNMENT 11.3, PAGES 241–242**

A Final Word

The ability to create music is partly a natural gift, but you can improve your skill as a composer with knowledge and experience. The information in this chapter concerning the length and contour of phrases, the nature of cadences, and form can guide you as you set about composing melodies. Your knowledge of harmonic rhythm and chord choice can help you to create effective accompaniments. The most important ingredient, which only *you* can supply, is your creative imagination, which will blossom if you let it. A positive mental attitude is absolutely essential as you begin to compose. Seek the advice of experienced musicians, polish your creative work, and you can compose music that will give you personal satisfaction and enjoyment. I wish you every success in this and all your musical endeavors.

KEY TERMS

Define the following terms in your own words:

Nonharmonic tone _____

Harmonic rhythm _____

Common tone _____

Phrase _____

Melodic contour _____

Cadence _____

Authentic cadence _____

Plagal cadence _____

Half cadence _____

Form _____

USING WHAT YOU HAVE LEARNED

1. Write a melody in C major, in $\frac{3}{4}$ time, consisting of four 4-measure phrases. Using the following form:

A   A   B   A

If you want to make any of the repeated **A** phrases slightly different (**A'**), feel free to do so.

Choose chords to accompany your melody, bearing in mind the advice about chord choice, harmonic rhythm, and cadence. Write your song on the staves below.

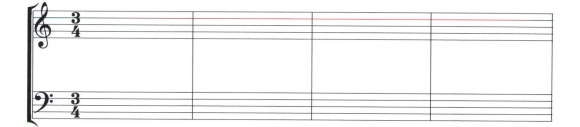

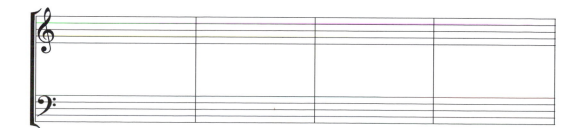

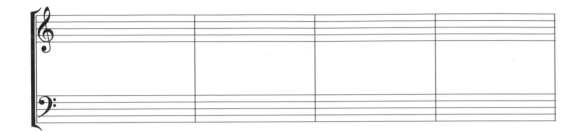

2. Write an accompaniment for "Goodby, Old Paint," using this accompaniment pattern as a model:

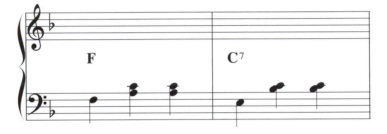

Start the accompaniment on the first full measure and change chords whenever the popular-music chord symbols tell you to. Play the completed song with a friend.

Goodby, Old Paint

3. Write an accompaniment for "Down in the Valley," using this accompaniment figure as a model:

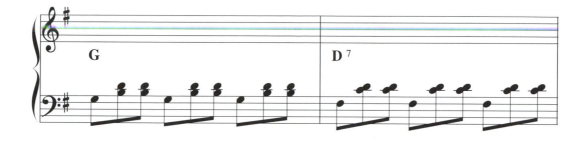

Start the accompaniment on the first full measure and change chords whenever the popular-music chord symbols tell you do. Play the completed song with a friend.

Down in the Valley

Go to the Online Learning Center and click on Chapter 11. Here you will find a number of activities that support your understanding of the process of harmonizing and composing. Use these activities and you will discover concrete methods that will help you develop your own creative processes.

CHAPTER 11 — ASSIGNMENT 11.1a
Nonharmonic Tones

Name _____

Section _____

Date _____

Circle all tones that are not part of the indicated chords in "Lavender's Blue."

See the nonharmonic tone analysis of "My Bonnie" in figure 11.3 (p. 223) for an example of the proper procedure.

Lavender's Blue

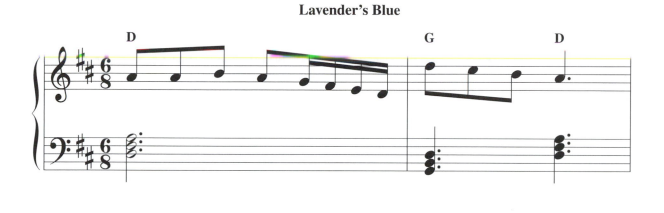

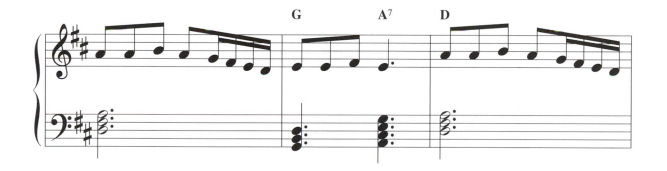

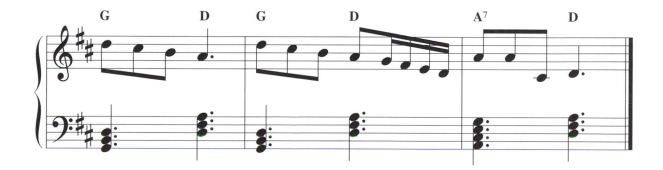

CHAPTER 11 — ASSIGNMENT 11.1b
Nonharmonic Tones

Circle all tones that are not part of the indicated chords in "Simple Gifts."

See the nonharmonic tone analysis of "My Bonnie" in figure 11.3 (p. 223) for an example of the proper procedure.

Simple Gifts

Writing Chords and Identifying
Nonharmonic Tones

Name _____

Section _____

Date _____

Write each of the suggested chords in "Barbara Ellen," using the correct rhythmic values to show the harmonic rhythm (see figure 11.7, p. 225). Now circle all tones that are not part of the indicated chords.

Barbara Ellen

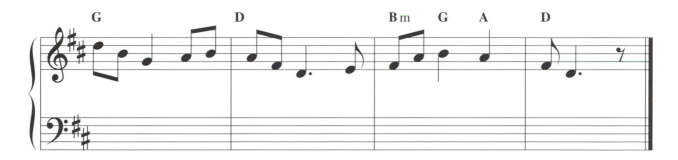

Write each of the suggested chords in "Crusader's Hymn" using the correct rhythmic values to show the harmonic rhythm (see figure 11.7, p. 225). Now circle all tones that are not a part of the indicated chords.

Crusader's Hymn

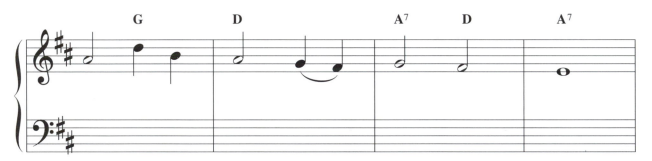

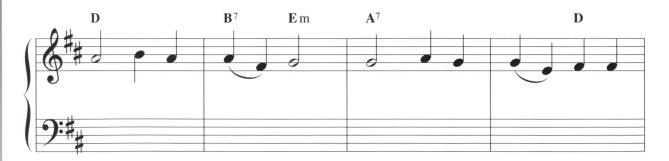

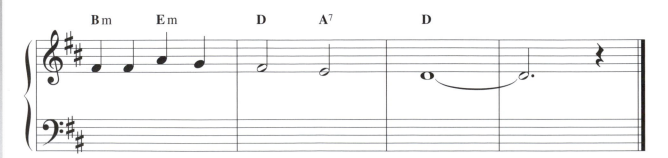

CHAPTER 11 — ASSIGNMENT 11.3a
Cadences and Phrase Analysis

Name _____

Section _____

Date _____

Divide the song *Auprès de ma Blonde* into phrases and draw the melodic contour of each phrase. Identify the cadence of each phrase by type: authentic, plagal, or half. (See figures 11.14, 11.15, 11.16, and 11.17 on pages 229–231 for the proper procedure.)

Auprès de ma Blonde

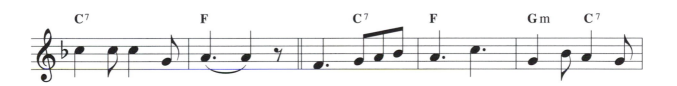

CHAPTER 11 — ASSIGNMENT 11.3b
Cadences and Phrase Analysis

Divide the song "I Saw Three Ships" into phrases and draw the melodic contour of each phrase. Identify the cadence of each phrase by type: authentic, plagal, or half. (See figures 11.14, 11.15, 11.16, and 11.17 on pages 229–231 for the proper procedure.)

I Saw Three Ships

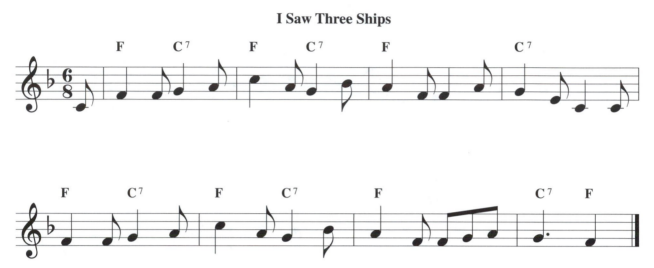

APPENDIX 1
Inversion of Intervals

An interval is inverted when the bottom tone is raised by an octave (or the top tone is lowered by an octave.

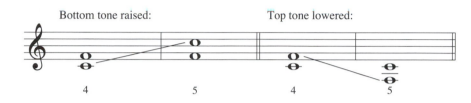

When a fourth is inverted, it becomes a fifth. Notice the effect of inversion on each of the intervals:

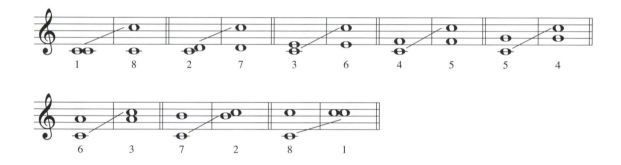

Notice that in each case, the sum of an interval and its inversion is equal to nine (1 + 8 = 9; 2 + 7 = 9; and so on).

To determine the specific quality of an inverted interval, study and play the following intervals and their inversions.

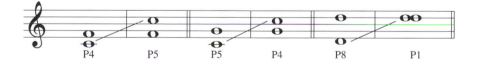

When Inverted, Perfect Intervals Remain Perfect Intervals

The situation with major intervals is different. Study and play the following major intervals and their inversions.

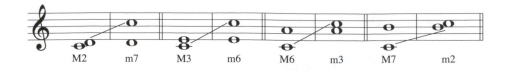

When Inverted, Major Intervals Become Minor Intervals

Study and play the following minor intervals and their inversions.

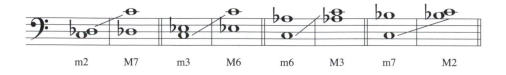

When Inverted, Minor Intervals Become Major Intervals

In Chapter 7 you learned one method for writing intervals below a given note. Now you can learn another method. To write an interval below a given note, first think of the inversion of that interval above the note and then write that note an octave lower.

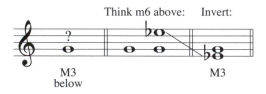

In effect, by writing the note an octave lower you are inverting the interval a second time.

APPENDIX 2
Popular-Music Chord Symbols

Notation of Bass Notes in Popular Music

Often, in popular music, chord symbols appear that are similar to fractions: **C/G** or **Cm⁷/F**. The symbol to the left of the slash indicates the chord to be played; the symbol to the right indicates the bass note. This bass note may or may not be a part of the chord:

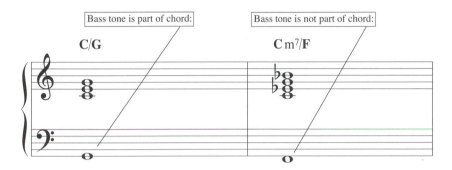

You will generally obtain the best musical effect in these cases by leaving considerable space between the chord and the bass note.

More Complex Chords

Many chord qualities are not explained in this book or listed on the chart on page 246. In most cases it is possible to substitute a simpler chord for these more complex sonorities; for example, if **G¹³** is specified, substitute **G⁷**. If you would like to figure out these more complex chords, bear in mind that chords are spelled in thirds. The more complex chords are generally the result of placing additional thirds above the seventh:

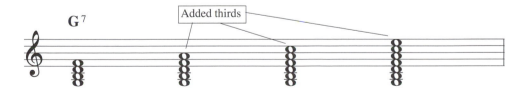

The chords are named for the interval formed between the root and the highest note:

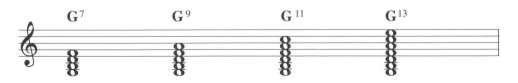

In this book we have used the more common chord symbols. However, a number of other systems for indicating chords in popular and commercial music are in use. The chart below presents a number of alternative symbols you may encounter.

	Common	Less Common
	C	CM–CMa–CMaj–C△
	Cm	Cmi–Cmin–C-
	Caug	C⁺
	Cdim	C°
	C6	CM6–CMa6
	Cm6	Cmin6
	C7	Cdom7
	CMa7	CMaj7–CM7–C△7
	Cm7	Cmi7–Cmin7–C-7

APPENDIX 3
Guitar Chords

The guitar chords on the accompanying chart assume a standard tuning of the instrument:

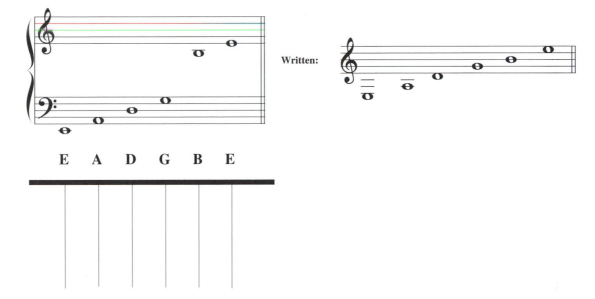

Written:

Tune the strings using a keyboard instrument. If a keyboard is not available, you can use the following method: Tune the lowest string as close to **E** as you can, then press at the fifth fret of the **E** string to get an **A** and tune the next string to that pitch. Continue in the same way with the other strings—except that the *fourth* fret is used on the **G** string to get the **B**:

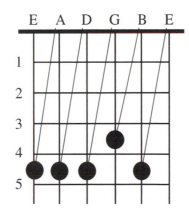

Chords are presented here in a circle-of-fifths order that places common chords in the various keys near each other on the chart. For example, in the key of **D** major the **A** and the **A**[7] chords are found immediately above the **D** chord and the **G** chord immediately below. Black dots ("•") indicate areas of each string that are to be pressed down.

F♯-G♭	F♯7	F♯ m	F♯ m7	F♯6	F♯ m6	F♯ dim
B	B7	B m	B m7	B6	B m6	B dim
E	E7	E m	E m7	E6	E m6	E dim
A	A7	A m	A m7	A6	A m6	A dim
D	D7	D m	D m7	D6	D m6	D dim
G	G7	G m	G m7	G6	G m6	G dim
C	C7	C m	C m7	C6	C m6	C dim
F	F7	F m	F m7	F6	F m6	F dim
B♭	B♭7	B♭ m	B♭ m7	B♭6	B♭ m6	B♭ dim
E♭-D♯	E♭7	E♭ m	E♭ m7	E♭6	E♭ m6	E♭ dim
A♭-G♯	A♭7	A♭ m	A♭ m7	A♭6	A♭ m6	A♭ dim
D♭-C♯	D♭7	D♭ m	D♭ m7	D♭6	D♭ m6	D♭ dim

APPENDIX 4
Playing a Keyboard Instrument

This appendix is a brief introduction to playing a keyboard instrument with both hands. If you can play the melody with one hand (usually the right hand), the other hand is free to play an accompaniment. The pieces you will play involve "five-finger position" in both hands. This means that the hands will be set in one position before you begin to play and will remain there throughout the piece. This allows you to concentrate on reading the music without worrying about where the keys are relative to your fingers. In fact, **it is important that you look at the music rather than your hands as you play.** Avoid the habit of looking back and forth from the music to your hands, because this will slow down your playing considerably. If you have taken a typing class, you will have heard similar advice given for the same reason.

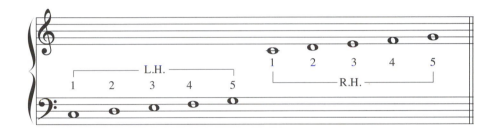

First set the two hand positions and play all the keys "under the fingers."

Now practice playing with each hand:

Warm-up Piece

Now you are ready to play "Aura Lee." Keep your eyes on the music and let your hands "do the walking."

Aura Lee

United States

You can play "Love Somebody" and "Lightly Row" with the same hand positions:

Love Somebody

United States

Lightly Row

United States

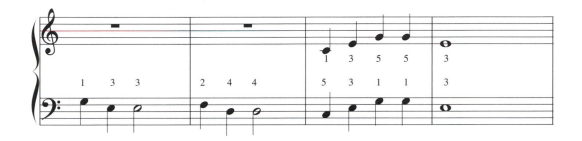

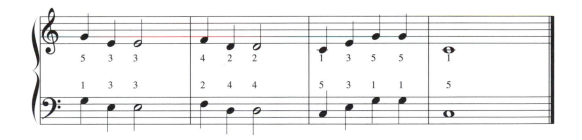

"My Hat" has the hands in different positions. Set the hand positions:

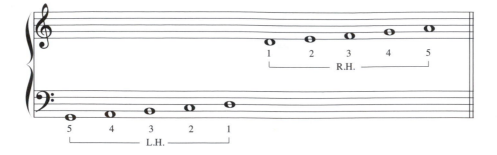

Practice playing these hand positions:

Warm-up Piece

Play through both the right-hand part (the melody) and the left-hand part, making sure to count the rhythm carefully. Then play the piece with both hands simultaneously. (Notice that the last note in the melody requires the right thumb to shift one key down. This is indicated by the circled "1" above that note.) It may take several practice sessions to be able to play the piece smoothly, but repeated practice will get results.

My Hat

Moderate waltz time

Germany

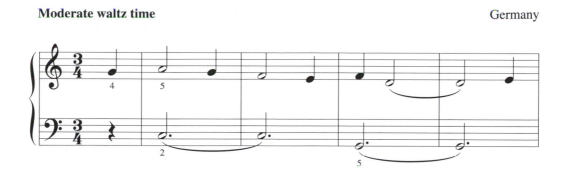

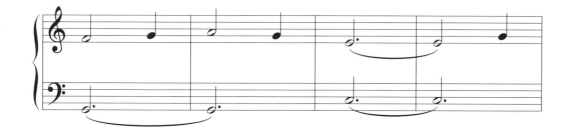

"Go Tell Aunt Rhody" has more activity in the left hand. Prepare the piece as you did "My Hat."

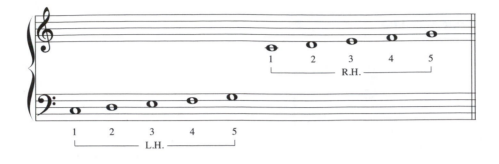

Go Tell Aunt Rhody

Moderately

United States

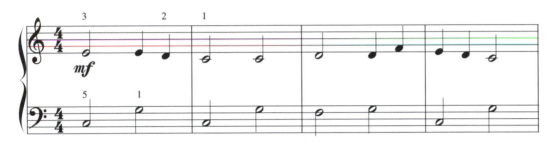

Answers to Selected Problems in the Assignments

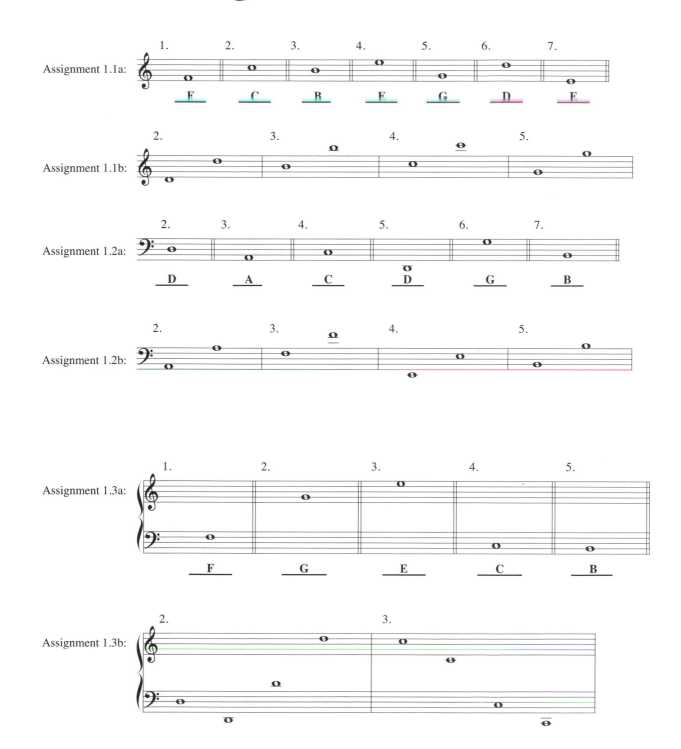

Assignment 1.1a:

1. F 2. C 3. B 4. E 5. G 6. D 7. E

Assignment 1.1b:

Assignment 1.2a:

D   A   C   D   G   B

Assignment 1.2b:

Assignment 1.3a:

F   G   E   C   B

Assignment 1.3b:

Assignment 2.1: 2. a is shorter by 2 beats.
   3. a is shorter by 2 beats.

Assignment 2.2a: 2.   3.

Assignment 2.2b: 2.   3.

Assignment 2.3a: 2.   3.

Assignment 2.3b: 1.

Assignment 3.1a: 1. 4 measures
   2. 4 measures

Assignment 3.2: 1.

   2.

Assignment 3.3: 1. $\frac{4}{4}$ or **C**   2. $\frac{3}{4}$

Assignment 4.1a: 1. 4 measures
   2. 4 measures

Assignment 4.1b: 1.

   2.

Assignment 4.2a: "Aura Lee" $\frac{4}{4}$ quadruple - simple

   "Barbara Ellen" $\frac{3}{4}$ triple - simple

Assignment 4.2b: 1. 3 measures
   2. 4 measures

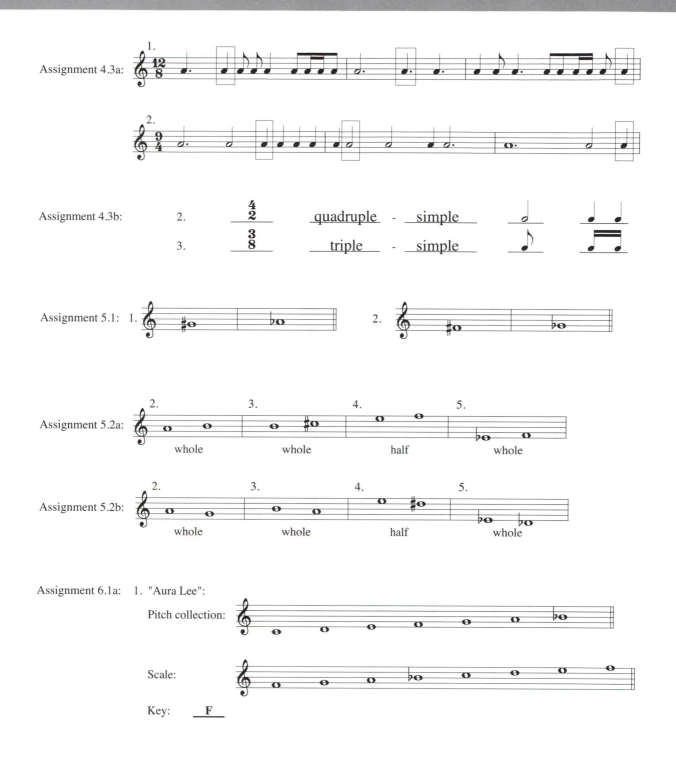

Assignment 4.3a:

Assignment 4.3b:
2. $\frac{4}{2}$ quadruple - simple
3. $\frac{3}{8}$ triple - simple

Assignment 5.1: 1. 2.

Assignment 5.2a:
2. 3. 4. 5.
whole   whole   half   whole

Assignment 5.2b:
2. 3. 4. 5.
whole   whole   half   whole

Assignment 6.1a: 1. "Aura Lee":

Pitch collection:

Scale:

Key: __F__

Assignment 6.1b: 1. "Barbara Ellen":

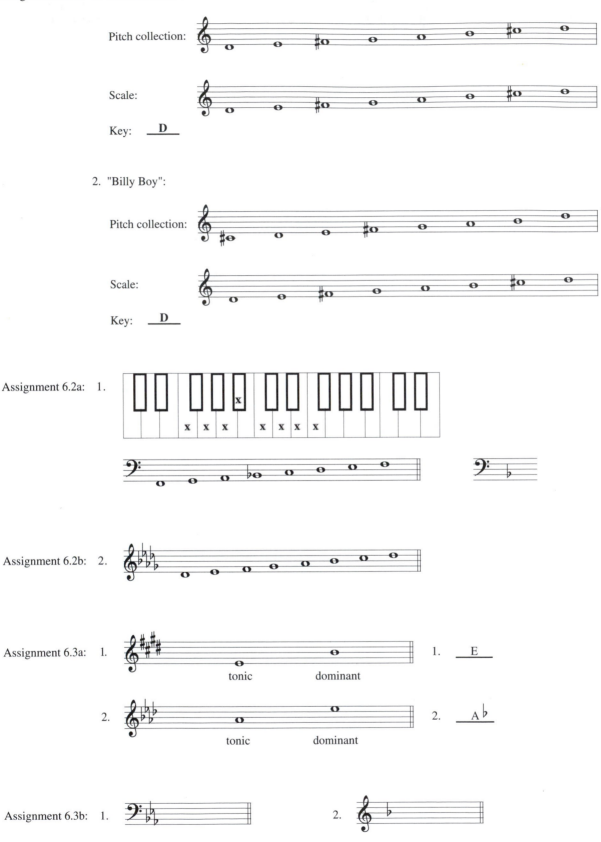

Pitch collection:

Scale:

Key: __D__

2. "Billy Boy":

Pitch collection:

Scale:

Key: __D__

Assignment 6.2a: 1.

Assignment 6.2b: 2.

Assignment 6.3a: 1.   1.   __E__

tonic   dominant

2.   2.   __A♭__

tonic   dominant

Assignment 6.3b: 1.   2.

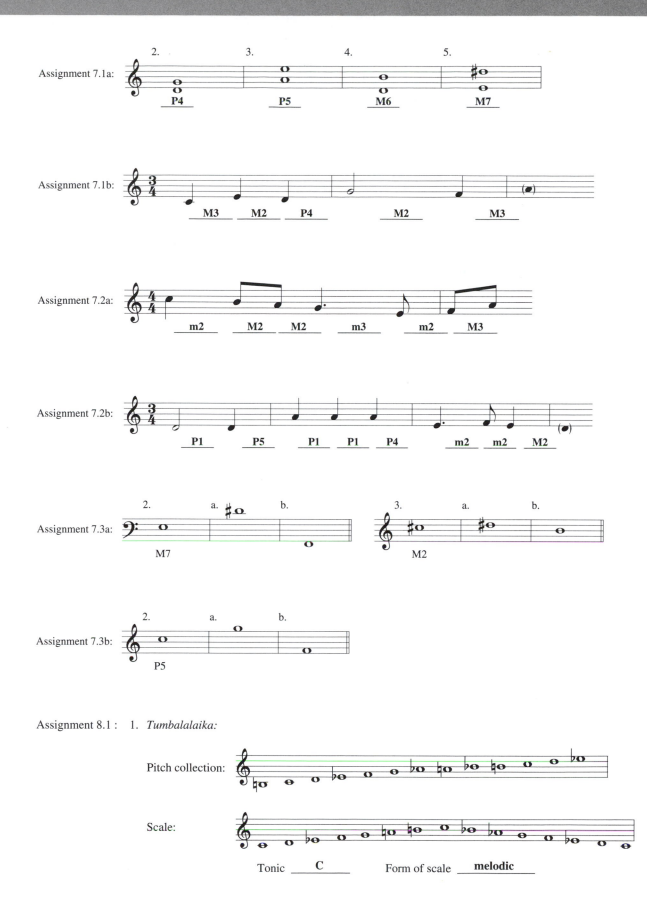

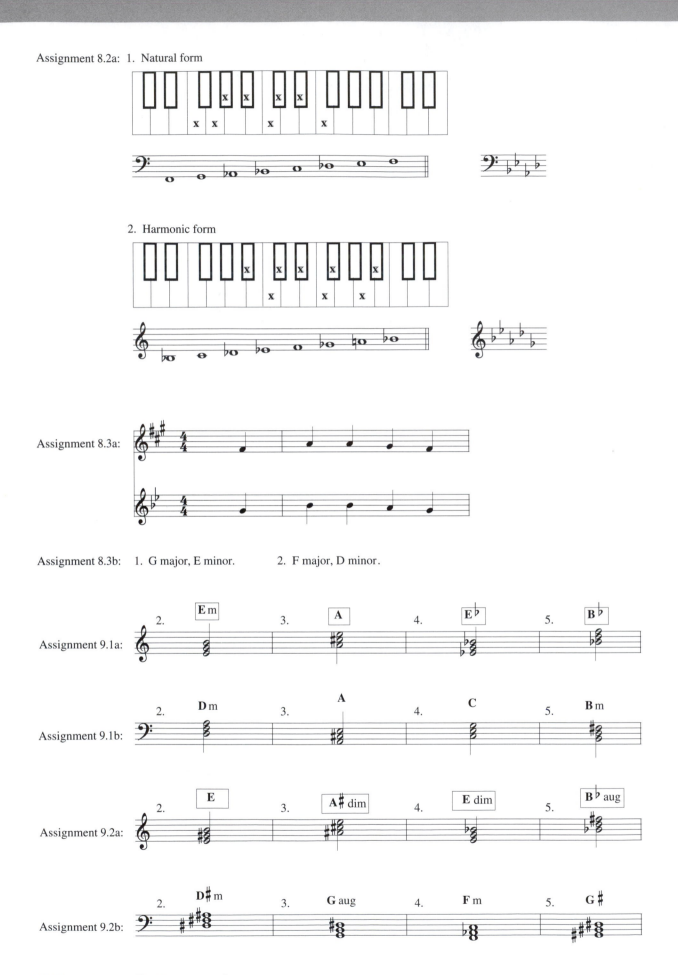

Assignment 8.2a: 1. Natural form

2. Harmonic form

Assignment 8.3a:

Assignment 8.3b: 1. G major, E minor.   2. F major, D minor.

Assignment 9.1a: 2. Em   3. A   4. Eb   5. Bb

Assignment 9.1b: 2. Dm   3. A   4. C   5. Bm

Assignment 9.2a: 2. E   3. A# dim   4. E dim   5. Bb aug

Assignment 9.2b: 2. D# m   3. G aug   4. F m   5. G#

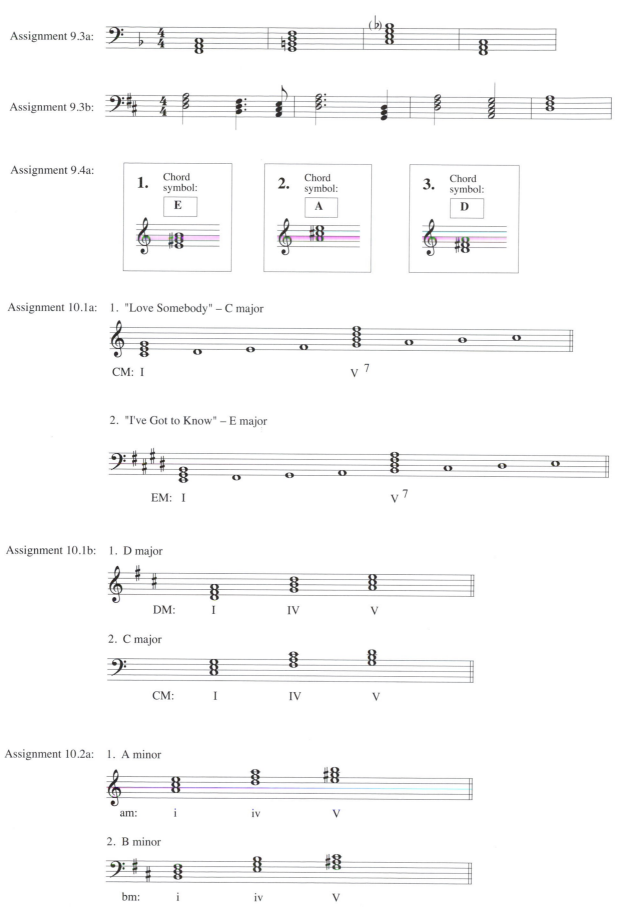

Assignment 9.3a:

Assignment 9.3b:

Assignment 9.4a:

1. Chord symbol: E

2. Chord symbol: A

3. Chord symbol: D

Assignment 10.1a:

1. "Love Somebody" – C major

CM: I   V⁷

2. "I've Got to Know" – E major

EM: I   V⁷

Assignment 10.1b:

1. D major

DM: I   IV   V

2. C major

CM: I   IV   V

Assignment 10.2a:

1. A minor

am: i   iv   V

2. B minor

bm: i   iv   V

Assignment 10.2b:

Harmonic Background:

F: V   I   I   I

Assignment 11.1a:

Assignment 11.1b:

Assignment 11.2a:

Assignment 11.3a:

Phrase one

Plagal cadence

Songbook

There are a number of ways you can hear musical backgrounds to accompany your singing of the songs in this songbook. In addition to the CD enclosed with the book, the Web site at www.mhhe.com/musicfirst5 contains complete accompaniments that are different from those on the CD. Also, there are a number of online sources of musical accompaniments to the songs. You will find a variety of styles from traditional to jazz and pop on the Web. Just enter the song name in your Web browser and check them out. You will enjoy having a variety of musical backgrounds for your singing.

Some URLs:

www.nieh.nih.gov/kids/music.htm
www.cyberhymnal.org

http://sniff.numachi.com/~rickheit/dtrad
www.ingeb.org

America the Beautiful (CD #10)

Katharine Lee Bates

Samuel A. Ward

With dignity

1. O beau - ti - ful for spa - cious skies, For am - ber waves of grain, For pur - ple moun - tain maj - es - ties A - bove the fruit - ed plain!
2. O beau - ti - ful for pa - triot dream, That sees be - yond the years, Thine al - a - bas - ter cit - ies gleam, Un - dimmed by hu - man tears!

Chorus

A - mer - i - ca! A - mer - i - ca! God shed His grace on thee, and crown thy good with broth - er - hood From sea to shin - ing sea!

Are You Sleeping (CD #11)

Moderately

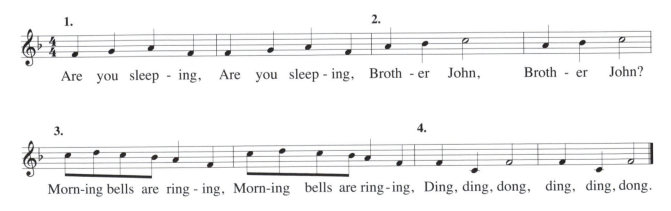

Are you sleep - ing, Are you sleep - ing, Broth - er John, Broth - er John?

Morn-ing bells are ring - ing, Morn-ing bells are ring-ing, Ding, ding, dong, ding, ding, dong.

Auprès de ma Blonde (CD #12)

France

Jauntily

1. With - in my fa - ther's gar - den the li - lacs bloom the best, ____ With -
2. Au jar - din de mon pê - re les lau - riers sont fleu - ris, ____ Au

in my fa - ther's gar - den the li - lacs bloom the best, ____ And
jar - din de mon pê - re les lau - riers sont fleu - ris. ____ Tous

birds of ev - 'ry feath - er go there to make their nest. ____
les oi - seax du mon - de s'en vont y fair' leurs nids. ____

Close, close to my dar - ling, oh, how good it is to be,
Au - près de ma blon - de, qu'il fait bon, fait bon, fait bon,

close, close to my dar - ling, it is good to stay. ____
Au - près de ma blon - de, qu'il fait bon dor - mir. ____

Aura Lee (CD #13)

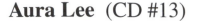

Sentimentally

United States

As a black-bird in the spring, 'Neath the wil-low tree,

Sat and piped, I heard him sing, Sing-ing Au-ra Lee.

(Chorus) Au - ra Lee, Au - ra Lee, Maid of gold-en hair,

Sun-shine came a - long with thee, And swal-lows in the air.

Barbara Ellen (CD #14)

Scotland

Sadly

1. In Scar - let town where I was born, There
2. It was in the mer - ry month of May, When

was a fair maid dwell - in', Made ev 'ry youth cry ___
green buds they were swell - in', Sweet Wil - liam came from the

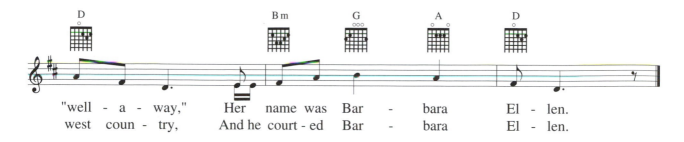

"well - a - way," Her name was Bar - bara El - len.
west coun - try, And he court - ed Bar - bara El - len.

Battle Hymn of the Republic (CD #15)

Excerpts from MUSICAL GROWTH IN THE ELEMENTARY SCHOOL PB. Fourth edition by
BERGETHON © 1979. Reprinted with permission of Wadsworth, a division of Thomson Learning:
www.thomsonrights.com, 800-730-2215.

Julia Ward Howe

William Steffe?

March

1. Mine   eyes have seen the glo - ry of the com - ing of the Lord; He is
2. I have seen Him in the watch - fires of a hun - dred cir - cling camps; They have

tram - pling out the vin - tage where the grapes of wrath are stored; He hath
build - ed Him an al - tar in the even - ing dews and damps; I can

loosed the fate - ful light - ning of his ter - ri - ble swift sword; His
read His right - eous sen - tence by the dim and flar - ing lamps; His

Chorus

truth is march - ing on. Glo - ry, glo - ry, hal - le - lu - jah!
day is march - ing on.

Glo - ry, glo - ry, hal - le - lu - jah! Glo - ry, glo - ry, hal - le -

lu - jah! His truth is march - ing on.

Bendemeer's Stream (CD #16)

Thomas Moore

Ireland

With longing

There's a bow - er of ros - es by Ben - de - meer's stream, And the night - in - gale
In the time of my child - hood 'twas like a sweet dream, To ___ sit in the

sings round it all the day long. That bower and its mus - ic I ne'er shall for -
ros - es and hear the bird's song.

get, But oft when a - lone in the bloom of the year, I think, "Is the night - in - gale

sing - ing there yet? Are the ros - es still bright by the calm Ben - de - meer?"

Billy Boy (CD #17)

Lightheartedly

England

Oh, __ where have you been, Bil - ly Boy, Bil - ly Boy, Oh, __ where have you
Did she ask you to come in, Bil - ly Boy, Bil - ly Boy, Did she ask you to come

been, charm - ing Bil - ly? _____ I have been to see my wife, she's the
in, charm - ing Bil - ly? _____ Yes she asked me to come in, There's a

joy _____ of my life, She's a young thing and can - not leave her moth - er. ____
dim - ple in her chin, She's a young thing and can - not leave her moth - er. ____

The Caisson Song (CD #18)

Words and Music by
Edmund L. Gruber

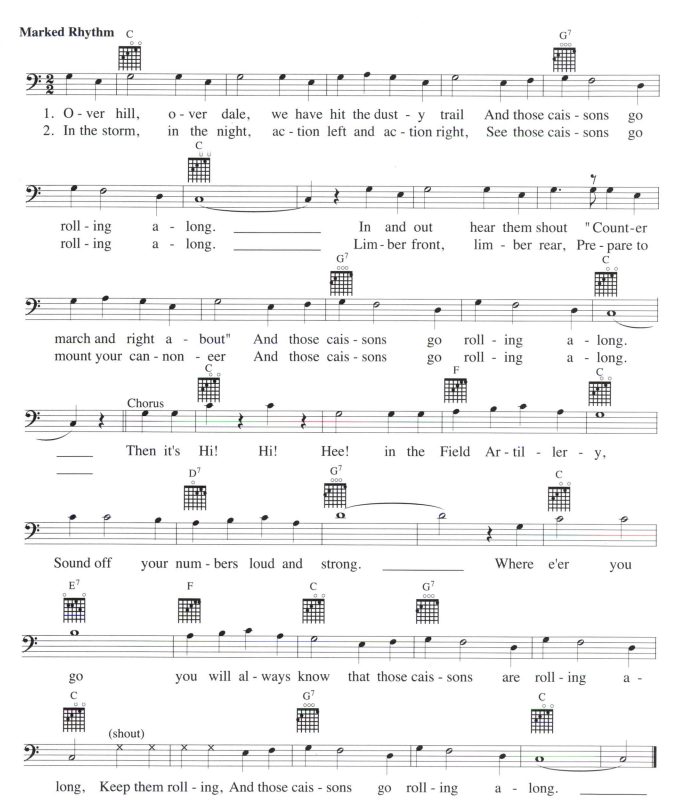

Marked Rhythm

1. O - ver hill, o - ver dale, we have hit the dust - y trail And those cais - sons go
2. In the storm, in the night, ac - tion left and ac - tion right, See those cais - sons go

roll - ing a - long. _____ In and out hear them shout "Count - er
roll - ing a - long. _____ Lim - ber front, lim - ber rear, Pre - pare to

march and right a - bout" And those cais - sons go roll - ing a - long.
mount your can - non - eer And those cais - sons go roll - ing a - long.

Chorus

_____ Then it's Hi! Hi! Hee! in the Field Ar - til - ler - y,
_____

Sound off your num - bers loud and strong. _____ Where e'er you

go you will al - ways know that those cais - sons are roll - ing a -

(shout)

long, Keep them roll - ing, And those cais - sons go roll - ing a - long. _____

Cantemus Hymnum (CD #19)

Text from second stanza of
"Beati, qui esuriunt"
Edited by Noah Greenberg

Anonymous (fourteenth century)

cto - ri - ae. Qui na - tus est de vir - gi -

cto - ri - ae. Qui na - tus est de vir - gi -

ne Si - ne vi - ri - li se - me - ne, Cum gau - di -

ne Si - ne vi - ri - li se - me - ne, Cum gau - di -

o _____ be - ne - di - ca - mus Do - mi - no.

o _____ be - ne - di - ca - mus Do - mi - no.

Children's Prayer (CD #20)

Adelheid Wette
(tr. Constance Bache)

Englebert Humperdinck

Prayerfully

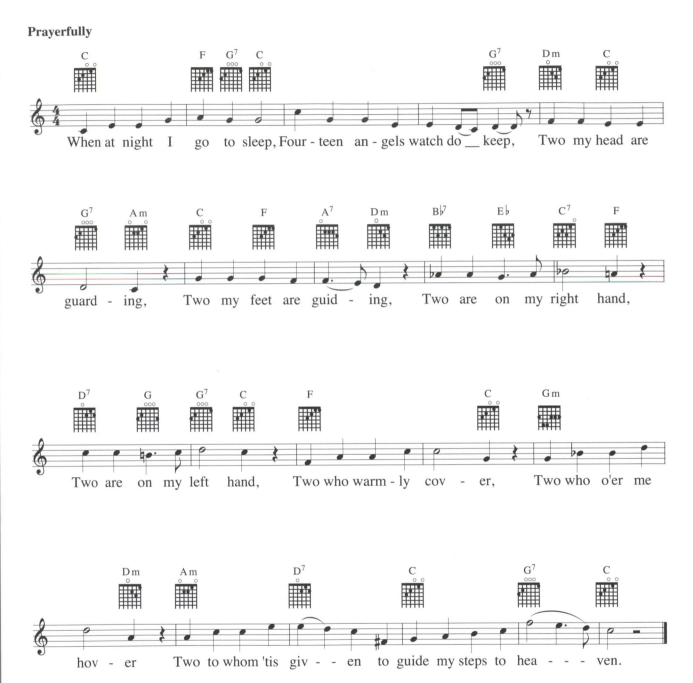

Cielito Lindo (CD #21)

Mexico

1. From Si - er - - ra Mo - re - na, Cie - - li - to Lin - do comes
2. De la Si - er - - ra Mo - re - na, Cie - - li - to Lin - do rien -

___ soft - ly steal - ing, _____ Laugh - ing eyes, ___ black and
___ en ba - yan - do, _____ Un par de ___ oji - tos

ro - guish, Cie - - li - to Lin - do, beau - - ty re - veal - ing. _____
ne - gros, Cie - - li - to Lin - do de ___ con - tra - ban - do. _____

Ay, ay, ay, ay! _____ Sing, ban - ish
Ay, ay, ay, ay! _____ Can - ta y'no

sor - row! _____ To pass the hours ___ light - ly sing - ing, Cie -
llo - res! _____ Por - que can - tan - do ___ se a - le - gran, Cie -

- li - to Lin - do, glad - - dens the mor - row. _____
- li - to Lin - do, los ___ co - ra - zo - nes. _____

Dona Nobis Pacem (CD #22)

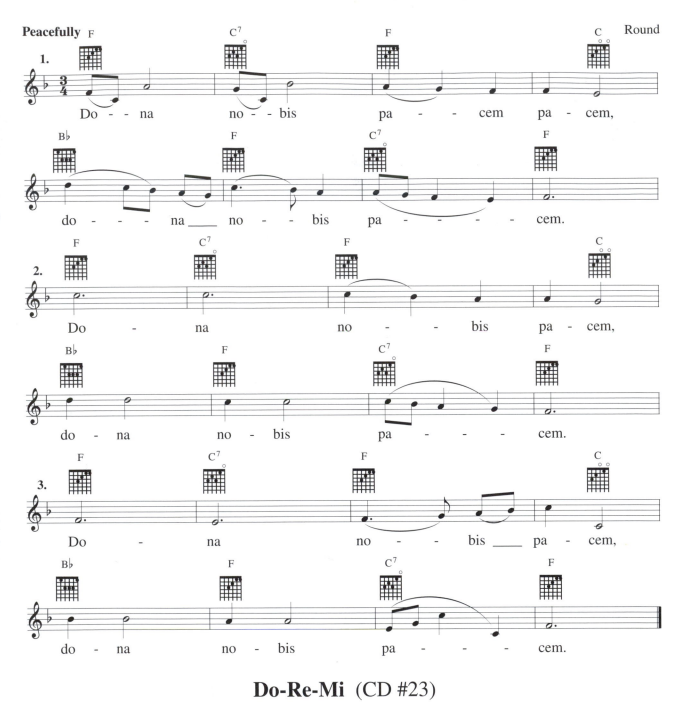

Peacefully

1. Do - - na no - - bis pa - cem pa - cem,
do - - na ___ no - - bis pa - - - - cem.

2. Do - na no - - bis pa - cem,
do - na no - bis pa - - - cem.

3. Do - na no - - bis ___ pa - cem,
do - na no - bis pa - - - cem.

Do-Re-Mi (CD #23)

From THE SOUND OF MUSIC. Lyrics by Oscar Hammerstein II. Music by Richard Rodgers. Copyright © 1959 by Richard Rodgers and Oscar Hammerstein II. Copyright Renewed. WILLIAMSON MUSIC owner of publication and allied rights throughout the world. International Copyright Secured. All Rights Reserved.

Oscar Hammerstein II   Richard Rodgers

Moderately

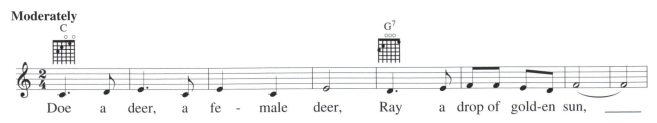

Doe a deer, a fe - male deer, Ray a drop of gold-en sun, ___

Me a name I call my-self, Far a long, long way to run. _____

Sew a nee-dle pull-ing thread, _____ La a note to fol-low sew, _____

Tea a drink with jam and bread, _____ That will bring us back to doe!

_____ Do re mi fa so la ti do! _____

Down in the Valley (CD #24)

Kentucky

Plaintively

Down in the val - ley the val - ley so low, Hang your head
Ro - ses love sun - shine vio - lets love dew, An - gels in

o - ver, hear the winds blow. Hear the winds blow, dear, hear the winds
heav - en, know I love you. Know I love you, dear, know I love

blow, Hang your head o - ver, hear the winds blow.
you, An - gels in heav - en, know I love you.

The First Noël (CD #25)

Traditional English carol

With joy

1. The __ first ___ No - ël the ___ an - gel did say, Was to
2. They __ look - -ed __ up and ___ saw ___ a star shin - ing

cer - tain poor shep - herds in fields as they lay, In __ fields __ where __
in __ the east __ bey - ond __ them far, And __ to __ the __

they lay __ keep - ing their sheep On a cold win - ter's night _____ that
earth it __ gave a great light And __ so it con - tin - ued both

Chorus

was _____ so deep. No - - ël, ___ No - - ël, No - - ël, No -
day _____ and night.

ël, Born is the King _____ of Is - - ra - el.

Go Down Moses (CD #26)

African-American spiritual

Deliberately

1. When Is - rael was in E - gypt's land, Let my peo - ple go. Op -
2. O let us all from bond - age flee, Let my peo - ple go. And

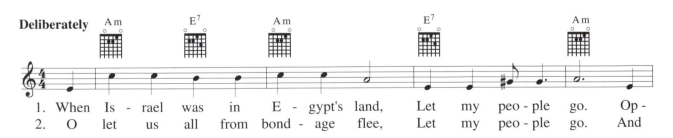

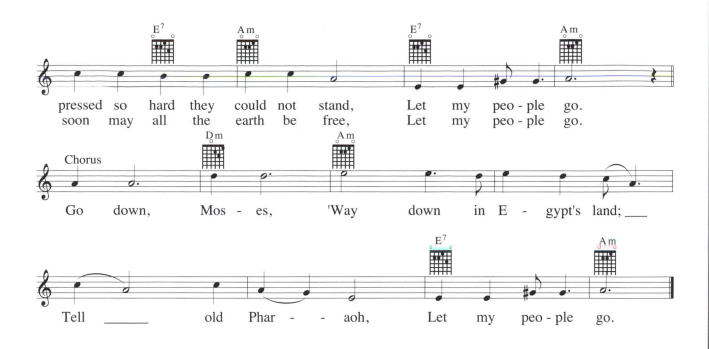

pressed so hard they could not stand, Let my peo - ple go.
soon may all the earth be free, Let my peo - ple go.

Chorus

Go down, Mos - es, 'Way down in E - gypt's land; ___

Tell _____ old Phar - - aoh, Let my peo - ple go.

Goodby, Old Paint (CD #27)

Cowboy song

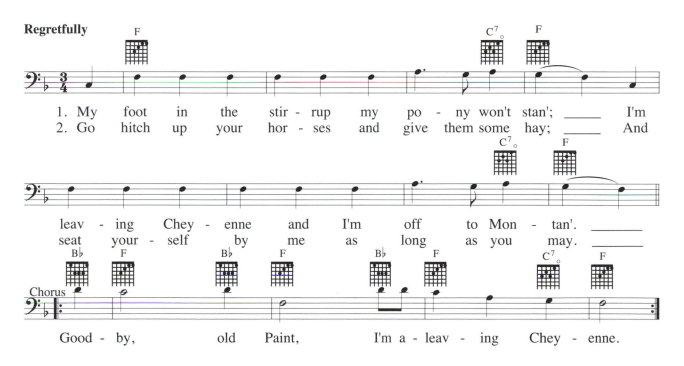

Regretfully

1. My foot in the stir - rup my po - ny won't stan'; _____ I'm
2. Go hitch up your hor - ses and give them some hay; _____ And

leav - ing Chey - enne and I'm off to Mon - tan'. _____
seat your - self by me as long as you may. _____

Chorus

Good - by, old Paint, I'm a - leav - ing Chey - enne.

Greensleeves (CD #28)

England

Quietly

A - las my love __ you do me wrong, __ To cast me off ___ dis - court - eous - ly; And

I have loved __ you for so long, __ De - light - ing in ___ your com - pan - y.

Green - sleeves __ was all my joy, _____ Green - sleeves __ was my de - light,

Green - sleeves was my heart of gold, __ And who but my lad - y Green - sleeves.

Hey, Ho, Anybody Home (CD #29)

England

Stoically

1. Hey, ho, an-y-bod-y home? **2.** Meat and drink and mon-ey have I none, **3.** Still I will be ve-ry mer-ry!

I Never Will Marry (CD #30)

Folk Song

I nev-er will mar-ry, _____ I'll ___ be no man's wife, _____ I ex-pect to live sin-gle _____ all the days of my life. _____

I Saw Three Ships (CD #31)

Festively   England

1. I saw three ships come sail - ing in On Christ - mas Day, on Christ - mas Day, I
2. And what was in those ships all three On Christ - mas Day, on Christ - mas Day, And

saw three ships come sail - ing in On Christ - mas Day in the morn - ing.
what was in those ships all three On Christ - mas Day in the morn - ing?

It Came Upon the Midnight Clear (CD #32)

Edmund H. Sears   Richard S. Willis

Gently

1. It came up - on ___ the mid - night clear, That glo - ri - ous song ___ of
2. Still through the clo - - ven skies they come, With peace - ful wings ___ un -

old, _____ From an - gels bend - ing near the earth, to touch their harps __ of
furled, _____ And still their heav - en - ly mu - sic floats o'er all the wea - ry

gold; _____ "Peace on the earth, ___ good will to men, From
world; _____ A - bove its sad ___ and low - ly plains They

hea - ven's all - gra - cious King"; ___ The world in sol - emn
bend ___ on ho - ver - ing wing, ___ And ev - er o'er ___ its

still - ness lay, To hear the an - gels sing. _____
Ba - bel sounds, The bless - ed an - gels sing. _____

I've Got to Know (CD #33)

I'VE GOT TO KNOW. Words and Music by Woody Guthrie. TRO-© Copyright 1963 (Renewed) Ludlow Music Inc., New York, N.Y. Used by permission.

Words and Music by
Woody Guthrie

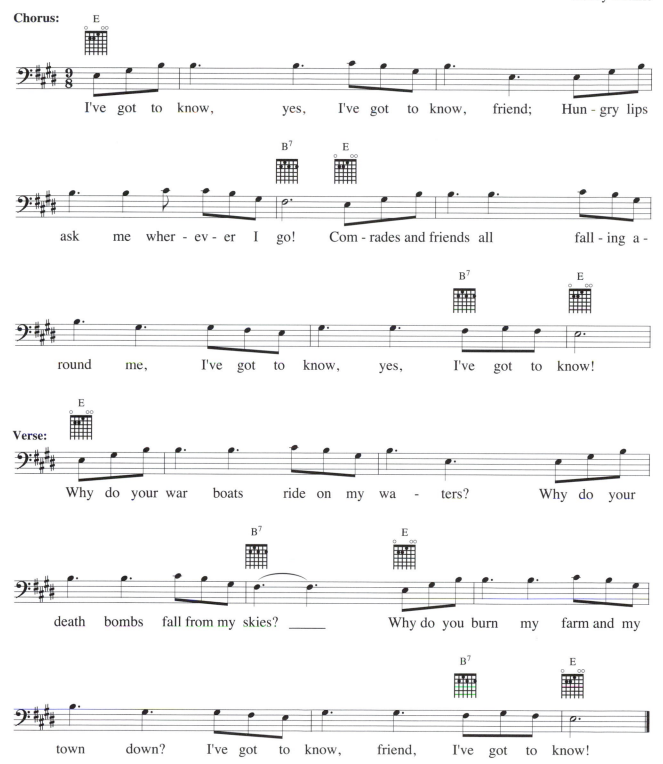

Chorus:

I've got to know, yes, I've got to know, friend; Hun - gry lips ask me wher - ev - er I go! Com - rades and friends all fall - ing a - round me, I've got to know, yes, I've got to know!

Verse:

Why do your war boats ride on my wa - ters? Why do your death bombs fall from my skies? _____ Why do you burn my farm and my town down? I've got to know, friend, I've got to know!

Jacob's Ladder (CD #34)

Excerpts from MUSICAL GROWTH IN THE ELEMENTARY SCHOOL
PB. Fourth edition by BERGETHON © 1979. Reprinted with permission
of Wadsworth, a division of Thomson Learning: www.thomsonrights.com,
800-730-2215.

African-American spiritual

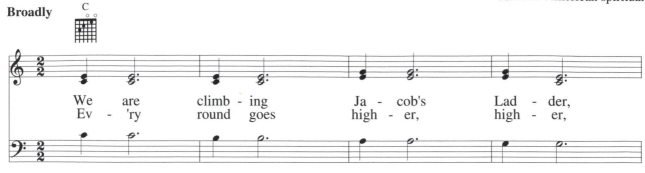

We are climb - ing Ja - cob's Lad - der,
Ev - 'ry round goes high - er, high - er,

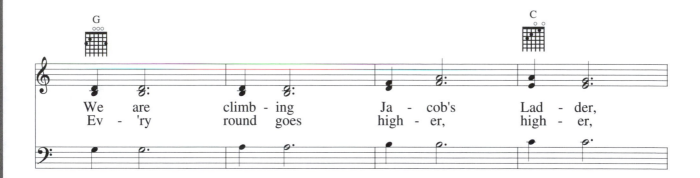

We are climb - ing Ja - cob's Lad - der,
Ev - 'ry round goes high - er, high - er,

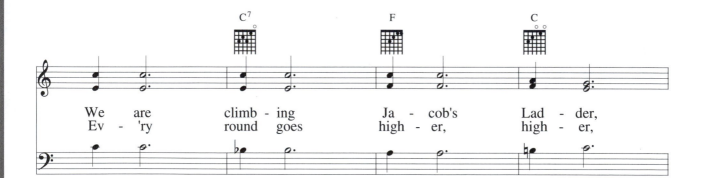

We are climb - ing Ja - cob's Lad - der,
Ev - 'ry round goes high - er, high - er,

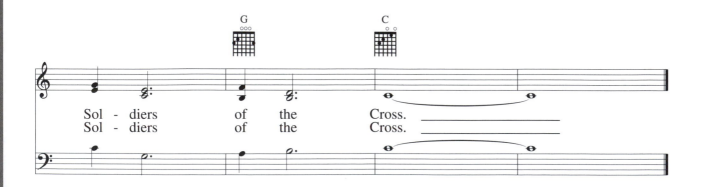

Sol - diers of the Cross.
Sol - diers of the Cross.

Lavender's Blue (CD #35)

England

Merrily

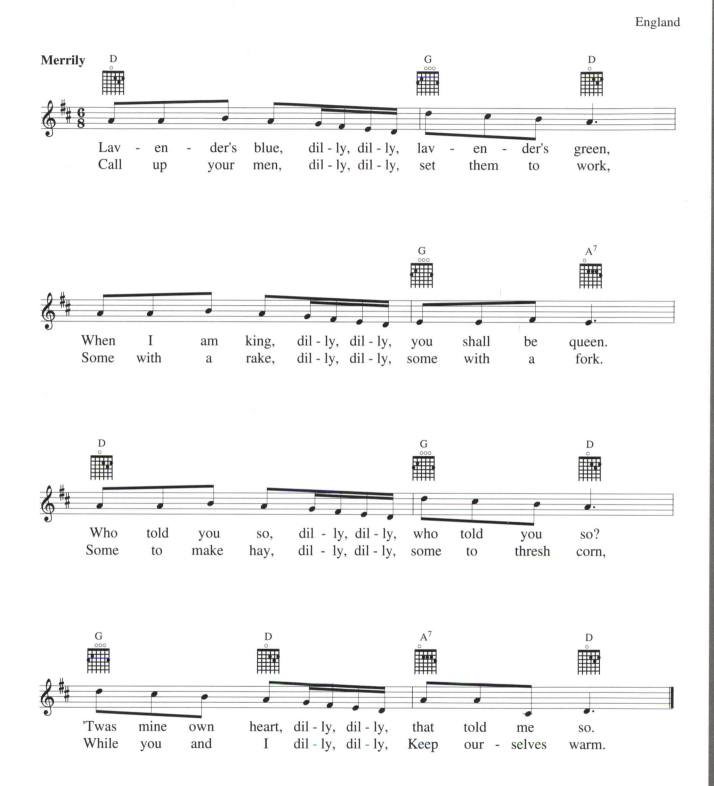

Lav - en - der's blue, dil - ly, dil - ly, lav - en - der's green,
Call up your men, dil - ly, dil - ly, set them to work,

When I am king, dil - ly, dil - ly, you shall be queen.
Some with a rake, dil - ly, dil - ly, some with a fork.

Who told you so, dil - ly, dil - ly, who told you so?
Some to make hay, dil - ly, dil - ly, some to thresh corn,

'Twas mine own heart, dil - ly, dil - ly, that told me so.
While you and I dil - ly, dil - ly, Keep our - selves warm.

The Linden Tree (CD #36)

Franz Schubert
Adapted by
Friedrich Silcher

Moderato

Be - side the gar - den foun - tain there stands a lin - den
And now great is the dis - tance from that old lin - den

tree. And of - ten in its shad - ows fond
tree. But still do I re - mem - ber the

dreams have come ___ to me. Up - on its bark I
com - fort there ___ for me. In dreams I hear its

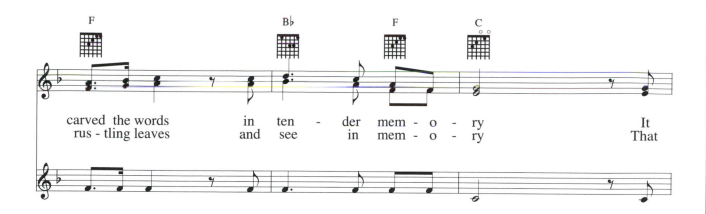

carved the words   in ten – der mem – o – ry   It
rus – tling leaves   and see   in mem – o – ry   That

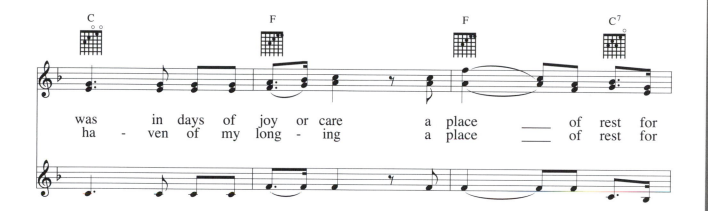

was   in days of joy or care   a place &rule; of rest for
ha – ven of my long – ing   a place &rule; of rest for

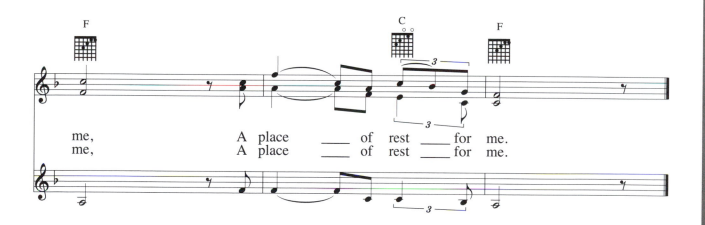

me,   A place &rule; of rest &rule; for me.
me,   A place &rule; of rest &rule; for me.

Lonesome Valley (CD #37)

White spiritual

With melancholy

1. Je - sus walked _____ this lone - some val - ley, _____ He had to
2. We must walk _____ that lone - some val - ley, _____ We must

walk _____ it by Him - self, _____ O, no - bod - y else could walk it
walk _____ it by our - selves, _____ O, no - bod - y else can walk it

for Him, _____ He had to walk it by ____ Him - self.
for us, _____ We have to walk it by ____ our - selves.

Love Somebody (CD #38)

United States

With zest

Love some - bod - y, yes I do, Love some - bod - y,

yes I do, Love some - bod - y, yes I do,

Love some - bod - y but I won't tell who.

Chorus

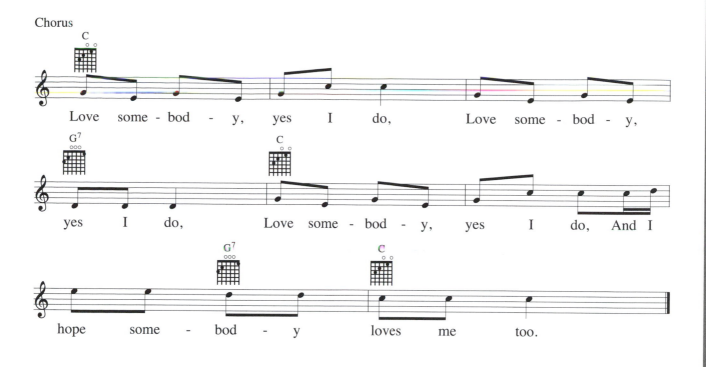

Love some-bod-y, yes I do, Love some-bod-y, yes I do, Love some-bod-y, yes I do, And I hope some-bod-y loves me too.

Lullaby (CD #39)

Johannes Brahms

Gently

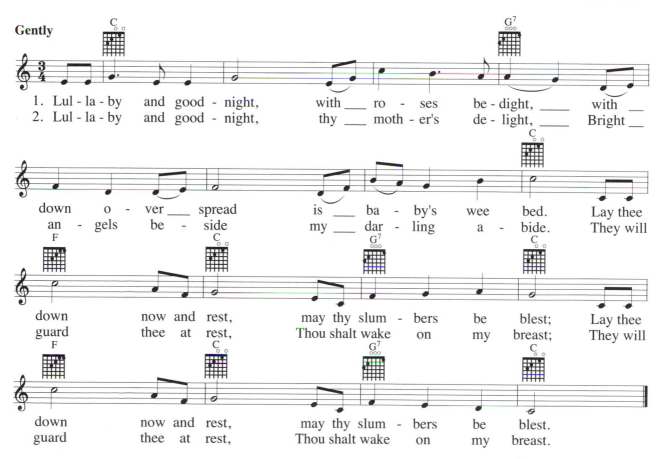

1. Lul - la - by and good - night, with ___ ro - ses be - dight, ____ with __
2. Lul - la - by and good - night, thy ___ moth - er's de - light, ____ Bright __

down o - ver ___ spread is ___ ba - by's wee bed. Lay thee
an - gels be - side my ___ dar - ling a - bide. They will

down now and rest, may thy slum - bers be blest; Lay thee
guard thee at rest, Thou shalt wake on my breast; They will

down now and rest, may thy slum - bers be blest.
guard thee at rest, Thou shalt wake on my breast.

Morning Has Broken (CD #40)

Traditional song

1. Morn - ing has bro - ken like the first morn - ing,
2. Sweet the rain's new fall sun - lit from heav - en,

Black - bird has spo - ken like the first bird. _____
Like the first dew - fall on the first grass. _____

Praise for the sing - ing! Praise for the morn - ing!
Praise for the sweet - ness Of the wet gar - den,

Praise for the spring - ing Fresh from the word. _____
Sprung in com - plete - ness Where His feet pass. _____

My Bonnie (CD #41)

Words and Music
by H. J. Fuller

With yearning

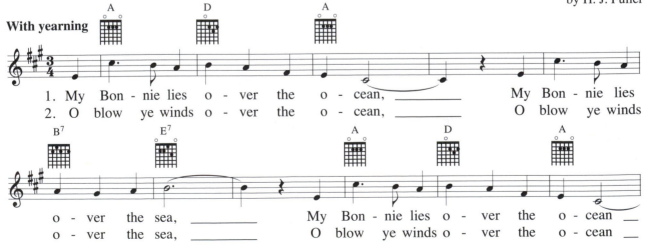

1. My Bon - nie lies o - ver the o - cean, _____ My Bon - nie lies
2. O blow ye winds o - ver the o - cean, _____ O blow ye winds

o - ver the sea, _____ My Bon - nie lies o - ver the o - cean _____
o - ver the sea, _____ O blow ye winds o - ver the o - cean _____

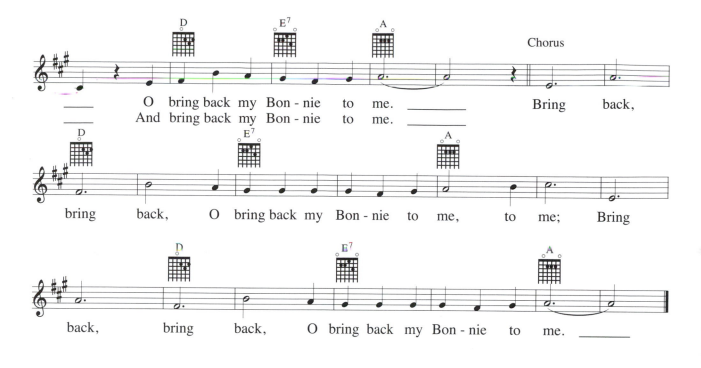

O bring back my Bon - nie to me. _____ Bring back,
And bring back my Bon - nie to me. _____

bring back, O bring back my Bon - nie to me, to me; Bring

back, bring back, O bring back my Bon - nie to me. _____

My Hat (CD #42)

Germany

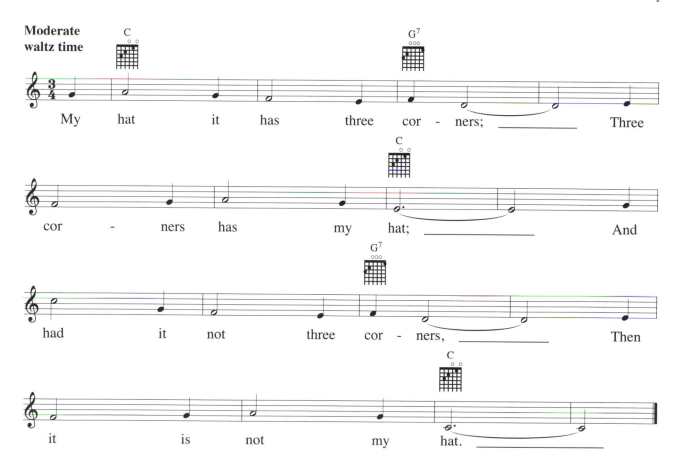

Moderate waltz time

My hat it has three cor - ners; _____ Three

cor - ners has my hat; _____ And

had it not three cor - ners, _____ Then

it is not my hat. _____

Oh, What a Beautiful Mornin' (CD #43)

From OKLAHOMA! Lyrics by Oscar Hammerstein II. Music by Richard Rodgers. Copyright © 1943 by WILLIAMSON MUSIC. Copyright Renewed. International Copyright Secured. All Rights Reserved.

Oscar Hammerstein II

Richard Rodgers

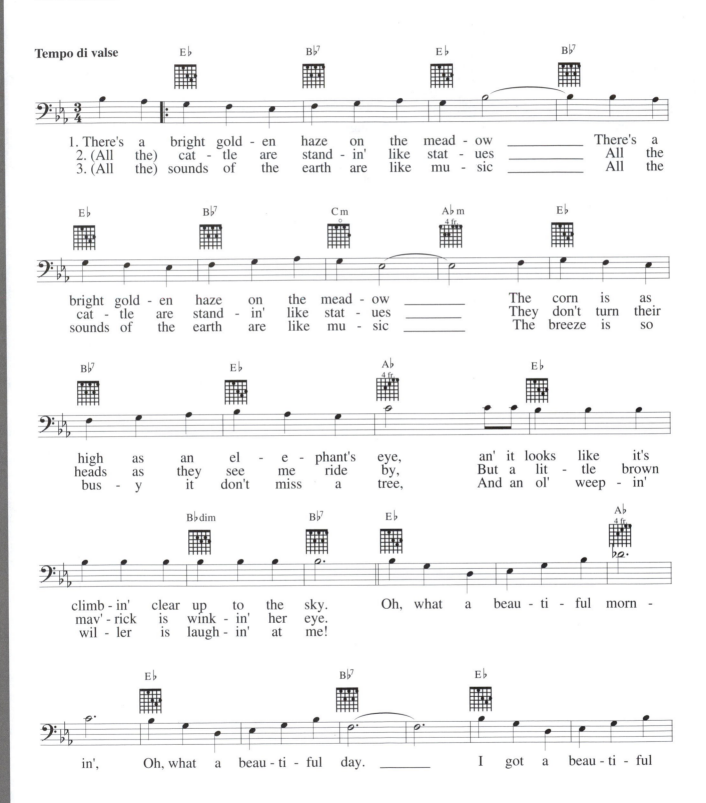

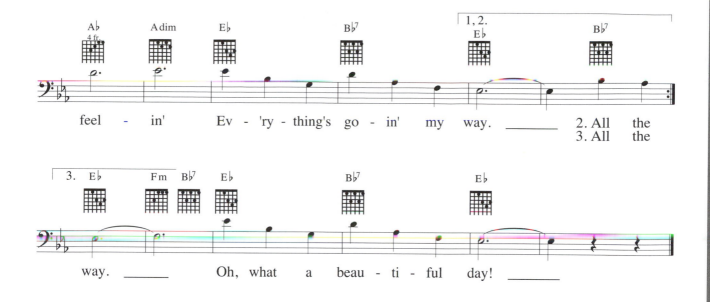

feel - in' Ev - 'ry - thing's go - in' my way. _____ 2. All the
3. All the

way. _____ Oh, what a beau - ti - ful day! _____

O Sole Mio (CD #44)

Neapolitan song

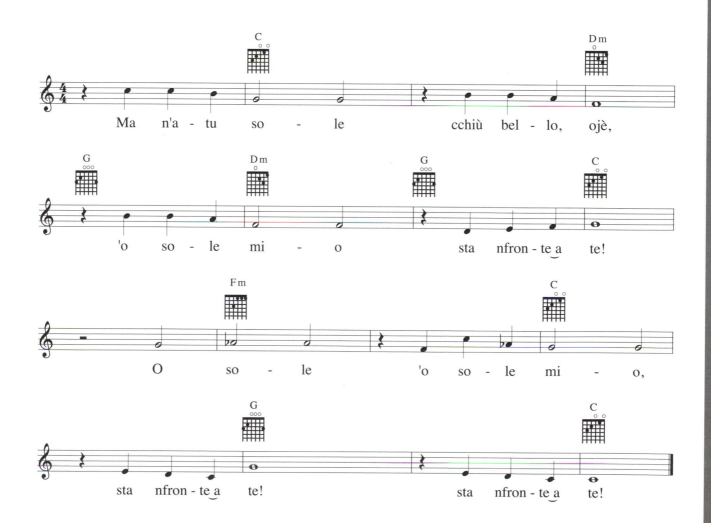

Ma n'a - tu so - le cchiù bel - lo, ojè,

'o so - le mi - o sta nfron - te a te!

O so - le 'o so - le mi - o,

sta nfron - te a te! sta nfron - te a te!

Over the River and Through the Wood (CD #45)

Lydia Maria Child

United States

With animation

O - ver the riv - er and through the wood, To grand - fa - ther's house we go; _____ The horse knows the way to car - ry the sleigh, Through the white and drift - ed snow. _____ O - ver the riv - er and through the wood, Oh, how the wind does blow! _____ It stings the toes and bites the nose, as o - ver the ground we go.

Pat-a-Pan (CD #46)

France

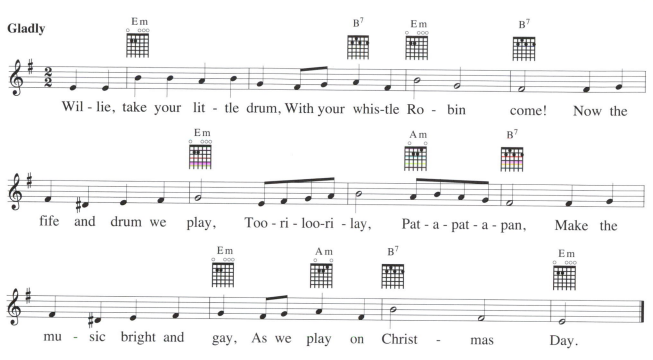

Gladly

Wil - lie, take your lit - tle drum, With your whis-tle Ro - bin come! Now the

fife and drum we play, Too - ri - loo-ri - lay, Pat - a - pat-a - pan, Make the

mu - sic bright and gay, As we play on Christ - mas Day.

Pawpaw Patch (CD #47)

Southern United States

Playfully

1. Where, oh where, is dear lit - tle Ma - ry?
2. Come on kids, let's go find her,

Where, oh where, is dear lit - tle Ma - ry? Where, oh where, is
Come on kids, let's go find her, Come on kids,

dear lit - tle Ma - ry? Way down yon - der in the paw - paw patch.
let's go find her, Way down yon - der in the paw - paw patch.

Pick a Little, Talk a Little and Goodnight Ladies (CD #48)

Words and Music
by Meredith Willson
(arr. Raymond J. Malone)

Moderately

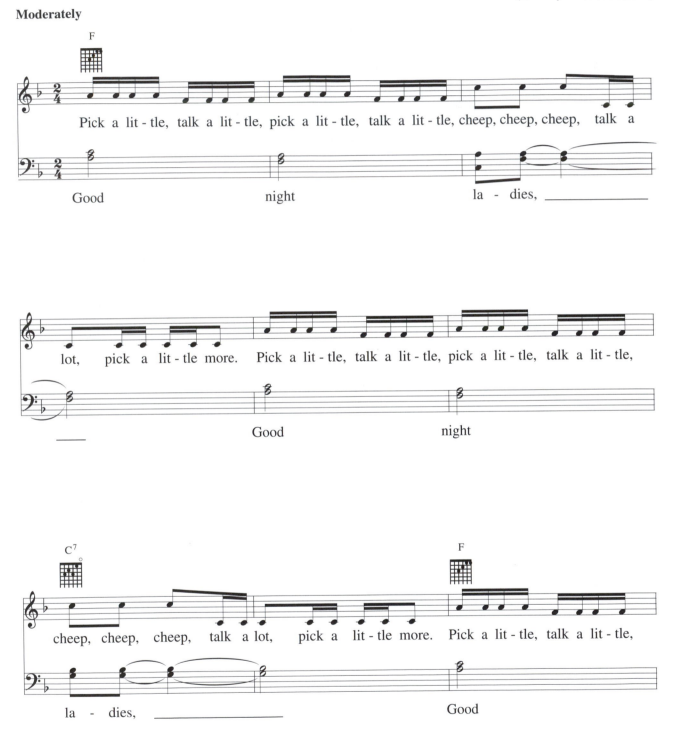

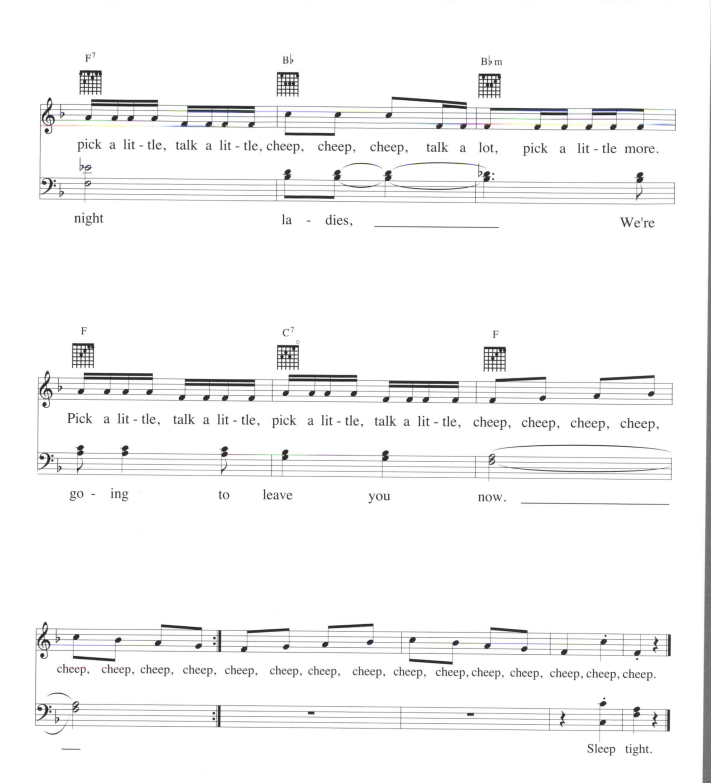

The Riddle Song (CD #49)

Kentucky

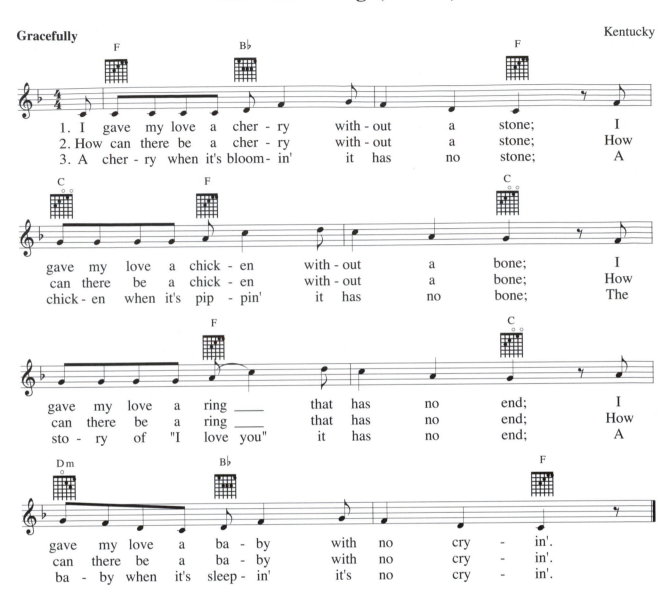

Row, Row, Row Your Boat (CD #50)

Round

3.

Mer - ri - ly, mer - ri - ly, mer - ri - ly, mer - ri - ly,

4.

Life is but a dream.

Santa Lucia (CD #51)

Words and Music by
Teodoro Cattrau
(tr. Thomas Oliphant)

Romantically

Now 'neath the sil - ver moon, o - cean is glow - ing,

O'er the calm bil - low, soft winds are blow - ing;

Here balm - y breez - es blow, pure joys in - vite ___ us,

And as we gent - ly row, all things de - light us.

Hark, how the sail-or's cry joy-ous-ly ech-oes nigh;

San - ta ___ Lu - ci - a, San - ta Lu - ci - a,

Home of fair po - e-sy, realm of pure har - mon - y,

San - ta ___ Lu - ci - a, San - ta Lu - ci - a!

Saturday Night (CD #52)

Nigerian folk song

Gaily

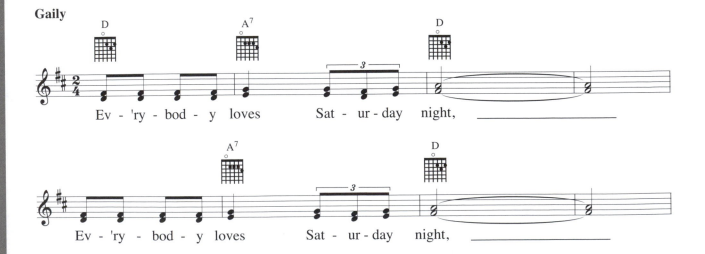

Ev - 'ry - bod - y loves Sat - ur - day night, _____

Ev - 'ry - bod - y loves Sat - ur - day night, _____

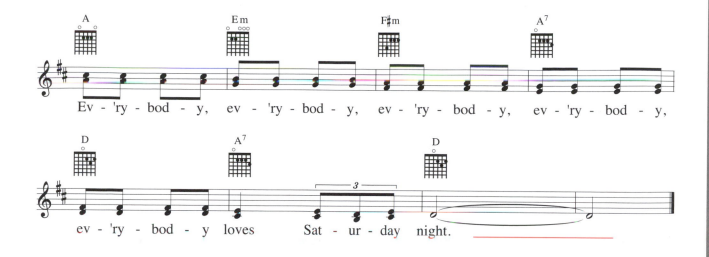

Ev - 'ry - bod - y, ev - 'ry - bod - y, ev - 'ry - bod - o - y, ev - 'ry - bod - y,

ev - 'ry - bod - y loves Sat - ur - day night.

Scarborough Fair (CD #53)

England

Liltingly

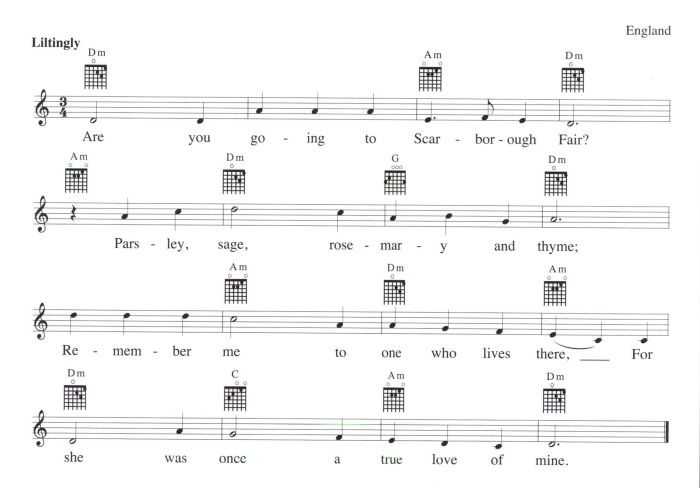

Are you go - ing to Scar - bor - ough Fair?

Pars - ley, sage, rose - mar - y and thyme;

Re - mem - ber me to one who lives there, _____ For

she was once a true love of mine.

Silent Night (CD #54)

Joseph Mohr

Franz Gruber

Peacefully

1. Si - lent night, ho - ly night! All is calm, all is bright.
2. Si - lent night, ho - ly night! Shep - herds quake at the sight.

Round yon vir - gin Moth - er and Child. Ho - ly In - fant so ten - der and mild,
Glo - ries stream from heaven a - far, Heav'n - ly hosts __ sing Al - le - lu - ia,

Sleep in heav - en - ly peace, _____ Sleep __ in heav - en - ly peace.
Christ the sav - ior is born, _____ Christ __ the sav - ior is born.

Simple Gifts (CD #55)

Shaker hymn

1. 'Tis the gift to be sim - ple, 'Tis the gift to be free, 'Tis the
2. 'Tis the gift to be sim - ple, 'Tis the gift to be free, 'Tis the

gift to come down where we ought to be, And when we find our - selves __ in the
gift to share our com - mon des - ti - ny, And when we find our - selves __ in the

place just __ right, 'Twill __ be in the val - ley of
place just __ right, 'Twill __ be in the val - ley of

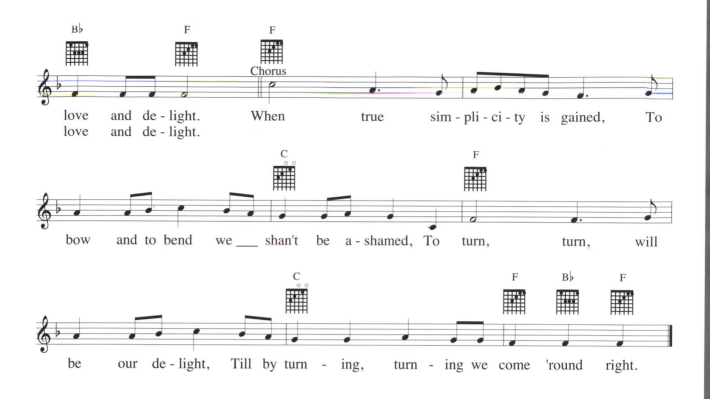

love   and de - light.   When   true   sim - pli - ci - ty is gained,   To
love   and de - light.

bow   and to bend   we ___ shan't be a - shamed, To turn,   turn,   will

be   our de - light, Till by turn - ing,   turn - ing we come   'round   right.

Six Rounds in Major Keys

1. (CD #56)

Germany

2. (CD #57)

3. (CD #58)

4. (CD #59)

5. (CD #60)

6. (CD #61)

Skip to My Lou (CD #62)

Skipping Pace

Southern United States

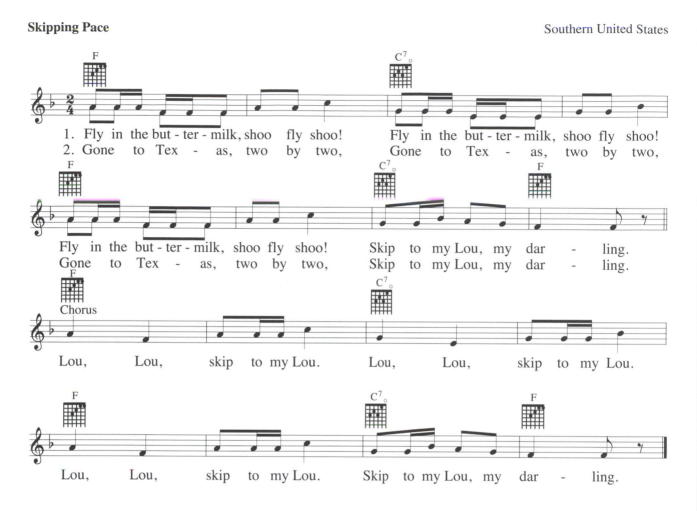

1. Fly in the but-ter-milk, shoo fly shoo! Fly in the but-ter-milk, shoo fly shoo!
2. Gone to Tex-as, two by two, Gone to Tex-as, two by two,

Fly in the but-ter-milk, shoo fly shoo! Skip to my Lou, my dar - ling.
Gone to Tex-as, two by two, Skip to my Lou, my dar - ling.

Chorus

Lou, Lou, skip to my Lou. Lou, Lou, skip to my Lou.

Lou, Lou, skip to my Lou. Skip to my Lou, my dar - ling.

Sweet Betsy from Pike (CD #63)

Crisply

Western United States

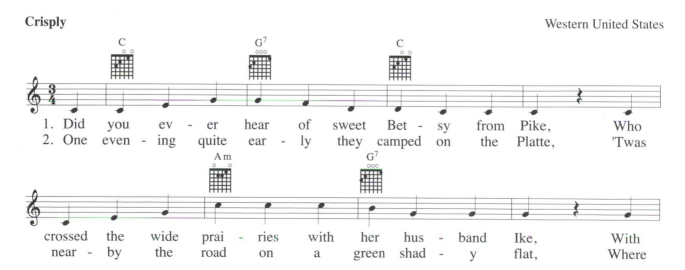

1. Did you ev - er hear of sweet Bet - sy from Pike, Who
2. One even - ing quite ear - ly they camped on the Platte, 'Twas

crossed the wide prai - ries with her hus - band Ike, With
near - by the road on a green shad - y flat, Where

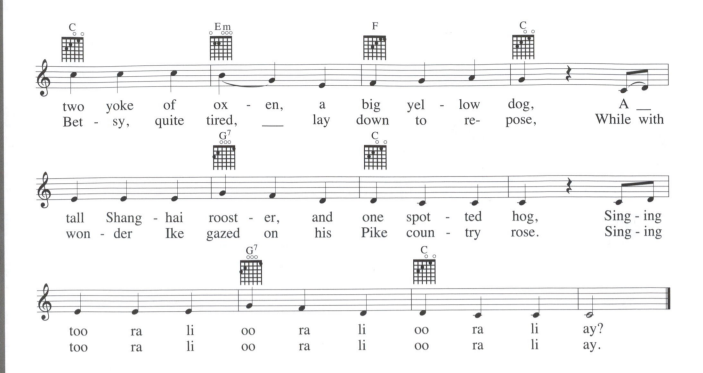

two yoke of ox - en, a big yel - low dog,
Bet - sy, quite tired, ___ lay down to re- pose,

tall Shang - hai roost - er, and one spot - ted hog,
won - der Ike gazed on his Pike coun - try rose.

Sing - ing
Sing - ing

too ra li oo ra li oo ra li ay?
too ra li oo ra li oo ra li ay.

Three Blind Mice (CD #64)

England

Zestfully

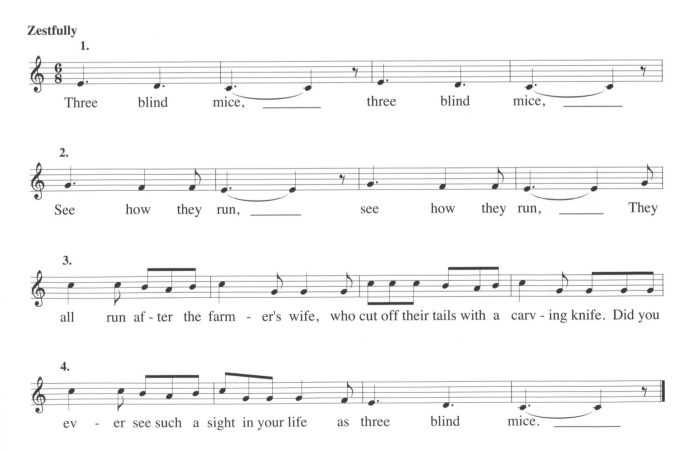

1.
Three blind mice, _____ three blind mice, _____

2.
See how they run, _____ see how they run, _____ They

3.
all run af - ter the farm - er's wife, who cut off their tails with a carv - ing knife. Did you

4.
ev - er see such a sight in your life as three blind mice. _____

Three Rounds in Minor Keys
1. (CD #65)

Praetorius

2. (CD #66)

Haydn

3. (CD #67)

England

Ah poor bird,   take thy flight Far a - bove the sor - rows of   this sad night.

Tumbalalaika (CD #68)

Verses 2 and 3 of "Tumbalalaika" from MAKING MUSIC YOUR
OWN Grade 8. Copyright © by General Learning Corporation.
Reprinted by permission of Pearson Education, Inc.

Margaret Fishback

Jewish Folk Song
(arr. Raymond J. Malone)

"Maid - en, maid - en, can you ex - plain _____ What can grow with -
"I - dle lad, you're jok - ing I know. A stone can grow with -

out snow or rain? What ___ can burn for end - less years, And
out rain or snow, love ___ can blaze and ne - ver die, A

what ___ can cry and shed ___ no tears?" Tum - bal - a, tum - bal - a,
heart ___ can weep and ne - ver cry."

tum - bal - a - lai - ka, Tum - bal - a, tum - bal - a, tum - bal - a -

lai - ka. Tum - bal - a - lai - ka, play bal - a - lai - ka, Tum - bal - a -

lai - ka, laugh and be gay.   laugh and be gay.

Twinkle, Twinkle Little Star (CD #69)

Smoothly

France

Twin - kle, twin - kle lit - tle star,

How I won - der what you are,

Up a - bove the world so high,

Like a dia - mond in the sky.

Twin - kle, twin - kle lit - tle star,

How I won - der what you are.

Wayfaring Stranger (CD #70)

United States

Patiently

We Shall Overcome (CD #71)

African-American spiritual

1. We shall o - ver - come, _____ We shall o - ver - come, _____
2. We are not a - fraid, _____ We are not a - fraid, _____

We shall o - ver - come some day. _____ Oh, ___
We are not a - fraid to - day. _____ Oh, ___

Deep in my heart _____ I do be - lieve that
Deep in my heart _____ I do be - lieve that

We shall o - ver - come some day. _____
We are not a - fraid to - day. _____

When the Saints Go Marching In (CD #72)

New Orleans

Andante

1. Oh, when the Saints _____ go march - ing in _____
2. And when the Sun _____ re - fuse to shine _____

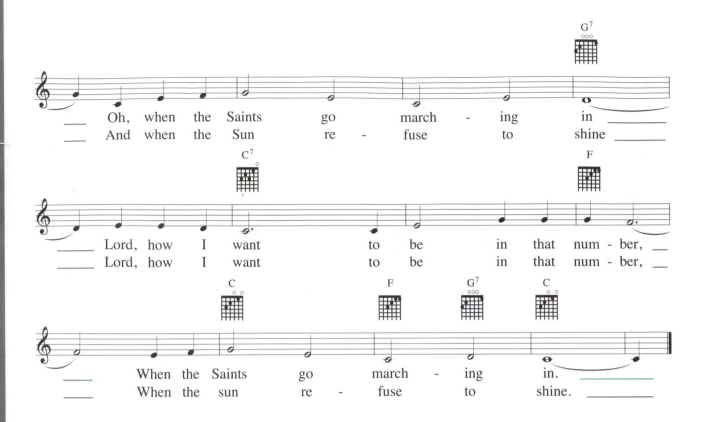

White Coral Bells (CD #73)

England

Clearly

1. White cor - al bells up - on a slen - der stalk,
Oh, don't you wish that you could hear them ring?

2. Lil - ies of the val - ley deck my gar - den walk.
That will hap - pen on - ly when the fair - ies sing.

Wondrous Love (CD #74)

Southern United States

Plaintively

1. What won-drous love is this, O my soul, O my
2. And when from death I'm free, I'll sing on, I'll sing

soul! What won-drous love is this, O my soul! _____
on, And when from death I'm free, I'll sing on, _____

_____ What won-drous love is this, that caused the Lord __ of
_____ And when from death I'm free, I'll sing and joy-ful

bliss To send this bless-ed gift for my soul, for my
be, Through-out e-ter-ni-ty I'll sing on, I'll sing

soul, To send this bless-ed gift for my soul. _____
on, Through-out e-ter-ni-ty I'll sing on. _____

Glossary

(Words enclosed by brackets are defined elsewhere in the glossary.)

a tempo Return to previous [tempo].

accelerando Becoming faster, accelerating.

accent Emphasis on one [note]. Accents are indicated by the placement of the [bar lines] or by various special symbols.

accidental Any of the symbols such as [sharps], [flats], and [naturals] that are used to raise or lower the [pitch] of a [note].

accompaniment The musical background of a piece of music, consisting of [harmony] and [rhythm].

adagio a slow [tempo].

alla breve A [meter signature] that is the equivalent of $\frac{2}{2}$ meter. (See [cut time].)

allegro A fast [tempo]. (It., lively or merry.)

anacrusis See [upbeat].

andante A moderately slow [tempo]. (It., "walking.")

animato Animated.

anticipation A [nonharmonic tone] that anticipates a member of the following [chord], often the [tonic] note.

appoggiatura A [nonharmonic tone] that is approached by leap and left by step, usually in the opposite direction.

arpeggiated chord A [chord] in which the pitches are sounded successively rather than together.

augmentation dot See [dot].

augmented interval An [interval] that is one [half step] larger than a [major] or [perfect] interval.

augmented triad A [triad] made of a [major] [third] and an [augmented] [fifth].

authentic cadence The most common [cadence] in tonal music consisting of the [dominant] [chord] (V) followed by the [tonic] [chord] (I).

bar line A vertical line drawn across the [staff] to indicate [measures] in a musical composition.

bass clef A common [clef] in music. The bass clef is a stylized letter "F" that indicates that the fourth line of the [staff] is named "F." 𝄢

beam A broad, straight line connecting two or more [eighth notes].

beat The steady pulse of music. Beats form the basis of the sense of musical time.

binary form A musical [form] consisting of two distinct sections, (AB), often with each section repeated.

block chord A [chord] in which the [pitches] are all sounded at the same time.

cadence A point of rest and the end of a [phrase], usually marked by a particular [harmonic progression]. (See [authentic cadence], [plagal cadence], [half cadence], and [deceptive cadence].)

calando Decreasing in loudness and often in [tempo]; waning or sinking.

canon A [melody] that can be sung against itself in [imitation].

cantabile In a singing style.

chord A combination of three or more [pitches] sounding at the same time.

chromatic scale The [scale] consisting entirely of [half steps], encompassing all [tones] on the [keyboard].

circle of fifths A clock face arrangement of the twelve [pitches] in the order of the number of [accidentals] in the [key signature].

circle progression A common [progression], consisting of a series of [chords] with descending [fifth] [root] relationships.

clef A symbol placed at the beginning of a [staff] to indicate the names of the various lines and spaces.

climax tone The point of greatest stress in a [melodic line], often the highest tone.

coda A section near the end of a piece of music that brings the work to a close.

common time Another name for a $\frac{4}{4}$ [meter signature]. This [meter] is often indicated with a large capital "C" as a [meter signature].

common tone A [pitch] that remains constant when the [harmony] changes.

compound division The division of the [beat] into three equal parts.

compound meter A [meter] in which the beats have a [compound division].

con brio With energy, fire, spirited. (It., with fire.)

consonance A combination of [pitches] (two or more) that are stable, not requiring [resolution]. (See [dissonance].)

counterpoint Music consisting of two or more independent [melodic lines]. (See [canon] and [round].)

crescendo Becoming louder, growing. (It., growing.)

cut time Another name for the $\frac{2}{2}$ [meter signature]. This [meter] is indicated with a large capital "C" with a vertical line drawn through it. (See [common time].)

da capo A term indicating that the performer should return to the beginning of a piece. (D.C.) (It., from the head.)

dal segno A term that directs the performer to return to a point in a piece that is marked by a special sign (§). (D.S.) (It., from the sign.)

deceptive cadence A [cadence] consisting of the [dominant] [chord] (V) followed by the [submediant] [chord] (vi), so named because the listener expects the [tonic] [chord] (I) rather than the [submediant].

degree One of the [notes] in a [scale]. Degrees are usually numbered starting with the [tonic] (the lowest [tone] of the [scale].

diatonic scale Any one of the common [scales] made of [whole steps] and [half steps] in a particular pattern. The white keys on a [keyboard instrument] form a diatonic scale.

diminished interval An [interval] that is one [half step] smaller than a [minor] or [perfect] [interval].

diminished triad A [triad] made up of a [minor] [third] and a [diminished] [fifth].

diminuendo Becoming softer, diminishing.

dissonance A combination of two or more [pitches] that are unstable, requiring [resolution]. (See [consonance].)

dominant The fifth [scale degree] of a [diatonic scale].

dominant seventh chord A [seventh chord] made up of a [major triad] and a [minor] [seventh].

dorian mode A [mode] with [half steps] between the second and third as well as the sixth and seventh [scale degrees].

dot A small symbol that is placed to the right of the [head] of a [note] that increases the [duration] by one-half.

double bar Two vertical lines drawn across the [staff], indicating the end of a section of a piece.

double dot Two small dots placed to the right of the [head] of a [note] that increases the [duration] by three-fourths.

double flat A symbol written to the left of a [note head] that lowers the [pitch] by a [whole step]. ♭♭

double sharp A symbol written to the left of a [note] that raises the [pitch] by a [whole step]. ✗

doubling The practice of giving the same [melody] or [chord] tone to more than one part.

duple meter A [meter] that consists of two [beats].

duration The time that a sound (or a silence) lasts in music.

eighth note A [note] with half the [duration] of a [quarter note]. ♪

enharmonic Two [pitches] or [chords] that sound the same but are spelled differently, for example G-sharp and A-flat.

expanded position A spacing of [chords] that involves duplicating [tones] in more than one [octave] and/or spreading the chord tones over more than one octave.

fermata A pause, indicated by the sign ⌢

fifth An [interval] that contains five [scale] [degrees].

fifth (chord) The [tone] that lies a [fifth] above the [root] of a [chord].

first inversion A [triad] in which the lowest-sounding [pitch] is the [third] of the [chord].

flag The curved shaded line extending from the end of a [stem] that is used to indicate an [eighth] or shorter note.

flat A symbol written to the left of a [note head] that lowers the [pitch] of a [note] by a [half step]. ♭

form The underlying design of a piece of music, consisting of [sections], [phrases], and [periods].

forte Loud, strong. (*f*) (It., loud.)

fortissimo Very loud. (*ff*) (It., loudest.)

fourth An [interval] that contains four [scale] [degrees].

giocoso In a playful or joking manner. (It., joyous.)

grand staff The combined [treble] and [bass] [staffs] that is commonly used to notate [keyboard] music.

grave Very slowly; solemn, stern.

half cadence A [cadence] whose final [chord] is the [dominant] (V).

half note A [note] with twice the [duration] of a [quarter note].

half step The smallest [interval] on the standard [keyboard]. The interval between two adjacent [keys] (including both black and white keys) is a half step.

harmonic minor scale A form of the [minor scale] that has [half steps] between the following [scale degrees]: 2-3, 5-6, and 7-8. The [interval] from 6 to 7 is an [augmented] [second].

harmonic progression The motion from one [chord] to another in a piece of music.

harmonic rhythm The [rhythm] formed by the [harmonic progressions] in a piece of music.

harmonization The practice of adding [chords] to a [melody].

harmony The study of [tones] sounding together.

head The round part of a [note] that is used to indicate the [pitch] of the note.

homophonic The most common [texture] in tonal music, consisting of a [melody] and an [accompaniment].

imitation The statement of a [melody] by several parts in succession.

interval The "distance" or relationship between two [pitches]. The smallest interval on the standard [keyboard] is the [half step].

inversion Reversal of the position of two musical elements; applied to a [chord] when the lowest tone is not the [root] and to [intervals] when the lower and higher [tones] are exchanged.

key Music that is based on a [major] or [minor] [scale] is said to be in a key. Keys are identified by their [tonic]. A single lever on a [keyboard].

keyboard/keyboard instrument A set of levers (called [keys]) arranged in [scale] order that allow a performer to actuate the tone-producing mechanism of a musical instrument. A musical instrument that is controlled from a keyboard.

key signature An arrangement of [sharps] or [flats] at the beginning of a [staff] that indicates the [pitches] that will be most common in a piece of music. Key signatures are associated with particular [major] and [minor] [scales].

keynote See [tonic].

larghetto A [tempo] slightly faster than [largo].

largo A very slow [tempo]. (It., "broad.")

leading tone The seventh [scale degree] in the [major] and those [minor] [scales] with a [half step] from the seventh to eighth degrees.

ledger line A small line written above or below the [staff] to extend its range.

legato Smoothly; linked together. (It., bound.)

lento Slowly, with a sense of laziness. (It., slow.)

lower neighbor A [nonharmonic tone] that descends a step from a [chord] [tone] and returns to the same [tone].

lydian mode A [mode] with [half steps] between the fourth and fifth as well as the seventh and eighth [scale degrees].

major interval One of the [intervals]; a [second], [third], [sixth], or [seventh] that is the size found in the [major scale] between the [tonic] and another [scale] [degree].

major key A term that refers to [tonal] characteristics of music based on a [major scale] and includes common [pitch] relationships that establish the [tonic].

major scale A [diatonic] scale with [half steps] between the third and fourth and the seventh and eighth [scale] [degrees].

major triad A [triad] made of a [major] [third] and a [perfect] [fifth].

marcato Marked, stressed.

measure One unit of [meter], consisting of a number of [accented] and unaccented [beats]. A measure is indicated in music notation by [bar lines].

melodic minor scale A form of the [minor scale] that has [half steps] between the following [scale degrees] in its ascending form: 2-3 and 7-8. The [natural minor] is used in the descending form.

melody/melodic line A succession of [tones] that create a coherent musical impression.

meno mosso Slower. (It., less motion.)

meter A regular pattern of [accents] in the [beats] of a piece of music. Meter is indicated by the [meter signature].

meter signature A symbol placed at the beginning of a composition to indicate the [meter] of the piece. Meter signatures usually consist of two numbers, the lower of which indicates a [note value] (2, 4, 8), and the upper the number of these notes per [measure].

mezzo forte Moderately loud. *(mf)* (It., medium loud.)

mezzo piano Moderately soft. *(mp)* (It., medium soft.)

middle C The C nearest to the middle of the piano [keyboard]. This [note] is an important point of reference because it is on the [ledger line] between the [treble] and [bass] [staves] on the [grand staff].

minor interval An [interval] that is one [half step] smaller than a [major interval].

minor key A term that refers to [tonal] characteristics of music based on a [minor scale] and includes common [pitch] relationships that establish the [tonic].

minor scale A [diatonic] family of scales that share the common characteristic of a half step between the second and third scale degrees. (See [natural minor], [harmonic minor], and [melodic minor].)

minor seventh chord A [seventh chord] made up of a [minor triad] and a [minor] [seventh].

minor triad A [triad] made up of a [minor] [third] and a [perfect] [fifth].

mixolydian mode A [mode] with [half steps] between the third and fourth as well as the sixth and seventh [scale degrees].

mode A term referring to one of the diatonic scales other than [major] and [minor]. (See [dorian mode], [phrygian mode], [lydian mode], and [mixolydian mode].)

moderato Moderate [tempo]; neither fast nor slow.

modulation A move to a new [key] or [tonal center] within a piece of music.

monophonic A [texture] consisting of a single [melody].

morendo Fading, dying away, becoming softer.

motive A short melodic or rhythmic idea that is used repeatedly in a composition.

natural minor scale The basic form of a [minor scale] with [half steps] between the following [scale degrees]: 2-3 and 5-6.

natural sign A symbol written to the left of a [note head] that cancels a previous [sharp] or [flat]. ♮

neighboring tone A [nonharmonic tone] that moves a step away from a [chord] [tone] and returns to the same [tone]. (See [upper neighbor] and [lower neighbor].)

nonharmonic tone A tone (often in the [melody]) that does not fit into the surrounding [harmony]. (See [passing tone], [neighboring tone], and [suspension].)

note A symbol placed on the [staff] to indicate the [pitch] and [duration] of a sound in music.

note head See [head].

octave The [interval] between two adjacent [notes] of the same name. The name comes from the Latin word for eight, denoting the eight [pitch classes] contained within the [interval].

ostinato A repeated melodic [motive] that usually occurs in an [accompaniment]. (It., obstinate.)

parallel keys The [major] and [minor] [scales] that share the same [tonic].

part singing The addition of one or more [melodic lines] to a [melody] to create the impression of [harmony].

passing tone A [nonharmonic tone] that moves by step from a [chord] [tone] to another of different [pitch].

pentatonic scale A [scale] (consisting of five [tones], usually in the relationship of the black keys on the piano) that is common to many folk songs.

perfect interval One of the [intervals]: a [unison], [fourth], [fifth], or an [octave] found in the [major scale] between the [tonic] and another [scale] [degree].

period A group of [phrases] with the final phrase having a stronger [cadence]. The phrases often have the character of a "question" phrase followed by an "answer" phrase.

phrase A complete musical thought.

phrygian mode A [mode] with [half steps] between the first and second as well as the fifth and sixth [scale degrees].

pianissimo Very softly. *(pp)* (It., softest.)

piano Softly. *(p)* (It., soft.)

piano staff See [grand staff].

pitch The "highness" or "lowness" of a musical [tone].

pitch class All [notes] of the same name on the [keyboard].

plagal cadence A common [cadence] in [tonal] music consisting of the [subdominant] [chord] (IV) followed by the [tonic] [chord] (I).

polyphonic A musical [texture] consisting of two or more [melodic lines] of equal importance.

prestissimo As fast as possible. Faster than [presto].

presto A very fast [tempo]. Faster than [allegro].

primary chords The [chords] built on the first, fourth, and fifth [scale degrees] in [major] or [minor] [keys].

progression See [harmonic progression].

pulse See [beat].

quadruple meter A [meter] consisting of four [beats].

quarter note A basic [note] value in music. Often used to indicate the [beat].

rallentando Gradually slowing; relaxing.

relative major The [major scale] that shares the same [key signature] with a [minor scale].

relative minor The [minor scale] that shares the same [key signature] with a [major scale].

repeat sign Any one of the symbols used to indicate the restatement of a musical idea or section.

resolution The movement (usually by step) from a [dissonance] to a [consonance].

rest A symbol used to indicate silence in music.

rhythm The movement of music in time. A pattern of uneven [duration] over the steady background of the [beat].

ritardando Gradually slowing; delaying. (It., slowing down.)

roman-numeral analysis A system for labeling [chords] to show how they function within a [key].

root The lowest [tone] in a [chord] when written in [simple position].

root position A [chord] with the [root] as the lowest sounding [pitch].

round A [canon] at the [unison]. One singer begins the round and, upon reaching a certain point, is joined by a second singer who begins at the beginning. Rounds are usually in three or four parts.

scale A summary of the [pitch] material of a piece of music arranged in order from the lowest to the highest pitches.

scherzando Joking, whimsical. (It., joking.)

second An [interval] that contains two [scale] [degrees].

second inversion A [chord] with the [fifth] as the lowest-sounding [tone].

secondary chords The [chords] built on the second, third, sixth, and seventh [scale degrees] in [major] or [minor] [keys].

semicadence See [half cadence].

semitone See [half step].

sentence See [period].

sequence The repetition of a melodic [motive] on a different [pitch].

seventh An [interval] that contains seven [scale] [degrees].

seventh (chord) The [tone] that lies a [seventh] above the [root] of a [chord].

seventh chord A [chord] made up of a [triad] and a [seventh].

sforzando With a forced accent; coerced. *(sf)* (It., forced.)

sforzato Forced, heavy accent. *(sfz)* (It., forced.)

sharp A symbol that is written to the left of a [note head] to raise the [pitch] one [half step].

simple division The division of the [beat] into two equal parts.

simple meter A [meter] that has a [simple division] of the [beat].

simple position A [chord] in its most basic position, with the [root] at the bottom and the other chord tones written in order above the root.

sixteenth note A [note] with half the [duration] of an [eighth note] or one-fourth the [duration] of a [quarter note].

sixth An [interval] that contains six [scale] [degrees].

smorzando Dying away, becoming extinguished.

solfeggio A system used to help singers to remember the [pitches] of the various [scale degrees] in a [diatonic scale].

sperdendozi Fading away, disappearing. (It., fading.)

staccato Detached, separated. (It., detached.)

staff A group of five horizontal lines on which music is notated.

stem The vertical line extending from the [head] of a [note].

subdivision The division of the [beat] in [simple meter] into four equal parts or in [compound meter] into six equal parts.

submediant The sixth [scale degree] of a [diatonic scale].

suspension A [nonharmonic tone] that remains from a previous [chord] and moves down by step.

syncopation A [rhythm] with accents on [notes] that are not usually stressed.

tempo The speed of the [beat] in music, which may be expressed in general terms or in [beats] per minute. (It., time.)

tempo giusto Strictly in [tempo]. (It., just time.)

tempo rubato Free or elastic [tempo]. (It., stolen time.)

ternary division See [compound division].

ternary form A [form] consisting of three sections (usually ABA).

texture A general term describing the relationships among [melody], [harmony], and [rhythm] in a piece of music.

third An [interval] that contains three [scale] [degrees].

third (chord) The [tone] that lies a [third] above the [root] of a [chord].

tie A curved line connecting two [notes], which indicates that they are to be played as a single [note].

tonal/tonal center The organized relationship of [tones] in a [major or minor scale] to the [tonic] of the [scale].

tone A musical sound of definite [pitch].

tonic The [keynote] of a piece of music. The [tone] that is felt to be a point of rest, where the music can logically conclude.

tonic ([parallel]) major The [major scale] that shares the same [tonic] note with a [minor scale].

tonic ([parallel]) minor The [minor scale] that shares the same [tonic] note with a [major scale].

transposition The process of rewriting a piece of music or a [scale] so that it sounds higher or lower in [pitch]. This involves raising or lowering each [pitch] by the same [interval].

treble clef The most common [clef] in music. It is a stylized letter "G" that indicates that the second line of the [staff] is to be G.

triad A [chord] consisting of three [tones] built in [thirds].

triple meter A [meter] consisting of three [beats].

triplet A group of three [notes] that are performed in the time usually given to two [notes].

tritone An [interval] that contains three [whole steps]: the [augmented fourth] and the [diminished fifth].

unison Two [pitches] that are the same. Performing musical parts at the same [pitch] or in [octaves].

upbeat The [note] (or notes) that occur at the beginning of a phrase before the beginning of the first full [measure].

upper neighbor A [nonharmonic tone] that ascends a step from a [chord] [tone] and returns to the same [tone].

vivace Lively, quick, full of life. (It., brisk.)

whole step An [interval] consisting of two [half steps].

whole tone scale A [scale] consisting only of [whole steps].

Index